USB Explained

ISBN 0-13-081153-X

9 780130 811530

90000

USB
Explained

by

Steven McDowell
Martin D. Seyer

Prentice Hall PTR
Upper Saddle River, New Jersey 07458
http://www.phptr.com

Library of Congress Cataloging-in-Publication Data
McDowell, Steven.
    USB explained / Steven McDowell, Martin D. Seyer.
      p. cm.
    Includes index.
    ISBN 0-13-081153-X (alk. paper)
    1. USB (Computer bus) 2. Computer architecture.
TK7895.B87M39   1999
004.6'4--dc21   98-3619
                                            CIP

Editorial/Production Supervision: *Craig Little*
Acquisitions Editor: *Bernard Goodwin*
Buyer: *Alan Fischer*
Cover Design: *Scott Weiss*
Cover Design Direction: *Jerry Votta*
Art Director and Interior Design: *Gail Cocker-Bogusz*
Marketing Manager: *Kaylie Smith*

© 1999 Prentice Hall PTR
Prentice-Hall, Inc.
A Simon & Schuster Company
Upper Saddle River, NJ 07458

The publisher offers discounts on this book when ordered in bulk quantities. For more information, call the Corporate Sales Department at 800-382-3419; FAX: 201-236-7141, email corpsales@prenhall.com or write Corporate Sales Department, Prentice Hall PTR, One Lake Street, Upper Saddle River, NJ 07458

Prentice Hall books are widely used by corporations and government agencies for training, marketing, and resale.

Printed in the United States of America

10 9 8 7 6 5 4 3

ISBN 0-13-081153-X

Prentice-Hall International (UK) Limited, *London*
Prentice-Hall of Australia Pty. Limited, *Sydney*
Prentice-Hall Canada Inc., *Toronto*
Prentice-Hall Hispanoamericana, S.A., *Mexico*
Prentice-Hall of India Private Limited, *New Delhi*
Prentice-Hall of Japan, Inc., *Tokyo*
Simon & Schuster Asia Pte. Ltd., *Singapore*
Editora Prentice-Hall do Brasil, Ltda., *Rio de Janeiro*

Contents

v

Chapter 5

Inside a USB Device 81

Chapter 6

On the Wire 103

Chapter 7
USB in the Windows World 123

Chapter 8
Frequently Asked Questions 133

▮ Listing of Figures

Preface

What Is This Book?

This is a book about the Universal Serial Bus, or USB. The USB was designed by the computer industry to replace the ailing and ancient RS-232 serial-port technology. The USB is bigger, faster, and better. It's built to handle the demands of audio and video. It's built to be hot pluggable. It's built to be plug-n-play. It's built to host a hundred or more devices at the same time, though it works wonderfully well with just a single device or two. Finally, it's built to be inexpensive enough to seamlessly become a part of the personal computer without burdening the PC owners.

This book explains exactly what the USB is and how it works. It does not explain how to write software for the USB. We'll leave it up to Sun, Apple, and Microsoft to tell us how to write code for their platforms. This is a "concepts" book. If you want to know how it works under the hood, then you picked up the right book. You will get a lot of detail about how the bus and its devices all communicate and keep things straight, but you won't see any state or timing diagrams that require an engineering degree to understand.

Who Is This Book For?

The book was written first and foremost with the curious end user in mind—someone who wants to understand how the USB works under the hood. It is technical enough, however, and explores the standard well enough that it will make an ideal companion to the USB specification for practicing engineers and software developers. In short, this book is for anyone who wants a complete treatment of the Universal Serial Bus in easy-to-understand terms.

Organization

The book takes a top-down approach to the Universal Serial Bus. The first two chapters provide an overview of the USB in general and the USB within a host computer in particular. Chapter 3 talks about setting up USB hardware and all the issues associated with that. Chapter 4 takes us inside a USB Hub. Chapter 5 takes us inside a USB Device. Chapter 6 is dedicated to explaining what actually happens "on the wire"—the USB protocols that keep everything communicating. The main part of the book is rounded out with chapters describing USB on the most popular computer operating systems (Chapter 7) and answering frequently asked questions (Chapter 8). Appendix A provides a comprehensive list of where to go for USB devices and software. Appendices C through F cover some of the more technical aspects of the USB protocols.

Readers are encouraged to read and understand the material in Chapter 2, "USB Concepts," and then go to the part of the book that describes what is of particular interest to them. A complete treatment of the subject, though, should include review of each chapter.

Universal Serial Bus Standards and Terminology

This book describes the Universal Serial Bus as described in version 1.0 of the Universal Serial Bus Specification from the USB Implementers Forum. Even though the book does not mirror the organization of the specification, every attempt is made to be consistent with the terminology and concepts used in the specification. Inconsistent terminology is used in a few instances when it makes a concept or technique easier to understand; terminology from the standard is included also. The terms "Universal Serial Bus" and "USB" are interchangeable within this work.

Acknowledgments

A book like this one isn't possible without the personal contributions of a number of people. We would like to thank the early and on-going reviewers of this book who gave invaluable feedback on both the style and substance: Doug McDowell, Lee Parsons, and Lazlo Bodine. For their support, encouragement, and on-going feedback during the process, special thanks must go to Vicki, Karen, and Denise (the breakfast club). Rita Anderson allowed the book to happen in the face of more important, company-driven, deadlines and commitments; thank you to her. Thank you to Michelle for her encouragement and dedication. Special thanks should go to Cheryl for providing the table on which this book was started.

The authors would like to acknowledge Mark Sokos for his assistance in the description of the other buses available in the industry. Much of the information is available on the worldwide web at http://www.gl.umbc.edu/~msokos1 and is presented here with his permission. The reader is encouraged to visit his sites, as there is a wealth of information about these subjects. We would also like to thank Joakim Ogren for providing the pin-out information for a number of the different ports and buses. Further information can be found at the web site, http://ftp.sunet.se/pub/etext/hwb/menu_Connector.html, should the reader desire more information. We would like to acknowledge the effort of Jonathan Bearfield at Texas Instruments for his efforts in securing material for us. Texas Instruments has a good USB program and we encourage every reader to visit their USB site on the worldwide web at http://www.ti.com/sc/usb.

Introduction

Why a Book about USB?

The Universal Serial Bus was invented and standardized in early 1995 by a group of computer manufacturers and peripherals vendors under the auspices of an organization called the Universal Serial Bus Implementers Forum (USB-IF). The aim was to bring serial-port (and serial-bus) technology into the twenty-first century. There are many existing standard and proprietary serial-port and serial-bus technologies for communication between peripherals and host computers, each with its own purpose and its own drawbacks. The goal of this group of manufacturers was to develop a low- to high-speed technology that would provide a shared-access, highly available, robust, self-configuring, extensible, and easy-to-use serial bus to computer owners. This bus was to be host-computer independent and consistent across computer architectures. The USB-IF met these goals and published a specification for a serial technology that was called the Universal Serial Bus, or simply USB.

This book describes and explains the Universal Serial Bus. It attempts to clearly and concisely explain the USB protocols and data flow. It even delves into the physical properties of the bus and devices on the bus. It describes the functionality of the USB host and USB devices, talks a bit about software issues on some of the more popular computer operating systems, and explores the detection of USB problems and device configuration in an attempt to diagnose these problems. Rather than dryly translating the USB specification, the book gives real-world examples in explaining the protocols and data flow.

Just What Is the Universal Serial Bus?

The Universal Serial Bus is one of the fastest-growing and most widely accepted expansions to the personal computer in recent memory. It is impossible to buy an Intel-based PC (which makes up 94% of the personal-computer market) without a Universal Serial Port bus. This is not to say that the USB is limited to the PC world, not by any stretch. Every computer hardware manufacturer is now acting to implement the Universal Serial Bus on its own platform.

Why the sudden interest in something as seemingly trivial as a serial port? The answer is that the Universal Serial Bus is much more than a serial port—it's a serial bus. This means that a single port on the back of your computer can be the window (no pun intended) into a myriad of devices. Devices can be daisy-chained together. Groups of devices can be separated by concentration hardware called on a hub. When you think of the Universal Serial Bus, it's best to think of it as a "network" of devices, much as you would think of the ethernet network. Figure 1–1 illustrates what a typical network of USB devices might look like.

Chaining a bunch of devices together might not seem like such a good thing at first glance. In fact, it might seem like a downright bad idea for a lot of devices to share what little bit of bandwidth serial devices have traditionally had to work with. After all, there is barely enough bandwidth on an RS–232 port to get a decent connection to a printer. There certainly isn't enough to talk to a digital camera to download images.

The answer lies in providing a fast bus. We have to be careful with our terminology, though, because the Universal Serial Bus is considered in the

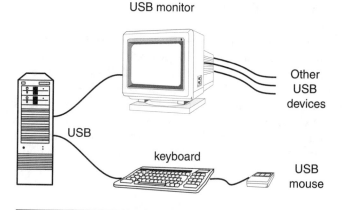

Figure 1–1   Typical USB configuration

computer industry to be a "mid- and low-speed" bus. The Universal Serial Bus operates at over 10 *million bits per second*—this is the speed of the computer network in most businesses.

The Universal Serial Bus is not considered "fast" when compared to things such as the Fibre Channel serial bus, which clocks in at about 300 million bits per second, or to upcoming bus technologies such as the IEEE 1394 "FireWire" bus to control audio and video sources that are "broadcast quality." So we will accept that the USB is a "mid-speed" bus and move on.

What Can I Do with It?

The Universal Serial Bus was designed with the thought of providing pure digital audio, video, and telecommunications to the modern computer user. The speed of the bus is more than sufficient to support these types of devices.

A big problem with personal computers has always been connecting to the peripherals that you want to use. Everything always seems to need its own adapter card plugged into the bus. There are video cards for high-resolution video. There are game cards to drive your joysticks. There are sound cards to drive speakers and there are video-input cards to bring video into the computer. The list goes on and on.

Computers are shrinking. Every year there are fewer slots for adapter cards. The goal of the personal-computer industry truly is to make the computer as ubiquitous and unobtrusive as possible. At the same time, the computer now contains sufficient technology and raw "horsepower" to run the types of applications and drive the types of tasks that are requiring precision digital input and bandwidth-intensive peripherals. Video conferencing on personal computers is today a reality. Surround-sound stereo from your personal computer is a standard function.

The computer industry is striving to enclose a technology that is expanding—to the point that mid- and high-speed digital peripheral devices are required—into an ever-shrinking footprint. This is where the Universal Serial Bus comes into play. Just put all of the input and output to peripherals outside "the box" and don't use any slots. Put the intelligence into the devices, rather than into the computer.

Peripherals designers are now freed up to implement solutions that are in "one piece"—they don't have to split the functionality of a peripheral between a device and an interface card. This is a win for them. As this happens, the internal bus on your computer ceases to be saturated with traffic and information flowing between these interface cards. This is a win for you; you'll find that you achieve better overall system performance with this type of configuration.

Speaker designers are incorporating the functions previously performed by your sound card directly into the speaker. Video-input folks are building video digitizers to plug into the Universal Serial Bus. Even monitor manufacturers are putting Universal Serial Bus interfaces into the backs of their monitors, making the video card obsolete. There are digital joysticks that offer superhigh resolution

Laying It All Out

You might be wondering: won't this clutter up my workstation or desk? The simple answer is "maybe." Configuring the layout of your Universal Serial Bus will require some thought on your part. Laying out your USB device will be as important as laying out a computer network—after all, they have the same basic purposes and components.

Just as when laying out a computer network, almost everything will work if you just plug all the cables in and have the right software loaded. What makes the USB better than your local-area network, though, is that there is no software to configure to run a device (apart from your operating system maybe asking you to put a CD in so *it* can load a driver).

The basic components of a Universal Serial Bus (and we'll get into this in excruciating detail throughout the rest of this book) are the host (your PC), the devices you choose to put on your bus (e.g., speakers, monitor, etc.), and the hubs that tie the pieces together.

Your PC will probably have two Universal Serial Port plugs. They will most likely be on the back of your computer where you would expect to find the RS–232 serial port and printer port. The USB ports are recognizable as the only small rectangular plugs on the computer. The cables for them only fit one way—it's impossible to plug in a Universal Serial Bus cable the wrong way. This is illustrated in Figure 1–2.

Figure 1–2   Back of a typical PC w/ USB ports

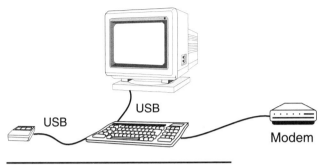

Figure 1–3   USB layout w/ keyboard hub

If you have only one or two USB devices, then simply plug the devices into the ports, and you should be done. If, on the other hand, you have multiple devices, then you might want to think a little before blindly plugging devices in.

If you have more devices than ports, then you obviously need a hub. This hub may stand alone, or it might be integrated into the a device. For example, many of the USB keyboards have an integrated single-port hub into which you can plug your USB mouse or joystick. This configuration is shown in Figure 1–3.

To take things further, almost all of the USB monitors shipping today have integrated 4- and 8-port hubs. This allows the monitor to be the center of the USB universe on your desktop. Having the monitor as hub makes the most sense, in that you won't have long runs of cable snaking to, and behind, your computer. This sort of setup is shown in Figure 1–4.

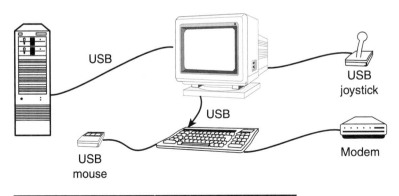

Figure 1–4   USB layout w/ monitor & keyboard hub

It doesn't really matter which devices are attached to which ports in a Universal Serial Bus system. There is no performance difference between a device that is 4 hubs away from the computer and one that is attached directly. The important thing is to lay them out in a way that makes sense for your environment. For example, it makes sense to have your USB keyboard, joysticks, mouse, and speakers attached to the multiport hub integrated into your USB monitor. It might make sense in this example to have your USB modem, or the subwoofer in your speaker system, attached directly to your computer's USB port and sitting under your desk.

The choice is up to you when working with the Universal Serial Bus, because it's next to impossible to make a mistake. If you plug in the cables, and you have the software that supports your devices, then your system will work. This book will describe to you how it all works.

What Kinds of Devices Are There?

A multitude of devices are available to attach to you Universal Serial Bus system. Some are what you might expect: modems, keyboards, and mice, to name a few. Some might surprise you—for instance, companies are making solar panels to keep the USB devices attached to a sleeping laptop computer alive. In this section we'll talk about a range of devices that are available for the Universal Serial Bus.

■ Monitors

A natural fit for the Universal Serial Bus is in embedding into the video monitor a USB hub (Figure 1–5). After all, the monitor sits on your desktop and provides a natural point at which to attach other USB peripherals. With a USB hub built into your video monitor, there is no need to awkwardly run cables to the back of your computer. And with a digital connection between your computer and the monitor, you can control directly from your PC such things as contrast, screen sizing, brightness, and all of the other aspects you used to have to adjust with manual buttons on the monitor.

The bandwidth required for PC video, however, is too great for the Universal Serial Bus to bear. For this reason, you will still have a video card inside your computer. This allows you the flexibility of choosing the video card that works best for your application and keeps the price of the monitors stable.

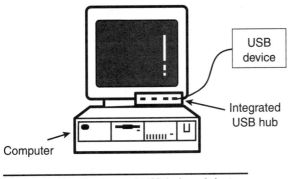

Figure 1–5   Monitor w/ USB hub and devices

■ Modems

A natural device to attach to the Universal Serial Bus is a modem. A tricky element of dealing with existing modems is interfacing to the computer's RS-232 port: there is a multitude of signals that you must be concerned with. There is also a speed limitation with RS-232 devices—you have a maximum data-transfer rate of about 119 thousand bits per second (Kbps).

While 119 Kbps is plenty fast for existing dial-up modems, and even seems to work fairly well for ISDN lines, it is inadequate for future tele-communication technologies. Fast approaching are technologies that promise to deliver Internet and other communication over your cable television paths, your small-dish satellite, and even a new type of phone connection call DSL (direct subscriber loop).

In the computer server space, people are already hooking computers up to dedicated phone lines running at 1 million bits per second and faster (T1 line speed). Today, they use a piece of equipment that sits between the server and the dedicated line. With the Universal Serial Bus, you will be able to plug a T1 or T3 line directly into your server.

■ Video Camera and Input Devices

Bringing video into a computer has always required the use of a dedicated video-capture card. The capture card shares your PCI and ISA bus slots with the rest of the peripherals on the system. Capture cards take an analog signal and turn it into a digital signal.

The problem with existing technologies is that the signal degrades with each conversion between analog and digital. A secondary problem is that a high level of system bus (PCI or ISA) activity limits the amount of traffic that the video adapter can put on the bus to the computer. For example, if your disk controller is on the same PCI bus as your capture card, then you have bus contention. There is only so much bandwidth, and with PCI any device that wants to control the bus pretty much can control the bus— there are no guarantees.

Putting video-capture devices directly on the Universal Serial Bus eliminates a number of problems. First, there is no dedicated capture card taking up slots on the computer. Second, by using a digital camera you can avoid any signal degradation caused by converting video signals between analog and digital. Last, the Universal Serial Bus provides for guaranteed reserved bandwidth for devices that ask for it. There will also be enough room on the bus for the video signals if the capture device was told that it's available.

■ Keyboards, Mice, and Joysticks

The most obvious connection that you'll make with your Universal Serial Bus will be with input devices: keyboards, mice, and joysticks. For these three classes of devices there are three distinct jacks on the back of your computer that computer manufacturers would like to get rid of.

You will see keyboards with integrated hub devices, so that you can plug your USB mouse directly into your USB keyboard. There will be no more confusion of two identical-looking ports on the back of your computer having two different functions, as there is today with the mouse and keyboard ports.

Joysticks will be the biggest win with Universal Serial Bus. Digital joysticks will have an amazing amount of granularity and control when compared with existing analog joysticks. A new class of joysticks falled *force-feedback joysticks* also are increasing in popularity among game players. Force-feedback joysticks reflect vibration and other feedback into the joystick. For example, if you were playing a game where you were flying a plane, then you would feel the motion and resistance of the aircraft in the joystick. This provides a much greater degree of realism. With a digital link between the joystick and the computer, these devices will work much better and will proliferate. The other benefit with USB joysticks is that you can have as many of them as you want, whereas with traditional game ports the user needs to buy a new interface card for every joystick (or pair of joysticks).

▌ Power Devices

The Universal Serial Bus, by specification, provides power to the devices attached to it. Some devices require more power than the bus provides, so they have their own power source (these are called "self-powered devices"). If the Universal Serial Bus is attached to a portable computer, the latter might put itself into a power-suspended mode, which might not be desirable for all of the attached peripherals (for example, an ISDN modem connection may be dropped if the modem is powered off). Another concern is that the USB will be a larger drain on the portable computer's battery.

To forestall these problems, vendors are working on a number of innovative methods of keeping the USB powered in a mobile environment. There are USB "power sources," which are basically battery packs that live on the Universal Serial Bus and provide power to the entire bus. There is even a solar panel that attaches to the bus to keep peripherals alive when a laptop computer goes to sleep. Desktop computers probably won't need such devices, but you may want to look into them if you have USB on a laptop and you have peripherals you want to keep alive.

▌ Hubs

The core component in a Universal Serial Bus system is the USB hub. Hubs concentrate USB devices into a single cable that can be plugged back into the host computer. The computer has a small hub built into it called the "root hub." Most computers' root hubs support two ports. If you have more than two USB peripherals, then you will probably want an external hub. As we've already discussed, devices such as keyboards and monitors will include hubs within them, making it easy to attach more devices. There are also a number of stand-alone external USB hubs. If you have more than a couple of devices, and you don't buy a device with a built-in hub, then you will probably want to buy a hub. The functionality they offer is fairly consistent across the range of available hubs.

▌ Bus Converters

Serial-bus converters provide a bridge between existing RS-232 and parallel-port devices and the Universal Serial Bus. Using these converters protects your investment in existing technology. There is no need to rush out and buy a new USB modem, for example, if you already have a modem. You simply need to purchase a serial-bus converter.

A serial converter enumerates as a PC COM port, so to your system's software it's treated as just another serial port. You can continue to use your existing software, since this USB device looks like the COM port the software is expecting to see. The converters ship with device drivers to ensure that this is true. Using a converter is the easiest, fastest, and cheapest way to get up and running with the Universal Serial Bus.

■ Audio Speakers

Embedded USB technology within your computer's audio speakers may eliminate the need for sound cards. Then again, it may not. It depends upon your application. If you are a studio musician, then USB speakers may not be for you. If you're a business user, then you probably don't care much about the quality of sounds coming from your speakers. Most of us computer users live somewhere in the middle.

Speakers that attach to the Universal Serial Bus are a convenient way to get sound out of your computer without buying an expensive sound card. Most USB speakers are self-powered with built-in amplifiers. The quality is good. If you don't already have speakers on your system, or you simply want to free up a bus slot inside your computer, then USB speakers may be a good investment. As with any audio (or video) device, quality varies, so do some comparison shopping.

Wrapping It Up

In this chapter we provided a brief introduction of the Universal Serial Bus. We talked a bit about what USB is and what you can do with it. We discussed briefly a number of devices that are available today to plug into the USB. This list is far from definitive but represents some of the more common device classes. We demonstrated that configuring a USB system is as simple as plugging things together. There are not many considerations for the average user.

The remainder of this book will get into the technical underpinnings of the Universal Serial Bus. We will delve into each subject area a piece at a time, until we understand how and why USB works.

USB Concepts

Why a New Serial Port?

The Universal Serial Bus (USB) comes to us at a time when serial-port technology has hit a brick wall, in terms of both how much information can be sent to serial devices and how many serial devices one can attach to a modern PC. The advent of multimedia and the proliferation of relatively inexpensive processing power have left the venerable RS-232 serial port that you are used to working with a relic of times past.

Today, technology can deliver digital joysticks for high-precision game playing. Today's technology can also deliver digital audio peripherals, eliminating sounds cards and other analog audio equipment from within the PC. It can provide high-resolution "live" video input and output devices. Modern PCs can attach to data networks and telephony equipment at speeds faster than the RS-232 serial port was designed to handle. In adding these types of functions and peripherals to a modern personal computer, the problem arises as to *where* such things should live. Computers are shrinking, and plug-in peripheral slots are becoming fewer. The traditional RS-232 serial port certainly cannot handle these kinds of technology. The ideal would be a moderate-speed serial *bus* technology that would allow the capacity and feature set needed to support new technology.

With these thoughts in mind a group of computer and peripherals manufacturers gathered in early 1995 under the auspices of the "Universal Serial Bus Implementers Forum" (the USB-IF) to define a high-speed serial-bus technology to replace, or phase out, the existing RS-232 serial-port technology.

The Universal Serial Bus was designed with the following goals in mind:

- Easy peripheral expansion
- Data-transfer rates up to 12 Mbs
- Economical implementation
- Support for real-time devices
- True "plug-n-play" device support
- Bus-powered devices

The USB-IF met their goals and created a specification defining the USB. Devices are being built, software is being shipped, and systems are coming equipped to handle USB right out of the box. Every indication is that the Universal Serial Bus is here to stay.

What Are the Advantages of Using the USB?

The Universal Serial Bus provides a number of inherent features that easily make it the choice for low- to medium-speed digital peripherals (other solutions are on the way for those who need high-speed serial-bus devices). The USB is easy to use, easy to administer, and easy to design to. These features include:

- Details hidden from the user
- Broad application space
- Guaranteed bandwidth for multimedia applications (isochronous)
- Robust
- System-independent devices

An important aspect of the Universal Serial Bus is that details of the implementation and most of the configuration are hidden from the user. There is one cable type, and connectors fit only into the correct plugs. There are no visible electrical details. There are no terminators or other nasty electrical things that users must be aware of that plague other bus technologies (e.g., SCSI). The USB provides true and automatic plug-and-play configuration. (When we say "plug-and-play," we're talking about the ability of the computer to automatically detect and configure the USB device. In the old days of computing, you would have to set switches on every device indicating the addresses and interrupts used by the device. With plug-and-play, that is all done by the operating system.) The USB also allows for dynamic device configuration and the "hot plug" of devices.

Another important aspect of the Universal Serial Bus, and one of the overriding design goals, is that it supports a very broad application space. What this means is that you can have a USB digital speaker peacefully co-existing with a USB ISDN-line interface and digital joystick all at the same time. There is simultaneous support for both medium-speed (1.5-Mbps) and high-speed (12-Mbps) device connections. There is also simultaneous support for asynchronous bus traffic, from devices such as keyboards and joysticks, and isochronous (i.e., guaranteed) bandwidth for such things as audio and video devices. There is support for using up to 128 devices at the same time. Devices on the USB bus may even be compound ones—incorporating multiple USB functions into a single package.

For multimedia and other data streams that need a degree of certainty that space is available on the bus when transmitting or receiving data, the Universal Serial Bus provides an amount of guaranteed bandwidth. This is called **isochronous bandwidth**. Bandwidth that is not guaranteed but is used "as available" is called **asynchronous bandwidth**. As long as bandwidth is available, and a device must have that bandwidth, it is used. If a device requests some portion of the available isochronous bandwidth, and none is available, then he's denied. This is all done when the device is first added to the system.

The Universal Serial Bus is, above all else, extremely robust. It offers at the protocol level a very high degree of error handling and recovery. It allows you to plug and unplug devices at will, without turning off your computer. It also offers very easy identification of misbehaving devices.

Finally, USB devices are completely *system independent*. The same USB peripheral can be used on any computer architecture supporting the Universal Serial Bus, provided there is software available. This will hopefully serve to encourage manufacturers to build USB devices, since they can broaden their target markets immensely without building different devices for each popular computer type on the market.

What Is a Bus?

One of the misunderstood features of computers today is the bus. Today one hears about the system bus, the local bus, the SCSI bus, the ISA bus, the PCI bus, the VL-bus, and now USB. These terms are also confused with other terms for slots, ports, connectors, etc. What is a bus, then, and how do these buses, differ?

In general, USB meets a solution to the I/O needs of relatively slow devices, such as a mouse, keyboard, etc., solving a connectivity and performance issue. Other buses, such as PCI and ISA, are set up to solve a system performance issue. Still others, such as SCSI, are targeted specifically to solve a disk and tape I/O performance and connectivity concern. VESA is used to enhance video performance. The next section describes some basics about buses and highlights the differences between the concepts for each bus. The appendix gives detailed specification and pinout information about each bus.

▌ Bus Definition

First, what is a bus? Basically, it is a means of getting data from one point to another, point *A* to point *B*, one device to another device, or one device to multiple devices. The bus includes not only the actual capability to transfer data between devices, but also all appropriate signaling information to insure complete movement of the data from point *A* to point *B*. To avoid loss of data, a bus must include a means of controlling the flow of data between two devices, in order to insure that both devices are ready to send and/or receive information. Finally, both ends must understand the speed with which data is to be exchanged. A bus provides for all of these elements, and it includes a port definition to allow physical interfacing or connecting of two or more devices. Furthermore, there is general confusion about PCI, SCSI, ISA, and local bus versus USB. The sections that follow establish a few definitions about buses and protocols and then clarify the differences between the particular buses.

Serial vs. Parallel

One main aspect of a bus is whether the data is transferred in a serial or parallel fashion. In serial mode, the bits of each character are transmitted one at a time, one after another. For example, with each character containing 8 bits, the character is sent between devices, sending the first bit, then the second bit, third bit, and so on until the eighth bit is sent. Serial transmission is often easier to implement than the counterpart, parallel, and allows greater distances between devices. A single pipe, lead, or channel is used to transmit the data bits serially. The Universal Serial Bus, for example, uses serial transmission.

Contrast this with parallel transmission, where the bits of a character or data are transferred simultaneously. The parallel interface or transmission contrasts with the serial by allowing the devices to transmit all of a character's bits simultaneously instead of one at a time. Picture the runners in a 100-yard dash. They all start at the same time, and if all goes well, all arrive at nearly the same time. The data bits are transmitted in a similar fashion.

Whereas the bits in a serial interface are transmitted over a single channel, wire, or pipe, transmission of all of the bits at once in parallel requires eight separated data leads. For example, the Centronics parallel interface sets aside pins 2 to 9 for data transmission. Transmitting all the data bits of a character between devices at the same time allows for a very fast transmission of the data. Thus, the speed of the bus or interface is not always expressed in bits per second; rather, bytes per second or characters per second may be used. It is imperative that one clarifies whether bits or bytes per second is intended.

Generally—repeat, generally—most connections of systems over telephone wires, coaxial cable, via modem, etc. are made via serial interfaces and buses. Most slow-speed devices within a computer system, relatively speaking, are connected using a serial interface. Such devices include modems, some printers, mice, keyboards, speakers, etc. Most high-performance devices that are connected locally within a computer, such as the CPU, memory, video, disk drives, etc., are connected using parallel connections. *Caution:* Not all buses locally within a computer are parallel; for example, internal management buses or diagnostic buses are serial. With USB, even more internal buses will be serial instead of parallel.

Speeds of Buses

The speed of a serial bus (or interface) is generally expressed in bits per second (bps). For example, when a port, bus, or interface highlights 56-Kbps capability, the maximum throughput is 56,000 bits per second. To translate that into actual characters per second, we need to make a calculation. For a rough estimate of maximum throughput, one can add the start and stop bits of a typical character, totaling 10 bits per character, and divide the interface speed by the number of bits per character. In the case of a 56-Kbps bus or interface, the maximum throughput would be approximately 5600 characters per second. *Caution:* This is only an approximation. Each bus has what is referred to as "overhead" to provide the other highlighted functions of flow control, addressing, etc. The simplicity of the bus will dictate the amount of overhead required. Some interfaces, such as those of devices that are locally connected via RS-232, have little overhead. Hence the actual throughput is relatively close to the maximum speed rating. The RS-232 interface is NOT generally referred to as a bus, but it does have the elements of a bus. (For a complete description of RS-232, the reader is encouraged to refer to the book *RS-232 Made Easy* by Martin D. Seyer.)

The keyword here is maximum. Most buses are set up electrically to support a maximum (or burst) throughput rate, as well as a sustained throughput rate. When calculating throughput, use the sustained rate for a closer approximation of speed. The maximum rate is best-case rate that a pipe, bus, or interface can handle. The maximum rate is hyped by the marketing literature as a means to show competitive advantage versus the competition. For example, consider "56 Kbps" modems: 56,000 bits per second is their maximum rated throughput over a telephone wire. However, if the user were to transmit a file containing 5600 characters, with each character being 10 bits in length (8 bits, plus start and stop bits per character), it would take more than 1 second to transmit between two devices. Bus and interface overheads don't allow for one-to-one throughput numbers.

Protocols

What are some of the overheads that reduce the throughput from maximum to a sustained throughput rate? Bus protocols! A **protocol** is a set of rules that is instituted (or engineered) between devices to allow for the orderly flow of information. Protocols include rules or capabilities to support aspects such as when to send information, how to send it, how much information can be sent, confirmation that information has been sent, and means of confirming that the correct information has been sent. Protocols include the control mechanisms for two devices to properly communicate. Depending on the complexity of the information to be sent, protocols can be simple or very extensive. Generally, the more extensive the protocol, the greater the overhead, and the lower the sustainable throughput. Prominent protocols include binary synchronous communications (BSC), synchronous data link control (SDLC), Xmodem, Ymodem, Kermit, TCP/IP, PPP, and other Internet protocols.

Flow control is an important aspect of a protocol. Flow control is used to regulate the flow of information between the devices. When computers are communicating with other devices, flow control must be used to insure that data is not lost. For example, suppose that two computers are connected in order to upload and download data. Whether the connection involves modems, or the computers are connected back to back, at some point one of the computers will need to store the received information to a disk file. What happens to the incoming data while the file is being written? This defines the requirement for flow control.

Flow control is the ability of a receiving device to regulate the flow of data from the sending device. Protocols break the data into blocks or frames of data, hence the term *block size*. Some protocols support multiple block sizes, requiring the two communicating devices to agree on the block size before transmission. Typical block sizes are 128, 256, 512, 1024 (1 K), and 2048 (2 K) characters. The sending device will send the information a block at a time. In addition, the sending device will perform a calculation on the bits of the data in the block. The result of this calculation is some form of check character or frame-check sequence. The block-check character (BCC) is typically one or two characters appended to the block of data. The block and appended character(s) are then sent to the other device. The receiving device then performs the same calculation on the data block that it receives and computes a BCC. A comparison is made between the received BCC and the calculated one. If the BCCs are the same, then the block of data was received error free. The receiving entity then notifies the sending device that all was received "OK." If the BCCs are different, then the data was received with an error. The protocols allow for asking for a retransmission of one of more blocks of data.

At the time it receives a block, the receiving device can respond to the sender, asking it to send no more blocks until further notice. The receiving device uses the interlude to write to disk, display the received information, draw a screen, etc. The sending and receiving of blocks of data, with a corresponding acknowledgment of receipt, as well as a message for either continued or suspended transmission, is the flow control in a protocol. Flow control and other protocol components are components of a bus's efficiency or inefficiency, directly affecting bus overhead.

Sustained vs. Burst Throughput

What, then, is a sustained versus a burst throughput rate? A burst rate is the maximum rate at which data can be sent or burst over a bus. A sustained rate is the rate at which data can be continuously sent over the bus. Think here in terms of a sprinter versus a long-distance runner. The sprinter can achieve a high rate of speed in a short amount of time and get to the endpoint quickly. However, the sprinter cannot maintain this rate. A long-distance runner will hit a stride and then sustain it throughout the race. The same concept applies to buses. The sustained rate is the rate at which data can be sent over the bus in a consistent manner. It is a better metric than the burst rate for throughput expectations on a bus, as it reflects the typical transmission speed.

Factoring in the overhead, one can see where the block size will impact the sustained throughput on a bus. Small block sizes appear to be inherently less efficient, owing to their overhead for framing and flow control, but in reality they can be very efficient in terms of memory usage. Depending on the cache, buffering, and memory sizes and speeds, small block sizes can improve throughput. Conversely, large block sizes require inherently less protocol overhead and may be great for bursts of data. However, improper memory management may take away the gains of larger block sizes. Furthermore, if error conditions exist, then retransmission must occur on a bus. The larger the block size, the longer it takes to retransmit the block of data. Throughput on buses and protocols is somewhere between a science and an art. This book will leave the debate on block sizes to the engineers who live and breathe it. The point here is to highlight factors that impact the performance of a bus.

Buses vs. Ports vs. Slots vs. Cables vs. Interfaces

Many terms are used in reference to buses, often expressed in confusing vernacular. Multiple possible configurations also create confusion. For example, a bus can be implemented using a port, a slot, a cable, or a combination. We now define the basics of ports, slots, cables, interfaces, and buses. As a general guide, the following descriptions are preferred.

Interface: Refers to a particular specification, or conformance to a published specification.

Connector: Refers to the physical means for connecting devices.

Port: Can refer to (1) conformance to a specification, (2) a physical connector. This term always is used in conjunction with the gender (M or F) of a connector. It will almost always require further clarification.

Slot: Always denotes the physical connector on the motherboard

Bus: Refers to the physical signal specification as well as the protocols (rules) for an orderly exchange of data. The bus can be implemented using a variety of slots, ports, and connectors.

With USB, the bus is intended to define all of the above. For other buses and ports, however, the definition is not so complete. Hence the next sections establish various definitions and provide more details on each.

A **port** is a connection point on a computer, peripheral, or cable end. There are many types of ports. The reader will hear references to RS-232 ports, SCSI ports, USB ports, etc. The term can apply to either a type or a physical size port—usually the former. For example, "RS-232" refers to the port's type, not its size, even though the EIA–232 standard originally called for a 25-pin connector. In today's environment, an RS-232 port can be implemented using a DB-25 25-pin, DB-9 9-pin, RJ-45 plugs, RJ-11 plug, or mini-DIN connectors. The fact that it is an RS-232 port highlight that it conforms to the electrical signal standard outlined by EIA-232 from the

Electronics Industries Association. Refer to Seyer's *RS-232 Made Easy* for total details about the interface, as well as a cable guide for designing cables using the various port sizes. On the Internet at, www.rs232.com you will find a complete online cable-design tool.

The terms *interface* and *connector* are often used with regard to ports. A reference to an interface should generally indicate the specification of a particular port, confirming that the port conforms to a defined specification for such a port. A reference to a SCSI-II interface, for example, should imply conformance to the then-current standard for SCSI-II. However, the reference might apply to the physical port. In most cases an interface refers to the pin definitions on a port, the signal statistics. Foregoing any the connector references, SCSI ports that confirm to the particular standard, such as SCSI-II, should work together from a signal and timing perspective. However, the ports aren't always physically the same. A SCSI interface can be implemented using multiple types of ports, as is true for RS-232, etc. This is the source for some confusion around connectors.

The gender issue further complicates connectors. Some vendors use opposite genders for ports, causing cabling issues. When they provide a particular port, such as RS-232, SCSI, or mini-DIN, they don't always highlight the gender or conform to the standard recommendation. So a device may have a port of either male or female gender. Cables that connect such ports usually have a connector at each end (though not always). A male port requires a female connector at the cable end, and vice versa. The gender match-up adds complexity for the uninformed.

The exception to having connectors at each end occurs when a cable is hardwired at one end to the motherboard. This can cause confusion when connecting to another device. The user may, or may not, need another cable to connect the device to the computer.

Local Buses

What is a local bus? It is a bus that is local relative to the CPU, hence the name. Unlike USB, however, it is not used to drive the relatively slower devices such as a mouse, keyboard, or speakers.

Computers have had buses in them forever, but recently there has been movement toward industry-standard buses, away from the proprietary buses that existed in computers prior to the advent of the PC. In the early days of the AppleII computer, the bus was Apple designed, driven by Apple, and maintained by Apple. With IBM's introduction of a PC, using the XT and AT buses, the move was begun toward open buses. Refer to the appendix for more information about these buses. VME and other buses were introduced with a similar aim of providing an industry-standard bus, allowing devices to communicate. The buses mentioned here tended to focus on relatively slower-speed devices, such as modems, video (early days), networking cards (early days), and expansion cards. The speed requirements of such devices were not that demanding. The situation is dramatically different today. The advent of Windows sparked the need for greater video performance, which remains pressing today. Higher-speed networking is placing greater demands on servers for network I/O. Disk drive demands extremely high performance.

Further demands have arisen with the constraint of space. The typical computer has gone way beyond the basic CPU, memory, and disk. It now includes a mouse, a keyboard (or two), speakers, scanner, printer, modem, and even home devices such as TVs. Users want smaller-footprint computers but expect all of these additional features. Consequently, even lower-speed buses are called for to replace a multitude of ports on computers. USB is set to fill that requirement. However, we need to highlight the other buses in a computer before explaining the USB architecture.

In the early 1990s PCs began to incorporate what is called a *local-bus I/O*. Actually, there were at least three different types of buses—*i486 local bus*, *VL-bus*, and *PCI Bus*. The VL-bus is an extension to the 486 bus and has been used mainly for video. The 486 has been replaced by the Pentium line of processor subsystems from Intel. Furthermore, the PCI Bus has taken over as the dominant high-performance local bus due to its openness, performance, and support within the industry. Even though all these different buses have some similarities, each is distinguished by technical differences, as summarized below. The position of the local buses on a typical PC is illustrated in Figure 2–1.

PC Board

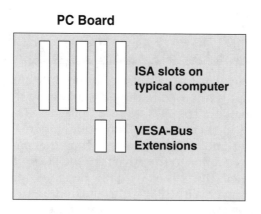

ISA slots on typical computer

VESA-Bus Extensions

Figure 2–1   Typical Bus Arrangement on Motherboard

▌ Why Local Buses?

The motivation behind these buses is higher I/O performance, which is demanded by the ever evolving PC operating systems, applications, and user interfaces such as Windows. Before the advent of some of these new local buses, the I/O performance of systems was based on older technology, originally introduced in the original IBM PC/AT.

Because the rest of the PC system had improved substantially, I/O performance needed a jolt and improvement. For example, looking at Intel's performance improvements alone, processor performance has improved by many multiples (6-MHz 286 versus 300-MHz Pentium processors); typical memory size has increased (256 KB versus 32 MB), typical disk size has increased (20 MB versus 2 GB); typical display resolution sizes have increased ($320 \times 200 \times 4$ bits versus $1024 \times 768 \times 8$ bits and larger), and so on.

ISA/EISA/Microchannel Architecture

To address this requirement, the industry launched multiple efforts to improve buses. The original bus in the IBM PC/AT became the ISA bus (Industry Standard Architecture). IBM and Compaq also pushed other buses. IBM introduced a totally new bus in 1987—the Microchannel (MCA). Due to incompatibility with the then-prevalent ISA bus, Microchannel achieved limited acceptance and has given way to PCI. Largely driven by Compaq in 1988, PC system vendors developed an extension to the ISA bus called the *EISA bus,* for *Extended ISA.* EISA-based systems began to appear in mid–1989. Use of EISA tended to be limited to servers and high-end desktops. Despite these efforts, ISA remained the dominant I/O bus in PCs. ISA and EISA I/O performance simply could not keep up with the performance demands of PC evolution. For example, VGA display subsystems were inadequate for the extensive use of the Windows graphical user interfaces (GUIs). Overall system performance tended to be limited by none other than the video performance, which was limited by the I/O bus used by VGA. Servers with disk-array subsystems and multiple network connections were limited by the then-current I/O bus bandwidth.

▌ VL-Bus (VESA Local Bus)

Approaches to improving performance included narrowing in on particular technology areas such as video performance. The VESA organization

(Video Electronics Standards Association) suggested an extension to the i486 bus to address video performance. The extension consists of using a standard connector on the i486 processor bus. VGA chips were typically mounted on removable cards and attached directly on the 486 local bus. This setup became known as the VL-bus, for Vesa local bus. The connector for the VL-bus is placed directly in line with the normal ISA connector, allowing a single slot to be shared by either an ISA card or a VESA card.

∎ PCI Bus (Peripheral Component Interconnect Bus)

The PCI Bus emerged as the answer to the performance bottleneck. The PCI bus is being used to address all of the aforementioned problems— video, disk (SCSI and IDE), network, etc. However, it is a high-performance bus that is used for peripherals requiring CPU-like performance. PCI is not targeted toward solving the needs of relatively slower devices like a mouse, keyboard, speakers, etc. This is where USB fits.

The typical computer system consisted of a processor chip with an optional high-performance cache memory. This bus consisted of 32 address signals, 32 data signals, and associated control signals. It had a 66- or 100-MHz clock rate and could transfer 32 bits of data every clock cycle. A bridge chipset allowed the connection of the system I/O bus, typically ISA. Data was transferred on the ISA bus in 8- or 16-bit increments. EISA supported 8, 16, or 32 bits. Depending on the bus cycle rate, typically 8-MHz, the maximum rate on ISA was 8 MBps, while EISA was 33 MBps. These buses were simply not designed to assume the performance responsibility placed on them by the increased video, disk, memory, and network capabilities.

The PCI local bus with great performance capabilities met these demands. The benefits included high-performance I/O, standardization due to wide industry support, and low cost based on volume. The PCI Bus is a high-performance I/O bus using a PCI chipset to connect the PCI Bus to the local CPU bus. In this architecture, the system bus gets the performance benefit of the CPU bus. The PCI Bus is now a well-defined open standard. There are a massive number of PCI-based systems, PCI cards, and chipsets. Today you can find PCI video cards, networking cards, SCSI and IDE controller cards and chips, and others. Furthermore, PCI is processor independent and is used on a number of different CPU-based systems, such as Intel, DEC Alpha, etc. Most systems shipped today include a PCI bus with slots, or at least PCI-based peripherals.

With USB you can easily attach peripherals to a PC without having to re-boot the system or deal with complicated IRQ settings and addresses, similar to plug-and-play technologies. This book gives the in-depth details about USB.

What Is a Serial Bus?

A serial bus is a little bit different from the traditional serial port that you might be used to thinking about. The single biggest difference between a single-ended serial port (like RS-232) and a serial bus like the USB is that

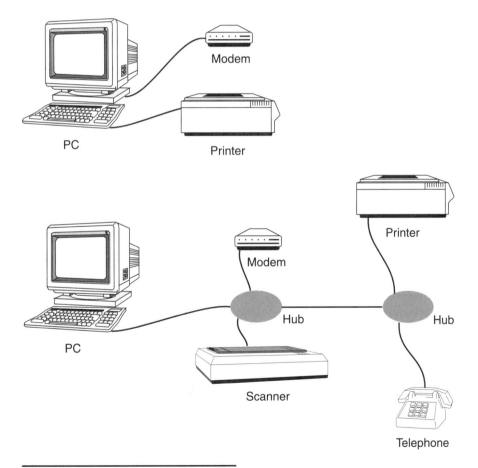

Figure 2–2 Drive Options with USB

the traditional serial port is a point-to-point connection between a computer and a device, whereas on a serial bus many devices can communicate and share the connection to the computer all at the same time. In the USB, up to 128 bus devices can simultaneously communicate with the host computer. This is illustrated in Figure 2–2.

Each device talks to other devices, or the host computer, through well-defined bus protocols. Each device on the Universal Serial Bus is individually addressable, and this is all controlled with software. In these respects, a serial bus is different from point-to-point serial ports.

What Are the Pieces of a USB?

As a bus technology, many different components must work together to allow multiple devices to share one connector on the computer. These components can be broadly separated into hubs (the connection between all of the components on the bus), USB devices, and the USB host. All of these will be described in more detail in subsequent sections of this book. Here we give you a good overview of the components and protocols.

USB devices allow a single port of entry into the host computer by attaching to **hubs**. These are like the hubs used in computer networking—they allow multiple devices to connect together, and they provide a single output to the host computer. Hubs are simply intelligent wiring concentrators, borrowing multiple access points into a single USB port on the host computer. The host computer may also include an integrated hub, providing multiple USB ports into the host computer itself. Typical PCs that are equipped with USB have 2 USB ports. This is typical when the computer is expected to have an integrated USB keyboard/mouse. The integrated keyboard/mouse combination would use one of the physical ports, and other USB devices would come into the system on the second port. Hubs connect to the USB host in the **upstream** direction, since data flows from the hub to the computer "up" the wire. Devices attach **downstream** of the hub, since the devices attach "down" the bus from the computer. Figure 2–3 shows a typical USB configuration using hubs.

A device on the Universal Serial Bus is defined as a physical entity attached to the USB. Devices include all USB components, including hubs, the host computer, and the actual USB peripherals. Each device contains some amount of logic on it, allowing it to be configured over the bus. A USB device may need power, or it may be bus powered, in which case the device takes the electrical power directly from the bus. Device implementers are allowed a tremendous amount of leeway in implementing their devices, provided they meet a minimum of functionality.

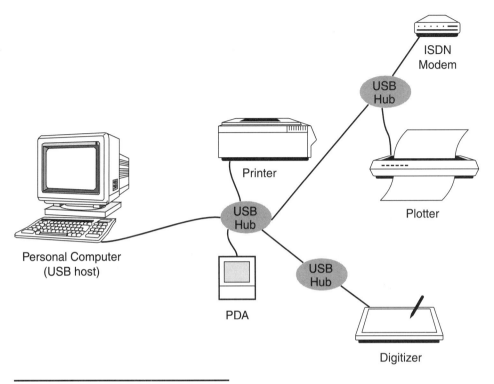

Figure 2–3   Typical USB Configuration

A device provides one or more **USB functions**. Most USB devices provide only one function, though a device may also be a **compound device.** Compound devices integrate multiple USB functions into a single package. USB devices may also be compound devices, integrating multiple USB functions into a single package. For example, a USB keyboard may contain a hub which a mouse might attach to, or a USB video device might provide functions for both capturing and playing back video; each of these is a compound device.

A device on the Universal Serial Bus never needs jumpers or dip switches or other relics from the "dark ages" of computing (of just a few short years ago!). The USB software configures each device when it is connected to the bus, much in the same way as PCI devices are automatically configured by software. It is truly plug-n-play.

The **USB Host** provides the central connection point between the Universal Serial Bus and the devices on the bus. The host functionality may be integrated onto the computer's motherboard, or it may be provided as an

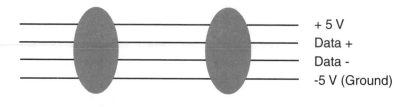

+ 5 V
Data +
Data -
-5 V (Ground)

Figure 2–4   Basic Cable Layout

add-in card. The USB host includes what is known as the **root hub**—that is, the central hub connecting the USB functionality within the computer to the external devices. The root hub may contain one or more physical USB ports. Coupled with the USB host device is some degree of software support. While the host software support on different operating systems may share common functionality, it is possibly quite different in the actual implementation.

Connecting the host computer, the hubs, and the devices together is the **bus interconnect**. This encompasses the physical medium, cables, the bus topology, and the protocol layers of the Universal Serial Bus. The physical medium is a 4-wired cable: there are 2 wires providing voltage to power bus-powered devices, and 2 wires for transmitting and receiving data. The cable is diagrammed in Figure 2–4.

The physical-bus topology is a tiered-star topology with the host computer at the top of the tier and a hub device at the center of each star. This is demonstrated back in Figure 2–3. The logical bus topology provides that the host has a direct path to each USB device; this is also demonstrated in Figure 2–3. The USB protocols govern how all of the devices peacefully coexist on the bus and are described in detail in Chapter 7.

The USB Protocols

Simplicity is the goal of the Universal Serial Bus. It is easy to plug components together. Figure 2–3 illustrates a typical USB configuration.

The devices all communicate over the bus via **packets**. A packet is nothing more than a small grouping of information. A group of packets that performs some useful function is called a **bus transaction**. The host always initiates transactions, and only a device that is selected by the host to communicate on the bus may do so. A device is given permission to talk on the bus when it receives a **token.** A token is a special packet that allows the holder to control the bus for as long as that device holds the token.

Transactions on the bus are governed by bus **protocol**. A protocol is simply the order in which packets on the bus appear to satisfy a given transaction. Each transaction involves the exchange of up to 3 packets. A transaction begins when the USB host issues a token packet to the device. The token packet contains all the information needed to select a function on a device.

If the host (through the token) is asking a device for data, then that device responds with either a data packet or a packet indicating that it does have data to send. If the device does not have any data to send, the host then issues the token to the next device. If the token is telling the device to expect data, then a packet of data follows it, from the host to the device. After a data packet is sent, the device that received the data generally responds with a handshake packet indicating the success or failure of the transaction. Once the data has been successfully transferred from the device to the host, the host issues a token to the next device to see if it has any data to send. This procedure is referred to as **polling**.

A typical sequence in a transaction is illustrated in Figure 2–5.

How Much Data Can the USB Handle?

The Universal Serial Bus was designed with multimedia and telephony applications in mind. It was also designed to provide for the efficient operation of lower-speed devices such as a mouse, keyboard, or joystick. This means that the USB must manage the bandwidth requirements of both low- and medium-speed devices. The USB manages the allocation of its available bandwidth on the bus in a couple of different ways.

Two different device speeds are supported on the Universal Serial Bus: 12 Mbps (million bits per second) and 1.5 Mbps. These different speeds are called **signaling modes**. The slower-speed devices can be constructed more easily and cheaply, since they depend less on electrical-noise shielding. Basically stated, the lower the speed supported on an electrical wire, the less expensive it will be.

The low-speed signaling mode keeps the bus free for the high-speed mode, since token packets are sent to these devices less often (one-tenth as often, by definition). It is important to note that both low-speed and high-speed devices can coexist in a given system. The USB hub will detect which signaling mode the device uses at device-attachment time and will notify the USB host appropriately. A low-speed device will never operate at high speed, just as a high-speed device usually can never operate in a low-speed mode.

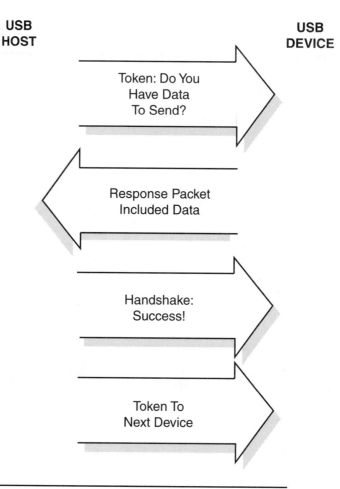

Figure 2–5   Typical USB Bus Transaction

Since the Universal Serial Bus must guarantee bandwidth to some devices and not to others, there must be some concept of bandwidth allocation. These are the **isochronous** and **asynchronous** methods of bandwidth allocation. This probably sounds much more complicated than it actually is. Isochronous means simply that a portion of the bandwidth is *reserved* for devices requesting it (if the bandwidth is available). Asynchronous, on the other hand, means that data is sent whenever it can be sent. Isochronous is used for **streaming** devices, such as video and audio multimedia devices. This is useful in cases such as streaming video which may

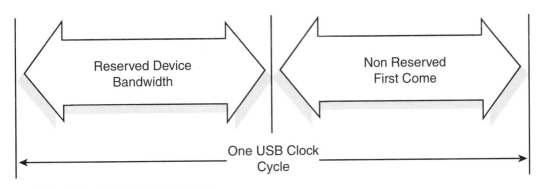

Figure 2–6   Bandwidth Allocation

use, for example, 2 MBps of bandwidth on the Universal Serial Bus. The streaming video device would reserve this bandwidth as isochronous bandwidth, guaranteeing that the bandwidth is always there. A typical bandwidth-allocated data stream is shown in Figure 2–6.

It is important to know that on an isochronous data stream, the system pays less attention to whether or not the data arrived on time. This is due to the fact that *most* isochronous traffic is digitized analog data, either audio or video, and this type of traffic has a great degree of tolerance for error. For example, if your home audio compact disk player dropped a bit or two, your ear would never notice the difference. This makes for a much more efficient implementation of the bus protocols.

What Are Pipes and Endpoints?

When you are dealing with the USB, you will hear time and again about pipes and endpoints. These are the basic communication primitives between the USB host and the various devices. Every concept in the world of the Universal Serial Bus eventually comes to pipes and endpoints.

An **endpoint** is simply a logical transmission path between the USB host and some function within the USB device. Each USB device has a certain number of distinct and unique endpoints that it supports. Endpoints exist to send data in one direction only, so two endpoints are required to do bidirectional data transfers between the USB host and a USB device. Endpoints are not very useful by themselves. They are used as building blocks for more advanced communication paths such as pipes.

A virtual connection between a software function that exists on the USB host and a given endpoint on a device is called a **pipe**. There are two types of pipes in the USB universe: **stream pipes** and **message pipes**. Stream pipes have no defined structure imposed on the underlying packets that flow across them. Message pipes, on the other hand, do have an imposed structure. Pipes also have associated with them bandwidth needs, transfer-service types, and endpoint characteristics (e.g., direction, buffer size).

Pipes are created by software living on the USB host when a device is attached to the system. There is one pipe, control pipe 0 (zero), that must exist for each device in the system. It is the job of the USB host to configure each device. It is also the responsibility of the device to provide access to device-configuration, status, and control information across control pipe 0. This matter will be discussed in detail throughout this book.

How Does Software Fit In?

The software that controls the Universal Serial Bus will be different on the various operating systems that must support the USB. Each will be structured similarly, however, and provide the same basic functionality. The operating system on the USB host computer will provide *device drivers* to control the physical aspects of the Universal Serial Bus. Communicating with the device drivers will be *client software*. The client software runs on the host computer, and it communicates with the USB devices through the underlying layers of the USB software stack. Client software will be provided to control each different type of device.

The device driver for the Universal Serial Bus directly controls the USB hardware within the host computer. It manages such things as processing errors, translating requests between the client software and devices into the proper bus transactions, moving data to and from devices and client software, and managing all of the bandwidth and plug-and-play aspects of the Universal Serial Bus. In short, it manages the Universal Serial Bus.

The client software, on the other hand, is concerned only with communicating and controlling the *logical* USB devices or functions. It communicates with the USB device driver via some set of defined application program interfaces (APIs) provided by the operating-system vendor. The actual API is operating-system dependent and will not be discussed further here. More information about the APIs can be found in your operating-system vendor's documentation.

How Do the Pieces Fit Together?

A complete picture of the software and communication flow between devices and the USB host is given by Figure 2–7.

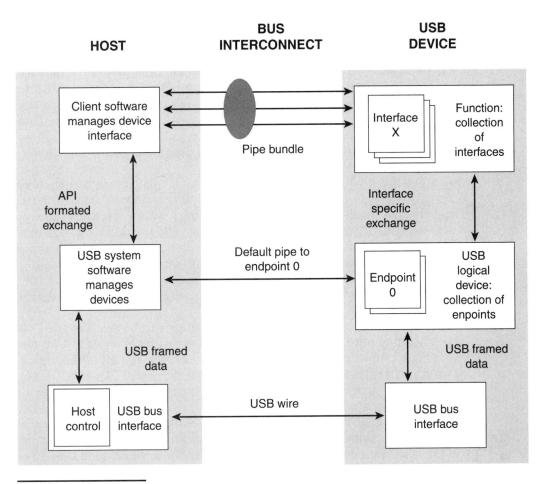

Figure 2–7   USB Flow

The first thing you might notice in this diagram is that most of the elements in it haven't been discussed in this book, or have only been mentioned briefly. Don't panic! Everything will be talked about in its logical place in due course. The important thing is to get a feel for how the parts of the USB flow together, and to start to understand on some level both the complexity and the simplicity in the design.

The next thing you might notice is that there are a lot of arrows between the USB host computer and the actual device. The "USB wire" is the physical connection—everything else is "logical." Having a logical pathway between the host computer and the device simply means that the different layers talk to each other, not to the other layers. Not directly, anyway.

For example, even though the USB system software layer on the host talks directly to the USB *logical* device layer in the physical device, the data still must be transmitted over the USB wire. Having a logical connection means that the *USB bus interface* (in this example) only moves the data for that endpoint zero; it makes no attempt to interpret it. That's left up to the logical layers that are communicating. It is easier to think in terms of logical communication paths than of the convoluted paths that the data sometimes really does take. Such thinking keeps things simple and allows us to take a "building-block" approach to understanding how the Universal Serial Bus really works.

Another thing you will undoubtedly notice in this picture is that there is no provision for talking to a hub. There are two reasons for this. First, a hub is just another device—the USB model works for every device, whether a hub or a joystick. Second, when the system talks to a device that is attached to a hub (and all devices are by definition attached to some hub), the hub is "invisible" in the sense that data passes right through it without the software having to do anything special. How the hub actually passes the data through is the subject of another chapter, which delves into the inner workings of the USB hub.

So, what is really shown in this picture? There are three layers to the USB host, and they tend to correspond to three equal layers on each USB device. Plug a USB wire between a USB host and device, and all of the logical connections that are demonstrated in Figure 2–7 occur. They occur for each and every device simultaneously; it's just that the devices don't really know about each other—the USB system software layer in the host takes care of hiding that fact. Client software is provided to actually make each USB device do something useful; leave it out and the device can live on the bus and the device can talk to the host, but it won't really do anything.

Next, let's take a look at what the actual hardware connections will look like. This becomes harder, as there are as many different pieces of hardware as there are peripherals manufacturers. The one thing they all have in common is the USB connector. If things are connected correctly in a USB system, then the odds are excellent that everything will work (at least from a hardware perspective—software is a whole different story!).

The Universal Serial Bus was designed to minimize errors when connecting devices together. In the last section we talked about *upstream* and *downstream* data directions. These aren't just for the diagrams; there are *upstream* and *downstream* connectors on each USB cable. The connector for the upstream direction will *only* connect into an attached hub (or the *root hub* on the USB host). The downstream connector will only plug into a device. This is readily apparent when you look at the actual plugs, as illustrated in Figure 2–8.

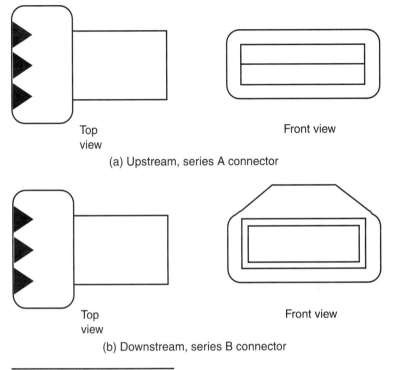

Top view   Front view

(a) Upstream, series A connector

Top view   Front view

(b) Downstream, series B connector

Figure 2–8   USB Connectors

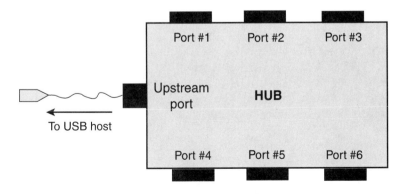

Figure 2–9   A USB Hub

Devices may have cables "hardwired" into them, as in a normal mouse today. In the case of devices that have permanently attached cables, there will be no downstream connector. It should be noted that the USB specification refers to downstream connectors as **Series A connectors** and to upstream connectors as **Series B connectors**.

When connecting hubs, the downstream side is the hub itself and the upstream side is the host computer, or a device port on the hub. A hub is diagrammed in Figure 2–9.

It really is as simple as it sounds: plug in the plugs where they fit. If a device isn't bus powered, then plug that device into the wall (or put in the batteries, or whatever the device actually needs for power). Load the client software for the device onto your computer, and you are ready to use the device. You don't even have to turn off your computer. There are no jumpers, no dip switches, and no reasons at all to break out a screw-driver.

Wrapping It Up

This chapter has demonstrated the basic principles behind the Universal Serial Bus. You have seen the basic pieces of the puzzle and encountered some of the basic terminology you will need to know when talking about the USB. You should be beginning to understand how the Universal Serial Bus works and that this bus, for the most part, runs itself. If not, keep reading, because you soon will.

In the chapters that follow, we will delve into the inner workings of each piece of the Universal Serial Bus, all in a great deal of detail. The next chapter will show us what happens inside the USB host.

USB Inside Your Computer

What Does a USB Host Do?

In a system built with the Universal Serial Bus, the host computer is the single most important element present—it acts as the hardware liaison between each of the separate components of the USB. It is the responsibility of the host to maintain the state of bus and all peripherals attached to it. In short, the host manages the whole thing. There is only one host in each system.

Within the host computer, there are a number of components (as is illustrated in Figure 3–1). The piece of hardware within the host computer that manages the physical part of the Universal Serial Bus is called the **host controller**. There is software on the USB host that is written to talk to the host controller, which in turn communicates with each of the attached USB devices (whether they are peripherals or hub devices). The Universal Serial Bus, from the host's perspective, is shown in Figure 3–1.

Each Universal Serial Bus system contains only one host; there are no provisions for host-to-host communication between machines in either the current specifications or implementations. There is talk within the USB standardization bodies and various USB implementers, however, of adding this support in future versions of the USB specification. Until that happens, this single-host limitation applies.

As we've already hinted, in a USB system the host manages data transfers between the client software and all the different and various USB devices that may be attached to the system. The USB host controller within the host computer performs a translation between the client's (client software running on the host computer) view of data transfers and the actual USB transactions appearing on the physical bus. The USB host controller is also

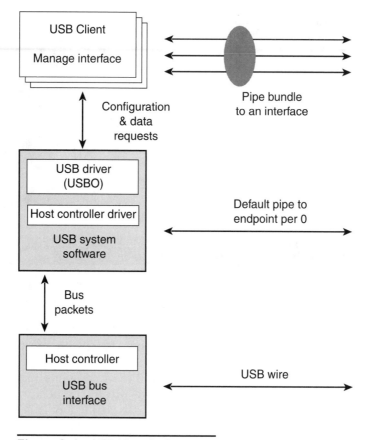

Figure 3–1 USB Host Architecture

the component that manages the various physical USB resources (such as bandwidth). We'll talk about the details as the chapter progresses.

The host system is divided into three major layers:

- The USB hardware interface
- The USB system software (device drivers)
- The USB client software (peripheral-device drivers and application programs)

The **USB host controller**, which is simply the physical-bus interface within the host computer, handles all the interactions between the host computer and the electrical and protocol layers of the Universal Serial Bus.

The bus interface contains the same connection types as a USB hub. In fact, the host's USB bus interface contains what is termed the **root hub**. This root hub provides attachment points to the host.

The system software on a Universal Serial Bus host system is divided into several different underlying pieces, and we'll talk about each of these pieces in the coming sections. What you should understand now is that the primary responsibility of the USB system software is to provide a layer of abstraction above the actual implementation of the Universal Serial Bus. This layer of abstraction provides a consistent interface to the underlying hardware and buses without the client software having to be aware of the actual implementation details. In this regard, the system software is much like a normal device driver (or set of application programming interfaces) that may be provided by an operating-system vendor.

The client software, on the other hand, lives just above the device drivers and other system software. The only thing that the client software should be concerned with is that the USB device it is managing is working correctly. The client software should let the system software and bus interface hide the details of the bus protocols, configuration, and arbitration issues (all things we'll cover a little later in this book). A properly implemented USB host system will make it a very easy job for people to develop client software that works well and easily with USB devices. That's the goal, anyway. You should understand early on that the client software we're talking about may be either a device driver or a simple user application running on host computer. The important thing, again, is that this piece of the puzzle is concerned only with the actual device, not the bus.

The host layers provide the following overall capabilities:

- The host detects when devices are attached and detached.
- The host manages data-flow control on communication between the host and the USB devices.
- The host manages data flow between the host and USB devices, collecting status and activity statistics.
- The host controls the electrical interfaces between the host controller and USB devices, including the provision of a limited amount of power.

The Host Software

The software in the host controller is itself divided into three logical components (see Figure 3–2). These are:

- The host controller driver
- The USB device driver
- The host application software

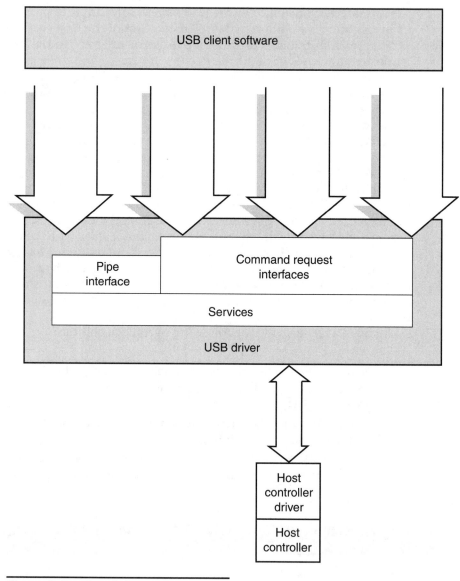

Figure 3–2   Host Software Organization

We will call the various pieces of the software inside the USB host (taken as a whole) the *software stack*. The modules in the software stack are may be physically distinct from one another, but they are logically connected and communicate with one another. This is shown in Figure 3–2.

If you are at all familiar with the device-driver architecture of Windows NT, then you will no doubt notice the obvious similarities between the software layers we talk about in the following sections and the overall NT driver architecture. This is no accident, as most of the members of the USB standardization group are PC hardware and peripherals manufacturers. The USB specification documents even talk in terms of "IRPs" and other such "NT-isms"—terminology that we'll spare you here. This isn't to say that computers outside the Windows NT universe won't embrace the USB standard, just that it was invented in the Windows world. Indeed, work is underway at Sun and other UNIX vendors to put the Universal Serial Bus on non-Windows platforms.

▌ Host Controller Driver

The function of the **host controller driver** (or **HCD** in USB parlance) is to map the various possible host controller implementations into a USB host system. This allows the client software to work with the USB device for which it's responsible without having to worry about the underlying hardware. With this model, both the USB driver and the client software can be written to work with an HCD-provided interface without having to deal with the actual hardware that the system builders put into the computer. This serves, in effect, to provide a hardware-independent abstraction layer.

▌ Universal Serial Bus Driver

The **USB Driver** (or **USBD** in USB terminology) provides an interface to the host controller driver to provide a basic and *generic* interface to the host controller driver (HCD). This interface is known as the USBD Interface, or **USBDI**. While they may seem overwhelming at first, these acronyms are important, because all you will see if you read documentation or specifications from the USB standardization organizations or hardware vendors are these acronyms. Just to keep you used to them, this book will use them a lot. This book will also define them many times over.

There is also a defined interface between the host controller driver and the Universal Serial Bus driver. This interface is known as the **host controller driver interface**, or **HCDI** in USB-speak. Since the interface between these components is not used by any client software, and is operating-system and HCD dependent, it is not provided as a part of the Universal Serial Bus specification. An operating system (such as Windows 98 or Windows NT) may provide a single HCDI that supports various host controller implementations. In this way, the hardware is hidden under a single OS-dependent layer, allowing a single USBD on all hardware platforms supported by that operating system.

The USBD, like all device drivers, is nothing more than a collection of software routines used to manage communication with underlying hardware—in this case Universal Serial Bus devices. There is no other direct access within a USB system to the underlying hardware than through the USBD. An operating system may provide "pass-through" commands that allow a programmer or application to directly manipulate a device (this is done often in the SCSI world), but even these pass-through commands go through interfaces provided by the USBD.

A single, operating-system dependent, Universal Serial Bus driver communicates, arbitrates, and manages communication with USB devices on behalf of the client software (which may include USB peripheral device drivers for specific peripherals). Just one USBD exists to control all of the host controller hardware that may be present in a given system. As far as the client software is concerned, the USBD with which it communicates manages all of the attached devices as well.

The USBD communicates with attached USB devices and hubs through transport requests. These requests flow across mechanisms known as *pipes*. We talked about pipes a little bit in the last chapter. As a quick reminder, pipes are nothing more than *virtual connections* across *virtual pathways* called *endpoints*. These are USB abstractions and should be considered only in that context. These pipes certainly shouldn't be confused with interprocess communication mechanisms (IPC) also called "pipes" that are provided by most modern operating systems.

Aside from providing a method for client software to transfer data to the USB devices, the USBD provides two groups of software mechanisms to clients: command mechanisms and pipe mechanisms. The command mechanisms provide the client software a pathway to configure and control general USB operation. The command mechanisms also allow the software a means to configure and generically control a USB device. In order to provide these services to the client software, the USBD owns what is known as the **default pipe**.

While the USBD uses pipe mechanisms to manage device-specific control and data transfers, client software is not allowed to communicate directly across a pipe. It is the absolute responsibility of the USBD to communicate over pipes and to translate requests and commands from the clients to the devices in order to send them over pipes.

This is a lot of information to digest about the USBD, but the important thing to remember is that the USBD is software that lives between the client software and the underlying hardware. A client cannot directly access the peripheral hardware or even the host's USB controller hardware.

Initialization

Let's spend a little time understanding what happens at system initialization time. Before we can do that we need to be consistent on what initialization is. **System initialization** happens when the computer system that is the USB host system is first powered on. **Device initialization**, on the other hand, occurs when a USB device is plugged into a Universal Serial Bus hub. It's important to remember that the USB is "hot pluggable." This means that devices can be added and taken off at the whim of the user, without powering the device or system down.

The steps that are taken to initialize the USB software stack during the initialization phase are completely operating-system dependent. There are as many different ways to initialize the host drivers and client software as there are software implementations. We'll leave this topic alone in this book.

We do know what happens in the overall *state* of the Universal Serial Bus system as a whole, and within the various pieces of the system. On the host system, this means that certain management information is accumulated and collected when each Universal Serial Bus managed by that host is initialized (remember that there can be multiple Buses attached to a given host). A part of this management information provides for the **default device address** and its **default pipe** (which we have already talked about in the preceding sections).

To elaborate a bit further on this: when a device is first attached to the bus, it doesn't yet know its device address—it is up to the host to give it one. Until this happens, the device responds to a special address known as the default address. In order for the host to communicate with the newly attached device, both the device's default address and the default pipe must be available at the time that a device is attached to the bus. The host software creates the default device address and its default pipe whenever a USB is initialized.

Pipe Usage

A pipe is an association between the endpoint on a device and the USB host software. It's a virtual connection of sorts. A pipe is also the perfect picture to have in your mind as you try to fathom the "plumbing" of a Universal Serial Bus system.

Each device has a unique set of pipes; they are not shared among devices. The endpoints that the pipes are constructed of are also unique to each device. Although the basic concept of a pipe is pretty much the same regardless of the device or the host software to which it is "connected," some specific capabilities do exist between two broad groupings of pipes:

■ Default pipes, which are owned and managed only by the USBD.
■ All other pipes, which are owned and managed by client software.

The default pipe for a device is never used directly by the client software. This does not mean, however, that the default pipe is not used by the USBD to satisfy some request on behalf of the client (the client issues requests to the USBD to achieve some device communication). The important thing to keep in mind here is that only the USBD driver uses default pipes, whether or not they're used because of some request that a client might have made.

Buffers are required in order to move data around within the host system. Buffers, in this context, are nothing more than storage locations within the host system that are managed by the software. When one software component, such as a USB client, wants to issue a request or ask for data from a USB device, it allocates a buffer and passes it to the USBD. The USBD passes the buffer, along with the request of the USB peripheral, to the host controller driver (the HCD). The HCD handles the communication with the device and returns data in the buffer. The buffer is then passed back up through the USB software stack until it reaches the client. Confusing as all this may sound when it you read it, the concepts of buffering are simple, as illustrated in Figure 3–3.

The USBD owns the responsibility of managing the buffers used to support transfers on the default pipe when, *and only when*, the client is not involved in the exchange of information with the device. An example of this occurs when the host needs to set the device address. If the client is involved in the transaction, such as when the host reads a device descriptor or asks for the device's vendor ID, then the client must provide any required buffering.

If the USB driver does not own a pipe, then it can be owned by one or more client pieces. From the perspective of the USBD, a single client process owns the pipe. It would be completely acceptable for a group of clients to pool their resources to manage a single USB device. Such cooperating client processes must behave at all times as a single entity. In actual practice you will rarely, if ever, see multiple clients coordinating the usage of a single pipe.

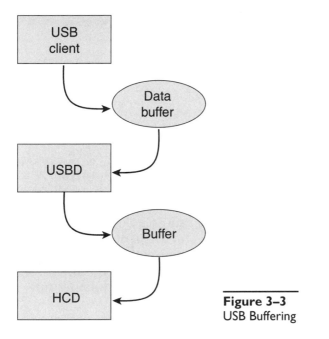

Figure 3–3
USB Buffering

One of the more important things to keep in mind when thinking about buffering is that USB devices can communicate at either low or full speeds. The buffers that hold the information used in bus transactions between the host and an attached device are used more frequently for a full-speed than for a low-speed device. This is only natural, considering that data is transferred much more quickly on a full-speed transfer. The client has to provide the appropriate amount of buffering to process the data-transfer speed of the pipe without losing pace with the device. The USB host software provides the client any additional buffering requirements for working space, or scratch space, that the client doesn't provide.

Talking to Devices

The USB host must provide a variety of services to both client software and the attached devices and hubs. These are broadly grouped as follows:

- Device and hub configuration (through command mechanisms)
- Basic data transfers (via both command and pipe mechanisms)

- Event notifications
- Status reporting and error recovery

These are basic USB services and, like all USB services, they're built around the ideas of pipes and endpoints.

Control and Command Mechanisms

Basic control transfers between the USB host and the USB devices are provided using something called a **command mechanism**. A command mechanism provides client software generic access to a USB device ("generic" meaning that the access is the same regardless of the type of attached device). A command mechanism is used to provide the client a means to read and write the control and data spaces within each attached USB device. To use a command mechanism, the client software simply tells the USBD which device to communicate with and, as we talked about in the preceding section, provides an empty buffer into which it puts the data.

An interesting aspect of the USBD command transfer is that a USB device does not have to be configured to use the mechanism. For example, many of the device-configuration operations used and provided by the USBD are command transfers.

Command mechanisms operate over pipes and, as with other types of pipes, the client can set the state of any given command pipe. These states are described in the next section.

Pipe States

A pipe can be in any number of valid configurations. These valid configurations are known as **Pipe States** (Figure 3–4). These states are **Active**, **Stalled**, and **Idle**. It's also important that you note that each pipe state has two components: a **host status** and a **reflected endpoint status**. Despite the complicated name, a reflected endpoint status is nothing more than the status *at* the USB device, while the host status is the status of the pipe at the host (of course!).

When a client asks for the status of a pipe, the host driver provides the statuses for both the host and reflected endpoints. The status of the pipe "reflected" from the device is the result of the pipe's endpoint at the device itself being in a particular state. The client software manages the pipe state on the host. If the client wishes to change the state of the reflected endpoint, it must directly interact with the USB device endpoint to change

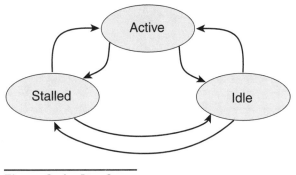

Figure 3–4   Pipe States

that state. If this all sounds convoluted and confusing, look at the simple example shown in the Figure 3–5. In this example, an endpoint is changed from the STALLED state to the IDLE state.

In the **active** state, the pipe's policy has been set up and data can be transmitted over the pipe; transactions can occur at this point. The client can also ask the USBD (the USB driver) whether or not there are any transactions waiting to be sent between the USB device and the USB host. Even if there are no outstanding transactions, the pipe is still considered active. In fact, as long as transactions are *possible,* the pipe remains active.

At the opposite extreme from the active state is the **stalled** state. A pipe is stalled if an error has occurred on it. A pipe is also stalled if there is an error on the USB device's endpoint. These are the only conditions for a stall.

A pipe is **idle** if it cannot accept further transfers. For a pipe to be truly idle, both the host and the USB device endpoint must agree that they are idle. An important point to consider when thinking about the idle pipe state is that nothing stands in the way of having that pipe transition back to the active state.

Except for error conditions, the state of a given pipe is controlled by the client software controlling the pipe. It's important to remember that the only USBD-controlled pipe, the default pipe, is always in the active state. All other pipe states are controlled by client software. The client can set a pipe to either *active* or *idle* from any of the states we've already discussed. The client can also set the endpoint on the USB device to either an active or idle state. Clients can also abort or reset a pipe.

When a pipe is **aborted**, all transactions that are waiting to occur are immediately taken off the list of things to do by the USBD and returned to the client. At this point, the client is told that the transactions have been

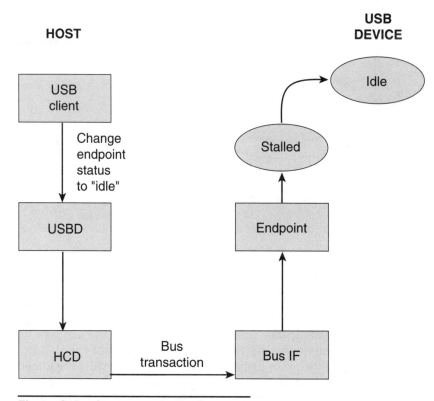

Figure 3–5   Changing Reflected Endpoints

aborted. Neither the host state nor the reflected endpoint state of the pipe is affected when this abort occurs.

In addition to aborting a pipe, the client can cause the pipe to **reset**. When a pipe is reset, all of the pending and active transactions are immediately aborted (just as occurs when an "abort" is requested) and returned to the client. The host state is also set to active. The reflected endpoint status is not changed, but nothing stands in the way of allowing the client software to change it.

The Host Controller

The **host controller** is a piece of hardware within a USB host system that has the great responsibility of ensuring that everything flowing across the Universal Serial Bus cable is correct and within specification. If the software within the host is incorrect, then the worst that can happen is that a device becomes confused. If the host controller, on the other hand, doesn't perform its actions correctly, then no device on the bus can be accessed.

Host controllers are independent of the attached devices and hubs. In every USB system, the host controller performs the exact same functional tasks. It serves both the USB host *and* the Universal Serial Bus itself. It brings the following functions to the system (all of which will be discussed further in this book):

- Handling all hardware and bus states
- Providing what is known as a *serializer/deserializer*
- Generating USB *frames* for transmitting data over the bus
- Processing the data sent across the bus
- Managing the physical-bus protocol
- Handling any transmission errors which may occur on the bus

Each of these host controller responsibilities is discussed in the following sections.

State Handling

As can well be imagined, a tremendous amount of information and states must be managed in a system as complex as the Universal Serial Bus. There are a large number of potential devices that can attached or removed at any given time. The devices can operate at one of two speeds. They may be bus powered or provide their own power source. It can get complicated fast. Fortunately, we have the host controller. It's the responsibility of the USB host controller to manage the state of the Universal Serial Bus.

We've talked quite a bit about state information in this chapter, and it could all become confusing. A simple thing to remember is that each layer of abstraction has state information that must be maintained to keep that layer functioning. For example, the USBD (the driver) maintains state information that is specific to the endpoints and pipes being used to talk to the devices. The host controller, on the other hand, is concerned only with what's happening on the wire at any given time; it does not understand such high-level concepts as pipes and endpoints. As such, it has only two primary things that it worries about: the **root hub** and **state-change propagation.**

If you recall from our discussions in the previous chapter, the *root hub* is a USB hub that is embedded within each USB host system (see Figure 3–6).

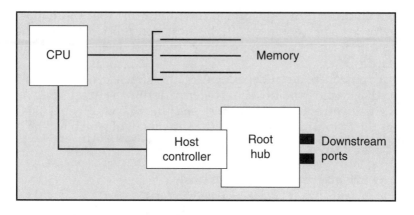

Figure 3–6   Root Hub's Place in a USB System

It is treated just like any other hub in the system, except that the host owns it. In fact, from a software perspective there is nothing special about the root hub. A full discussion of what hubs actually do is found in Chapter 4 of this book. What's important to remember about the root hub in this discussion is that the host controller is the one responsible for maintaining the root hub's state and state transitions.

The condition of the host controller at any given point in time is tied completely to that of the root hub. The condition of the root hub is intimately tied to that of the Universal Serial Bus. If there is a state change within the host controller, and that change is visible to devices attached on the bus, then those changes must be propagated to the attached devices (this is called, as you recall, *reflection*). The overriding goal is to maintain consistency between what the host controller thinks the system looks like and what the devices think the system looks like.

▍Serializer and Deserializer

Communication between devices and hubs on the Universal Serial Bus occur as a **serial bit stream**; i.e., bits flow down the wire one at a time (as opposed to a parallel bit stream, where many bits may flow simultaneously). Within the host controller lives a piece of hardware that turns the internal data flow into a serial bit stream. This is called the **serial interface engine** (or **SIE**). In addition to serializing the bit stream, the SIE must also "deserialize" the bit stream. What this means is that the incoming serial bit stream is converted into a data stream that the host computer

Figure 3–7 SIE in a USB System

can understand (usually a parallel data stream). This process is diagrammed in Figure 3–7.

▮ Frame Generation

Sending a serial bit stream down a wire, as the SIE does, is one thing. It is quite another thing for that data to be in a format that devices can recognize and synchronize to. This is where the concept of "frames" comes into play. It is the responsibility of the host controller to partition data flowing across the USB into small quantities called **frames**. Frames are defined as a specific bit pattern that occurs over a known time quantity—1 ms in the USB world. The layout of a frame is shown in Figure 3–8.

The host controller creates frames by first issuing a bit pattern called a **start of frame** (or **SOF**) at 1-ms intervals. This start-of-frame marker is called a *token*. The SOF delimits the frame and marks its starting point. A USB device knows that every 1 ms it should look for a valid SOF pattern on the wire. If it doesn't see one, then it waits another 1 ms until either it does see one, or it decides that there's an error on the wire.

The SOF token is just the first part of the USB frame. After issuing the SOF token, the host controller then places data and commands to actual

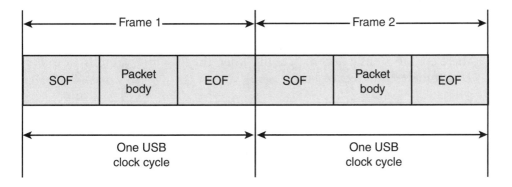

Figure 3–8 Inside a USB Frame

USB devices onto the bus. When the 1-ms time quantum has expired, it sends another SOF token and resumes the data transmissions. The only time that SOF tokens are not being sent down the wire is when the host controller is in a state where it is not providing power on the bus. There may be no power on the bus because the host has decided that, for some reason, it does not need to use the Universal Serial Bus. More likely, though, is that power-management functions on the host computer have put the computer into a "power-reduced" mode (this happens a lot on laptop computers).

The SOF token is the one thing on the bus that always holds priority. It is going to occur regardless of what else is occurring on the bus. In fact, there is an electrical circuit built into the hubs called "babble circuitry" that electrically isolates anything active on the bus between the end of a frame and the start of the next frame. This ensures an idle bus. We'll talk more about the babble circuitry in the next chapter.

After the SOF token, each frame has an associated **frame number**. This frame number is generated by the host, and each frame has a frame number that is one more than the one before it. In other words, the frame number is incremented after each frame is transmitted. The host controller is responsible for this. The frame number is encoded into the lower 11 bits of the SOF token in a given frame. This is illustrated in Figure 3–9.

This is a good time to define a couple of more terms. **Babble** is a phenomenon where a device speaks when it shouldn't be speaking. The "babble circuitry" discussed in the previous paragraph, then, simply squelches this unwanted transmission. Babble is usually caused when a device loses track of how much time it's spent on the bus ("lost the clock"), or is electrically unstable and is transmitting electrical noise down the wire (picture here static on your television set).

Another term is the **end-of-frame** interval (or **EOF**). This is the period of time between the last part of a frame transmission and the next SOF token. During the EOF interval, the host controller and all devices must cease transmission. When the EOF interval begins, any bus transactions that were scheduled for that frame are rescheduled for the next frame. If there is a bus transaction happening when the EOF interval rolls around, it is terminated and retried later.

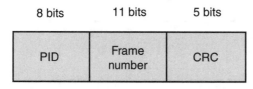

Figure 3–9   Layout of an SOF Token

▌ Data Processing

The host controller is responsible for a certain amount of **data processing**. What this means is simply that the host controller must receive data from the USB and put data onto the USB. The host controller must interpret that data only as much as necessary in order to know to whom to give the data. The particular format used for communication between the various devices on the Universal Serial Bus and the host controller is implementation specific, and we won't be discussing the host controller's role in that.

▌ Protocol Engine

We'll mention the **protocol engine** because it's a formal part of the host controller. It doesn't really do anything beyond what we have already discussed. It reads each frame and manages the SOF and EOF processing for the host. It inserts whichever appropriate frame-level protocol information is required for outgoing transmissions. It isolates and interprets incoming protocol information. Chapter 6 discusses all of the protocol issues in depth. We'll leave it alone as a topic until then.

▌ Resource Allocation

As you will recall from our overview discussion in Chapter 2, the Universal Serial Bus supports the concept of guaranteed bandwidth for devices that need it; this is called *isochronous* bandwidth. For nonisochronous data (or asynchronous data), the Universal Serial Bus has what are called *interrupt pipes*.

The decision of whether a particular transaction will fit into a given frame is left up to the host controller. This is provided by algorithms, called *heuristic algorithms*, built into the system to estimate the amount of time that a given transaction will take. If the actual transaction time in the host controller exceeds the estimated value, then the host controller must ensure that frame integrity is kept. If the transaction takes longer than a single frame would take, then the host controller will separate the transaction into multiple frames.

To determine if the bandwidth for a requested transaction can be allocated, or to see if the transaction can fit into a frame, the host controller must calculate the **maximum transaction execution time** (no acronym this time!). This calculation requires the host-system software to provide certain information. This information is:

- The number of data bytes to be sent to the device
- The type of transaction (e.g., data, control, etc)

- The depth in the topology (i.e., where's the packet going in the maze of devices?)

The calculation also uses items determined by the host controller. These variables are derived by the host controller. The variables used in the equation include things like the bit transmission time, the signal-propagation delay through the various layers of USB devices and hubs, as well as any implementation-specific delays such as preparation and recovery times required by the host controller.

Configuration and Plug-n-Play

An important concept in the Universal Serial Bus world is that of **plug-n-play**. That means just what you might think; devices should be able to be plugged in and immediately recognized without any help from the user. The proper client software should be automatically loaded by the operating system to communicate with the special feature on the device. The host software should give it a name, and the device should be configured to operate on the particular Universal Serial Bus. These things comprise plug-n-play, and this section will discuss the things that happen within the host environment to make it happen.

Getting the Current Configuration

Every device in a Universal Serial Bus system has a **configuration descriptor.** This configuration descriptor is built and maintained by the Universal Serial Bus driver and is accessed through the USBD interface (USBDI). If a device is not configured, then of course there is no configuration descriptor for the USBI to give to callers. If a device is configured—and it almost always is—a descriptor is returned to the caller. This descriptor contains the following basic information:

- The configuration information stored on each device (this includes any alternate settings for the interfaces)
- Which of the alternate settings, if any, are being actively used.
- Pipe handles for the endpoints associated with any alternate settings
- Actual maximum transfer sizes for any given endpoint on the device

In addition to this information, the configuration descriptor includes the maximum transmission size being used by the default pipe associated with that device. The maximum transmission size is the amount of data that a device can accept at once.

Configuration-management services are made available to client software as a set of commands. These commands, in turn, generate transactions on a device's default pipe. The only exception occurs when an additional interrupt pipe may deliver the status of a hub directly to the hub driver (which is just another client software piece in the USB software stack). When there is a change in the state of a hub port, the hub begins an interrupt transfer; this occurs most frequently when a device has been either plugged into or removed from a hub's port. Again, we'll discuss hubs more fully in the next chapter.

▌ Initial Device Configuration

A USB system cannot begin to configure a device until it knows that the device is present. The host is notified of a new device by the hub. It is the responsibility of the hub to ensure that this notification occurs. This happens as an interrupt transfer from the hub to the hub driver on the host. The hub driver on the host then notifies the USBD that there is a device that needs to be added to the list of available devices.

Each device on the Universal Serial Bus keeps a list of valid options and configurations that it will support. The configuration-management services accessible through the USBDI allow client software to initially set the device to one of its valid configurations. It is up to the USBD, however, to validate that the data-transfer rates given for all of the endpoints in the configuration do not exceed the capabilities of the USB with the current workload. It must also queue any pending transactions before allowing the new configuration to be set. If the host software decides that the selected configuration is unacceptable, it rejects it, and the device continues to be "not configured." It is up to the client software to select a different configuration that may be acceptable by the host software.

▌ Modifying a Device Configuration

As we've already mentioned, USB devices keep a list of valid configurations that they will accept. The configuration-management services allow software on the host to tell the USB to replace its current configuration with a valid configuration. The new configuration will come from the list of valid configurations for the device that the host maintains.

As with the initial device configuration, the host software must decide if the newly modified configuration will fit within the capabilities of the Universal Serial Bus. When this happens, the host must consider the current workload and schedule of transactions. If the new configuration is deemed inappropriate by the host software, then the previous (existing) configuration remains the one in use. Failing to modify a device configuration rarely causes the device to be put into the "not configured" state, though that is technically possible under the terms of the USB specification.

■ The Master Client

There is a concept in the USB host system that we haven't talked about yet: the **master client**. The USB bus and the device configuration-management services allow any client to become the "master client" on the bus. What this really means is that a client can directly control certain bus parameters that you would normally associate with either the USBD or the HCD, such as adjusting the number of bit times in a frame on the bus.

A client becomes a "master client" when the USBD yields control so that the client can control its associated USB device. A master client gives up its powers either by explicitly requesting that it not be a master any more, or when the device the client is controlling is detached or reset. There can only be one master client at a time in a USB system, and they share a **master token** to decide who can actually adjust the SOF token. This master token is nothing more than a "talking stick" whose bearer has permission to alter the frame bit patterns.

The SOF is modified only when the device that the client is talking to supports the change. If the USB device being controlled by the master client does not support the change, then the change is, naturally, invalid. This should cause the master client to relinquish the "master" status. In addition, you should note that adjusting the SOF more than once every 6 ms (or six frames) causes undefined results.

Pipe and Bandwidth Management

It is the job of the host in a Universal Serial Bus system to manage the bandwidth of each pipe, as well as managing the pipes themselves. This responsibility falls naturally to the host, since the use of each USB device is driven by client software. The client software understands the usage of the device and creates the pipes as it needs them (a device will never need a pipe without client software to talk to).

It is also natural that the host manages the bandwidth on the USB bus. After all, the host is talking with up to 127 devices at a time. It is the host that must make decisions about how to partition the Universal Serial Bus to most efficiently communicate with all of these devices crying out for attention.

▌ Service Capabilities

Pipe services provided by the USBDI offer clients the highest-speed, lowest-overhead transfer options available in the USB world. High performance is realized by shifting some of the management responsibilities to the client from the USBD (as we discussed earlier in the configuration section). The result is that pipes are implemented at a much more primitive level than the higher-level data-transfer services provided by the USBD command mechanisms. You should understand that pipe mechanisms through the USBDI do not allow direct access to a device's default pipe.

Pipe-transfer services are useful, but only if the USB has been configured. For that reason, no pipe-transfer services are available until all device and bus configuration tasks have been successfully completed. As part of the device configuration, the USBD attempts to allocate the resources required to support the device pipes required by the selected configuration. The clients are then allowed to modify the configuration within the boundaries of the configuration discussion in the previous section.

Clients communicate with underlying pipe-transfer services with a combination of buffer "hand-offs" and status codes. For example, for an outgoing transfer the client populates a buffer with data it wants to send to a device and passes this to the USBD. The USBD then returns a status code indicating the success or failure after the transfer has been attempted.

Conversely, to execute an incoming pipe transfer (a "read" of the device), the client passes an empty buffer to the pipe service. The USBD returns both a populated buffer (populated with the data transferred from the device) and a status code indicating whether or not the data is valid. The status code also can indicate the quality of the data on an isochronous stream. We'll talk more about quality of service in a later chapter.

▌ Isochronous Data Transfers

We've already talked quite a bit about isochronous transfer, and we'll continue to do so because it is one of the driving features of the Universal Serial Bus. As with other transfer services, all data is managed through the use of buffers. In an isochronous transfer each transfer buffer queued up for an isochronous pipe is a stream of data points (or samples). As isochronous transfers are used almost exclusively for digitized audio and video, this model makes sense. Remember that isochronous transfers are also called *streaming* transfers (and the pipes that carry these transfer are stream pipes).

As with all pipe transfers, the client decides what policies to use for the isochronous pipe, including the relevant service interval. If there are lost or missing bytes through the transmission process (detected when the data arrives), then these are noted to the client.

The client begins a streaming pipe transfer by first queuing a data buffer that will ultimately contain the data that is going to be transmitted over the bus. In order for continuous streaming to occur in an isochronous transfer, the client will queue an additional buffer of data before the currently queued buffer has been used and sent to the USB device. This type of scheme is known as "double buffering."

When a client uses streaming data pipes, it is concerned about moving a stream of bits (or bytes) either from or to the USB device under its control. The client is not interested (nor should it be) in the actual packetization of the data as it flows across the wire. This is usually invisible to the client software, and data for a transaction is always completely contained within some client data buffer. Note that while the packetization is normally invisible to the client, the USB specification provides that the "packet view" of the data is available should the client ask to see it. This occurs infrequently in practice.

■ Interrupt Transfers

Universal Serial Bus devices communicate asynchronously with the host system (i.e., when the host system least expects it!). When there is information to send that the host did not ask for, or did not want to wait for, devices on the Universal Serial Bus uses what are called **interrupt transfers**.

Interrupt transfers always originate in some USB device. They are routed through the host software to the client responsible for the device. The client is then notified by the pipe service component in the USBDI that there is an interrupt transfer for his device. The client should provide a buffer large enough to hold the interrupt-transfer data (the transfer is usually accomplished in a single USB transaction). Once the data is placed into the buffer, the USBDI then passes the buffer back to the client for processing.

■ Bulk Transfers

To move large amounts of data between a device and the client software living on the host system, the Universal Serial Bus uses **bulk transfers**.

These transfers can be initiated either by a USB device or by the client software on the host. No bandwidth or timing guarantees are made about the data exchanged in a bulk transfer. Data from bulk transfers are moved between the client and the USBD through buffers and the USBD Interface. As the data is pretty much application dependent, there isn't much more to say about such transfer here except that it occurs. Nothing in the Universal Serial Bus, excepting the client software, attempts to interpret any data flowing across the bus.

▌ Control Transfers

When software on the host system wants to set the configuration of a device, or otherwise control it, the host issues **control transfers**. Control transfers are bidirectional message pipes that are used in two stages. First, the client initiates a "setup stage" to the device endpoint, preparing it to use whatever data is about to follow. Then a data stage is executed to either bring data in from the device or send data to the device. Please keep in mind that the data stage is optional and depends upon the control function being exercised.

From the client's perspective, the client must prepare a buffer laying out the command phase and any data buffer space it might need to satisfy the command when using USBDI interfaces to initiate control transfers. The client receives notification from the underlying drivers when the control transfer is complete.

Handling Errors

In the normal case of operation for any complex system, errors will occur. The graces with which errors are tolerated and corrected mark the robustness of the system. The Universal Serial Bus is a complex system and as such will encounter errors.

The host controller will detect a number of transaction errors. These errors are defined and described from the host's point of view. The steps taken to address each error are the same for each type. These will be addressed at the end of this discussion.

The transaction errors that may be encountered in a Universal Serial Bus system are:

- Time-out conditions after a host-transmitted token or packet
- Data errors resulting in missed or invalid transactions
- Protocol errors

Time-out conditions occur when the host controller initiates a transaction and the device never responds. This can be caused when the device endpoint that is being used becomes unresponsive (e.g., the cable is disconnected, the power turned off, etc). A time-out condition can also occur when the structure of a transaction is so badly damaged that the targeted endpoint does not recognize it (e.g., this would be the case if electrical interference badly garbled the transaction).

On the Universal Serial Bus there can also be **data errors** resulting in missing or invalid transactions across the bus. An example would be the host controller's sending or receiving a packet shorter than what was expected. Another example would be an invalid checksum on the received data packet.

The final type of transmission error that can occur is a **protocol error**. Such errors arise from events such as invalid handshaking, false end-of-packet (EOP) delimiters, or even bit-stuffing errors. We haven't spent a great deal of time discussing the bus protocol just yet (we will do that in Chapter 7), so we'll leave these conditions unexplained for now.

We deal with each of these errors in a consistent fashion for each of the different transaction types. The host maintains a count of the errors for each transaction that occurs. This counter reflects the number of times the transaction encountered *each* error type. If the error count reaches three for a given error type, then the host aborts the transfer and returns an error to the client. A given implementation of a Universal Serial Bus host may allow the user to set the transaction-error threshold to a value other than three. Retransmission will handle most common and transient errors (such as would be caused by electrical interference on the cables).

It's important to remember that the error counter is directly related to the type of error. If you have multiple errors occurring on a transaction, then there will be multiple error counters. Only after you have three of the same type of error will the transaction be aborted.

Wrapping It Up

This chapter has covered a lot of territory. By now, you understand that responsibility falls upon the many varied layers within the host computer to manage the Universal Serial Bus. The host is divided into three pieces: the host controller, the USB driver, and the client software. Each manages its own piece of the USB puzzle.

The host detects when devices are plugged in (with a little help from the hubs, which we'll cover in the next chapter) and when they are removed from the bus. The host manages the bandwidth and flow control across that bus, as well. Finally, the host manages the pipes used for communication and provides the software that the bus actually uses.

The host cannot do any of this alone. It needs the complete cooperation of USB devices and hubs. We'll get into those areas next.

Chapter

Inside a USB Hub

What Does a USB Hub Do?

Hubs in the Universal Serial Bus world provide the connection point between devices and the host. All devices plug into hubs, and hubs plug into either the host or other hubs (creating a *tiered* layer of hubs). The host even has an integrated hub, known as the *root hub*. The hub supports many of the attributes that make the Universal Serial Bus easy to use, and it helps to hide the complexity of the USB from the end user. It should be noted up front that, as far as the USB is concerned, the hub is just another USB device (which we'll cover in the next chapter). While the hub may be just a device, it is a device with special responsibilities.

Among the functions that the hub provides to the USB are:

- Device connectivity
- Power-management functions
- Device attachment/removal detection
- Bus-error detection and recovery
- Full- and low-speed device support

As you can see in Figure 4–1, a hub consists of a **hub repeater** and a **hub controller**. It's up to the hub repeater to manage the setup and destruction of connections to and through the hub. It is also the responsibility of the hub repeater to support error handling and recovery (e.g., bus fault detection, etc.). The repeater, further, is the component within the hub that detects whether a device has been attached or removed.

65

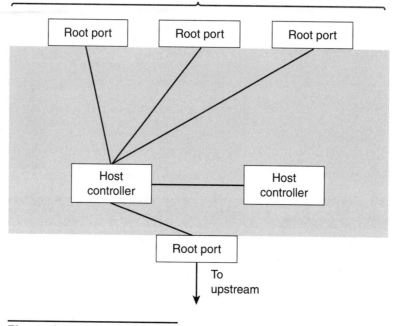

Figure 4–1   Hub Architecture

The hub controller, on the other hand, primarily provides the interface between the functionality of the hub and the rest of the Universal Serial Bus. It is the hub controller that formats commands to be sent across the bus and communicates with the host. There are hub-specific status registers and device-control requests on the hub that permit the host software to configure it through software commands sent over the USB. These status registers also allow the host system to monitor what is happening downstream of the hub, on its attached devices.

You will also notice, looking at Figure 4–1, a **root port** and some number of **downstream ports**. The root port points toward the host computer (in the *upstream* direction). Devices attached to the hub attach to the downstream ports. We'll talk about upstream, downstream, and the root port throughout this chapter (and the rest of this book), so you should be clear on what these directions are.

How Hubs Handle Packets

Unlike "normal" USB devices, which serve to provide some concrete function to client software on the host, a hub is more of a "middle man." The hub accepts packets and forwards them to an attached device that can use them. It also serves to move data from devices attached to it back to the host. While this is the primary responsibility of the hub, it also accepts and generates packets itself to make sure that the devices and host have a completely clear virtual pathway between them. Probably the biggest difference between the hub and devices that provide *function* is that hubs are controlled primarily by the host *system software*, while USB devices answer to client software that controls them.

The piece of the hub that handles packets is the hub repeater. While there may be any number of *downstream* ports for USB devices to attach to, there is at most one port in the upstream direction (called the *root port*) that sends data to the host. Remember, upstream is toward the host and downstream is toward the attached devices (away from the host). Figure 4–2 shows how packets move through the hub repeater in both directions.

The hub is constantly sending and receiving packets between the attached devices and the host system. The hub also has an **idle state** during

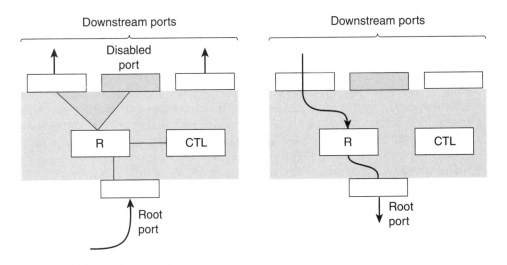

Figure 4–2   Hub Connectivity

which the hub does not pass packets. When in the idle state each port on the hub sits and waits for the start of the next packet.

When there is a device attached to the port in the hub, that port is considered *enabled*. Contrarily, when there is no device attached, the port is considered *disabled*. If a downstream hub port is enabled and the hub notices a start of packet on that port, then the hub opens the pathway to the host. The hub establishes connectivity upstream through the root port, but not to any other downstream ports. Devices can talk only to the host, not to other devices. Other devices downstream never see packets between the host and a device.

When the hub detects start-of-packet activity on an upstream port to a given port on the hub, all other downstream ports are locked. This ensures that nothing on the hub will be modified until the packet of data has been communicated to the device (detected by an end of packet, or EOP, on the wire).

When the hub detects an SOP on its root port, on the other hand, it operates in a *broadcast mode*. The hub establishes connectivity to all of the ports that have devices attached. Any port that is not enabled does not receive any packets from the root port (and doesn't send any either)—a policy that makes sense, since there's likely no device attached to the port!

Maintaining State on Ports

A downstream port on a hub is, at any given time, in one of several possible states. The port may be enabled, suspended, reset, or in any number of other defined states. The hub, since at heart it is just another USB device, maintains a device state that is hub specific. We'll talk about this device state in the next chapter. Our present discussion is focused on the possible states that the hub maintains on each individual downstream port. The root port is always "wide open" and does not support any of the states that we are talking about here. We are talking only about downstream port state. This is illustrated in Figure 4–3.

The states that a downstream port on a hub can be in are as follows:

- Powered off—no power applied to device
- Disconnected—device is not logically connected to the USB
- Disabled—device may be attached to port but it isn't being recognized
- Enabled—device is attached to the port and can be used
- Suspended—device is attached but is "asleep"

We'll talk about each of these states in depth in the sections below.

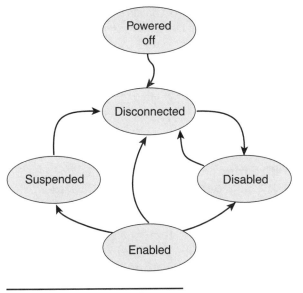

Figure 4–3 Hub-State Diagram

▌ Powered-Off State

Some ports on a hub have support for power switching, and some do not. **Power switching** means that the hub can selectively apply or remove power from each port. This switching is done because there is only a certain amount of bus power available, and intelligent hubs and devices can limit the amount of power they consume in order to give more power to other devices.

A port is set to the **powered-off** state at the request of the host. This setting is normally used when the host goes into a power-saving mode, such as a laptop going into a suspended state. The host sends a request, called ClearPortFeature (PORT_POWER), to set the port to a powered-off state. Also, the hub transitions the port from its current state to a powered-off state when it detects a reset signal on its root port. When the hub receives a reset signal, it reverts to its default power-on state. After a reset, the host must completely reconfigure each device and hub (remember, a hub is just a device) on the Universal Serial Bus. This procedure is called *bus enumeration* and is discussed at length in the next two chapters. Finally, a port becomes powered off when power to the hub is first applied (which seems counterintuitive, but isn't when you think in terms of the hub resetting itself).

All of the electrical signals from a port that is in the powered-off state are ignored by the hub (i.e., even signals from self-powered devices are ignored in the powered-off state). The port is treated as dead in this state, and all upstream activity from the host to that port is ignored. If there is upstream traffic, then you should worry about the coherency of your host software (it should know when it powers off a port and not try to talk to it)!

▊ Disconnected State

A hub port is in the **disconnected state** when the port has power but has no device attached. A port transitions from the *powered-off* state to the *disconnected* state when the host tells the hub to apply power to the port (via a SetPortFeature(PORT_POWER) request). If the hub doesn't allow individual power control on each port, then the disconnected state is the default state of each port of the hub. This means that each port will be put into the disconnected state when the hub is either reset or first powered up.

When a port is in the disconnected state, it doesn't communicate in either the upstream or downstream directions. The port can, however, detect a *connect event*. The connect event causes the port to transition to the *disabled state*. A connect event is triggered when a device is plugged into a port on the hub.

▊ Disabled State

A hub port is put into the **disabled state** when the hub detects a device being attached (a connect event). This assumes that the port is currently in the *disconnected* state, which means that it must be powered on (if the hub supports per-port power switching).

A device plugged into a port that is the disabled state cannot talk to the host, but the host can talk to it through the use of a *reset* signal. At all other times, the cabling to the device is electrically isolated from the rest of the hub. Certain events, though, may allow upstream signaling to be resumed. One such event is a *disconnect event*.

▊ Enabled State

A port transitions to the **enabled state** when the host tells the hub to put the port into the enabled state. This is done as a part of the bus-enumeration process, where the USB device is actually recognized by the host computer. This process occurs when the host sends either a PORT_ENABLE or PORT_RESET request to the hub (for a full discussion of these requests, see Chapter 6). Since the port can transition to the enabled state only from the disabled state, the port can never become enabled if there is not a device attached to it.

When the port is in the enabled state, packets may flow in both directions (upstream and downstream) from the attached device. The downstream traffic includes full-speed traffic, low-speed traffic (within the constraints described later in this chapter), and all reset signaling. The upstream traffic on an enabled port includes all full- and low-speed packets, as well as any resume signaling.

A port leaves the enabled state and reenters the disabled state if it the host tells it to (through a PORT_ENABLE request). This also happens if an error is detected on the bus. The hub will transition an enabled port to the disconnected state if the hub detects the port being removed (a *disconnect event*).

▌ Suspended State

A device can be temporarily put into a **suspended state** to keep power from being applied to it. This is different from the *powered-off* state. The suspended state is used for power management, whereas the powered-off state is used when no device is attached to the port. A hub port can be put into the suspended state by either the host requesting that it happen or the device deciding it wants to be suspended.

The hub will suspend a downstream port when it receives a PORT_SUSPEND request from the host. If this happens, the hub "holds" the suspend request until the current transaction to or from the device is complete. A hub may itself be suspended, but that state is maintained separately from each port's suspended state.

If the hub on which the suspended port lives is itself suspended, an attempt to communicate with the port will cause the hub to wake up before the port wakes up. If, on the other hand, the hub is already awake, then the port is awakened. This allows a chain of hubs to be suspended and then wakened up by means of a simple communication with a device at the bottom of the hierarchy, which in turn serves to simplify the host software design.

If a disconnect event occurs while a port is suspended, the hub will transition the port to the disconnected state. It is not possible to transition from a disconnected state into the suspended state.

Bus Signaling Behavior

As we discussed in the introductory chapters, devices can operate at either full speed or low speed. Packets can flow at very different data rates one right after another on the bus. There must be some mechanism in place to keep devices on the Universal Serial Bus from becoming confused and to keep everything synchronized.

To properly manage both full- and low-speed devices, the hub must detect the speed at which a device wishes to operate. The hub will detect whether a device is full or low speed when the device is first connected to its port on the hub, or when the device is powered up. This detection is done electrically, not through the software. If you remember from our brief hardware description in Chapter 2, there are two data lines in a USB cable, D+ and D–. One of these is pulled into the "low state." If the D– signal is high, then the device uses low-speed signaling. Conversely, if the D+ line is high, then the device uses full-speed signaling.

It is important, so as not to confuse low-speed devices, that full-speed traffic not be sent to low-speed devices. The reason is that a low-speed device might mistakenly respond to the signaling and create a bus conflict. On the other hand, low-speed traffic will never confuse a full-speed device, since a valid packet ID (PID) cannot be constructed from low-speed data patterns. The hub and the host always use full-speed signaling.

If a low-speed device is attached to a port, then the hub must generate something called a **low-speed keep-alive strobe**. Generated at the beginning of each transmitted frame, low-speed devices use the strobe to keep from going into the suspended state from lack of bus traffic. The hub repeater generates the keep-alive strobe from internal circuitry.

The keep-alive strobe is generated just one time per frame, and it must obey the following rules:

1. When entering the suspended state, the keep-alive strobe must not disappear before the last frame.
2. The hub is allowed to create only three strobes after the last frame.
3. The keep-alive strobe must happen no later than one frame after the hub is no longer suspended.

Fault Recovery in the Hub

Since the hub lives between the host and any attached devices on the Universal Serial Bus, it is in the ideal position to detect and correct errors on the bus. It is very important that any connectivity errors are detected and, if possible, prevented before the attached device (or host) sees them. This detection and correction is handled by the hub repeater function within the hub.

Besides connectivity errors, there may be packet errors caused by corrupted packets addressed directly to the hub. Since, as we keep saying, the hub is just another USB device, it must follow the same rules for corrupted packets as the devices that are attached to it. A full explanation of device error handling is found in the next chapter.

Corrupted Packets

There can be any number of different types of corrupted or missing packets. These include lost or corrupted tokens, data packets, or handshake packets. We talk about what all of these packets do, and describe their format, in Chapter 6. The accompanying table lists the possible packet errors that a hub should be equipped to detect, along with the expected response from the hub.

Packet Field	Error	Hub's Action
Packet ID (PID)	PID check or bit-stuff error	Ignore the packet
Address	Bit-stuff error, address CRC wrong	Ignore the packet
Data	Bit-stuff error, data CRC wrong	Discard the data

False End of Packet (EOP)

A false end of packet (EOP) is a phenomenon that occurs when a device detects the EOP marker before one actually exists. From a device's point of view, a false EOP makes a single packet look like two separate packets. This has the potential to confuse a device.

The hub will handle a false end of packet differently, depending on whether the hub is being accessed directly or is acting as a repeater forwarding data to attached devices. When the hub is acting as a repeater, it does not attempt to understand the data flowing through it. If it doesn't understand the data, then it cannot very well figure out whether the EOP is valid or invalid. In this case, a hub doesn't see the error, so it ignores it.

The hub can detect a false EOP when it's being talked to. If the hub detects a false end of packet, then the hub ignores all further traffic until the next start of packet (SOP). In this case, the hub manages false-EOP error-detection and recovery mechanisms just as any other USB device would.

■ Repeater-Fault Recovery

The hub must detect any condition that has the potential to cause the bus to wait "forever" or to be put into any state other than idle at the end of a packet transaction. If the hub does not catch these conditions, then the Universal Serial Bus, and all of the devices on it, will soon be in a confused and unreliable state.

Two of these conditions are defined by the USB specification: **loss of activity** (LOA) and **babble**. Loss of activity is defined as the detection of a start-of-packet token being followed by either no bus activity or no end-of-packet token before the end of the transmitted frame. Babble, on the other hand, is defined as bus activity continuing past the end of the frame. Because hubs have no notion of allocated bandwidth for isochronous devices, they must rely upon the frame timer to detect LOA and babble conditions. The hub will recover before the beginning of the next transmitted frame.

It's important to note that the hub recovers only from faults originating in the upstream direction. It is up to the host to detect and recover from its own downstream errors. There are really only two hard-and-fast rules that a hub must follow:

1. A device that puts illegal data on the bus after the end of frame (babbles) must have its port disabled.
2. A hub must always ensure that the bus is in the idle state at the end of a bus transaction.

When there are no faults, these requirements are met by having the hub receive an EOP token with every packet and having no bus traffic occur past the end of a frame. This is normal bus operation. Under non-fault conditions, these requirements are met by virtue of a hub receiving an EOP with every packet and having no bus traffic occur past the end of a frame.

Power-Management Functions

Every hub must support the *suspend* and *resume* power-management functions. At the very least, a hub must propagate these signals downstream. There are two types of suspend and resume functions: global and selective.

Suspend and resume functions directed toward specific port on the hub are known as *selective* suspend and resume. Conversely, suspend and resume functions to be propagated through the root port are known as *global* suspend and resume. Global resume may be initiated either by the host or through the hub's downstream port.

Global Suspend and Resume

Global suspend is implemented by causing the host to stop all downstream traffic to the entire Universal Serial Bus. When the root port on a hub is idle for more than 3 ms, then the hub goes into the suspended state. A suspended hub cleans up any pending bus transactions, maintains all per-port state and status, and preserves its own state and status. Since a suspended hub has its internal clock turned off, it has no concept of time. The hub can do nothing but watch the bus for transactions.

When the hub sees a transaction on the hub's root port, then it puts itself into the resume state. This also occurs if any traffic is being initiated by an attached device. Further, the hub will exit the suspended state if a device is either attached to a port or removed from a port.

Selective Suspend and Resume

A *selective suspend* occurs when a single device or bus segment is put into a low-power state. This depends upon the ability of the hub to selectively suspend an individual port at the request of the host (with a PORT_SUSPEND request). A hub that can do this is called a **disabling hub**, though in practice almost every hub is a disabling hub.

As with the global suspend, a port that is suspended is prevented from moving any data downstream (except for a PORT_RESET request). Further, the only traffic that can be sent upstream is the port's status, not any actual bus traffic from the device to the root port. The hub must ensure that a port is not put into the suspended state until any current bus transactions are completed. Rather than rejecting the suspend request from the host, the hub waits until the current packet is complete before suspending the port.

If there are ports further downstream of the port being put to sleep, it is only natural to assume that those ports will also be put into the suspended state. This is important behavior to note, since a device attached to a hub port may be another hub.

If a port on a hub is selectively suspended, but the hub itself is not suspended, then the hub must ensure that no traffic from the suspended port is reflected to the enabled ports on the hub. This reflection would have the potential of causing problems with the attached devices. Likewise, a resume message must be directed only to a specific port and not propagated to other suspended ports.

Hub-Reset Behavior

A fundamental function of a hub on the Universal Serial Bus is that it be able to respond to a host request that the hub reset itself. This is done, for example, when the host enumerates the devices on the bus. It must also be able to place any of its ports into the reset state, effectively resetting the device attached to that port. This section will talk about how the hub handles all this.

■ Hub Reset

A USB hub can be reset only by the host computer, or by resetting itself when it is first powered up. The hub is put into a *default configuration* when it resets. This default state includes the following properties:

- The hub controller default address is set to 0.
- The hub control bits are all set to power-up values.
- The hub repeater waits for an SOP.
- On a powered switched hub, all downstream ports are placed in the powered-off state.
- On a nonpowered switched hub, all downstream ports are placed in the disconnected state.

It should be noted that if a bus contains hubs that allow their ports to be power switched, then the host reset is not guaranteed to be sent all the way downstream to all devices. The host ensures that each level of USB devices, or tier, is reset when it goes through the bus-enumeration process (discussed in depth in the next chapter). Powered-off devices are reset. Self-powered devices and hubs reset both themselves and their downstream ports.

▌ Per-Port Reset

The USB host can ask that a particular port on a hub be reset. It does this by issuing a PORT_RESET request to the hub. The port number of the downstream port is included as a part of this request. In order to reset the port, the hub signals the device on the port that it is being reset before setting the port itself to the reset state. A reset request is ignored if the port that is being reset is either powered off or disconnected.

Hub Power Distribution

A USB hub, by definition, supplies power to devices that attach to its downstream ports. This power is provided for bus-powered devices. The hub may be able to supply a variable amount of power to the downstream components. To facilitate the management of this, each device knows its power requirement and reports it to the host during the bus-enumeration process.

Hubs, like other USB devices, can be any combination of self-powered and bus-powered. For example, a hub may get power for its root-port operation from the bus while, at the same time, powering its downstream ports with an external power supply. An important restriction is that a hub can supply power only in the downstream direction (toward the devices) and *never* put power on the bus upstream. This keeps things electrically "sane."

Every bus-powered hub has per-port power-switching capabilities on each of its downstream ports. Further, a bus-powered hub is required by the USB specification to power off all downstream ports when the hub first powers up. The hub is also required to power off all downstream ports when the host commands it reset.

As we discussed before, the host can cause power to be sent or withheld from a port under software control. While the bus-powered hub must have per-port power switching, it is acceptable to have the hub provide a single mechanism that switches power to all ports simultaneously.

It should be mentioned that a port-reset request does not affect the port's power status. In addition, a hub port must be powered on before it can detect the attachment of a device.

Hub Endpoint Configuration

Every device must have an endpoint zero for configuration and status reporting, and a hub is certainly no exception. The hub communicates over its endpoint zero to tell the host when a device has been attached or removed. The host accesses endpoint zero through the default pipe. This endpoint uses what are called *interrupt transfers*. Periodically the host polls endpoint zero on the hub to find out if anything has changed on the hub. If there has been a change, then the hub sends data informing the host of the specifics of the change. If there is no change, then the hub merely returns a NAK (negative acknowledgement). Hubs are logically organized as shown in Figure 4–4.

▮ Port Changes

One of the most important functions the hub provides, apart from moving data from the attached devices to the host, is detecting changes in the state of each port it owns. Devices attached to the ports can cause any

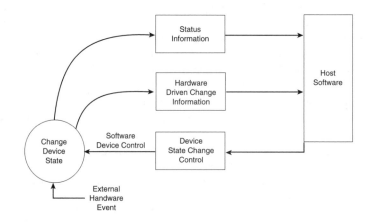

Figure 4–4   Relationship of Status, Status Change, and Control to Device States

number of hardware events. The host software can also request that the hub change the state of any port (or the hub itself). Since the hub can be can be changed by either an attached device or the host software, then the hub will report any changes for either of the hardware-initiated events. The hub continuously reports a change until the host acknowledges it. This report could indicate any state change, such as a device being inserted or removed from the Universal Serial Bus. This approach keeps the state information that both the device and the host must maintain on each hub. The host software uses its default pipe and endpoint zero to detect these changes. (See Figure 4–4.)

The status of a particular port on a USB hub is requested by the host on a per-port basis. When the host has been made aware of any change, then it informs the hub of the fact and the hub clears the "change pending" flag in the port status register. This keeps the hub from reporting the port as being changed after the host sees the change, and ensures that the host will not be notified again—at least until the port status changes once again.

▌ Hub Configuration

Hubs, like other devices, are configured through the standard USB device-configuration commands, which are described in the next chapter. A hub that has not yet been configured behaves like all other devices that have not been configured—it does not provide power to downstream ports, and it responds only to the default address.

A hub is configured by the host software with a set of configuration commands. These configuration commands operate on the hub's configuration *descriptors*. This is all done through the default pipe to endpoint zero. The host software will issue commands to the hub to put the hub's ports into powered and powered-off modes at the appropriate times.

One important difference between the configuration of a hub and the configuration of any other USB device is that the hub provides power to other devices. The host examines the hub's electrical characteristics and the power requirements of the attached devices to ensure that it will not violate the USB power topology.

Wrapping It Up

In this chapter we learned that a Universal Serial Bus hub is a fairly complex device. It maintains state on each connected device, as well as detecting misbehaving devices. It is the hub that ultimately drives the state of the attached devices, even if it is at the direction of the host computer.

It's important to remember that a USB hub is nothing more than a USB device with a few special capabilities. Think of it as a "super" USB device. We'll discuss the general case of devices in the next chapter. After reading this chapter, however, much of the next should seem very familiar to you.

Inside a USB Device

What Does a USB Device Do?

The first thing that you should understand about a Universal Serial Bus device is that nearly everything within a USB system *is* a device. The root hub is a device, as is every hub connected to the system. The peripherals that you attach to the Universal Serial Bus are all known as devices. The only part of a system that isn't a USB device is the actual host controller (and the controlling system software).

Each USB device is divided into three distinct and individual layers. The bottommost layer is the part of the device that is responsible for communicating on the physical bus by sending and receiving packets. The next layer up is the **protocol engine** that is responsible for translating bus communications from the lowest layer and sending them to the topmost layer: the endpoint.

The topmost layer of a device is the device endpoint. The **device endpoint** is the part of the device that actually deals with the data that's being sent around the bus. It uses information from the host, and it sends information to the host—every other piece of the device exists only to serve the device endpoint.

This chapter talks about the topmost layer of the device: the device endpoint. Certain attributes and operations are common to all device endpoints. The device in performing its defined functions uses all of these attributes and operation.

USB Device States

Before we can really begin to talk about what happens inside a device and why, it's important to understand what different **device states** there are and how the device transitions between the various states. These states and transitions are what all of the device actions depend upon (e.g., a device can not send data if it's in the powered-off state).

Each USB device has a finite number of states in which it can be. It can be in one (and only one) of those states at a time; i.e., states are *mutually exclusive* of one another. A USB device can also maintain a state apart from its USB state that is not visible to the host software (or other downstream devices) and is specific to its internal functionality. When we talk about *state* in this book, we're dealing only with those defined states that are visible outside of the device. Internal states are device dependent and not a part of the Universal Serial Bus proper.

Figure 5–1 diagrams the various states and the transitions between them. It may appear complicated at first glance, but revisit it as you read the rest of this section and it should become clear. Like many things technical, it's really much simpler than it looks.

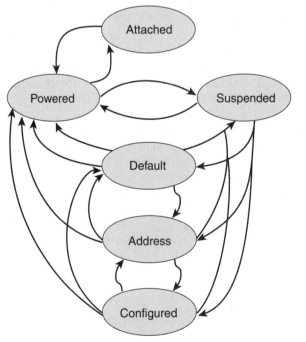

Figure 5–1
Device-State Diagram

Six device states are defined by the USB specification. These are:

- Attached state
- Powered state
- Default state
- Address assigned state
- Configured state
- Suspended state

We'll discuss each of these in depth in the following sections.

Attached State

Like most of the states, the **attached state** is named to convey exactly what it means. At any given time, a USB device connected to a bus either is attached to the Universal Serial Bus or is detached from it. Don't confuse the attached state with whether or not a USB device is plugged into the bus. The attached state is a *logical* state that is only related to what the device and the host believe to be true, not what may be physically true. For example, a device need not be physically powered off for the host to consider it in the powered-off state. It will be in the powered-off state until the hub tells the host differently, not when the device is powered.

A device is put into the attached state by the host as part of the *bus-enumeration* process that we will talk about a little later on in this chapter. A USB device may be attached to or detached from the bus, but the USB specification only discusses what happens on a device when it is attached. If a device is detatched, then it should not be putting data on the bus (or, rather, the hub shouldn't be allowing it too). From a USB perspective, we don't care what the device does when it's detached.

Powered State

The developers of USB devices must make an important decision: where to get the power for the device. If you recall from our earlier discussions, devices have the option to receive power directly from the Universal Serial Bus. Alternatively, each device can get its power from an external power source. In addition, as we will see a little later in this chapter, a device can offer the user the choice of using either bus power or external power.

Why would someone want to use external power when there's "free" power on the bus? Take the example of a USB speaker. While you can certainly drive sound out of a speaker with the 5-volt, low-amperage power on the USB, you can drive "bigger and better" sound when using powered amplifiers. The same is true of the output from your sound card. The option is there because it can make sense for some devices.

The USB term for an externally powered USB device is **self-powered**. These devices may already be powered before the device and the host "know" that they're powered—remember, these states are logical and only reflect what the device and the host agree on.

The USB terminology for a USB device that derives its power from the bus is, naturally enough, **bus powered**. Devices report how they are powered through an abstraction called the *configuration descriptor,* which we will talk about later in this chapter. The type of current power source is maintained as a part of the device's current status.

Another thing that the device keeps track of in its configuration information is the maximum amount of power that the device can use. This is used by the USB host to decide if there's enough power flowing across the bus to support the device. It's also used to make proper decisions about what to do should there not be sufficient electrical current flowing around for everyone who wants it. An important note is that the device must observe this maximum, regardless of whether the device is drawing its power from the bus or from an external power supply. If the configuration supports only one source of power and the host software changes the source of the power (and this is legal), then the device will lose its current configuration and revert to the *attached state.*

▋ Default State

While all of the states are relatively simple to understand, the **default state** is probably the easiest. The default state is achieved when the device first receives power. The device sits doing nothing until the host sends it a command to reset. After the host resets the device, then the device can be talked to, but only at the device's default address. A better name for the default state might have been the "idle state."

▋ Address-Assigned State

When a USB device is being first configured, the host software addresses it through the use of its **default address**. One of the first things a host does, if you recall our discussion in Chapter 3, is assign a unique address to the device.

The device uses the default address at the time that it is first powered on. It also uses the default address any time the device receives a "reset" command from the host controller. Once assigned an address, the device remembers it, even if the device is put to sleep with a suspend command. The USB device only reverts to the default address if the device loses power, or a reset command comes from the host.

One thing you might want to remember in order to avoid confusion: the default address has nothing to do with the *default pipe*. The default pipe is used for configuration regardless of the address used for the device. We'll talk about that later, as it's not completely relevant to the discussion on device states.

▌ Configured State

A logical thing to believe is that a USB device cannot be used until it is configured, that is, put into the **configured state**. As far as the device is concerned, the procedure to do this may be as trivial as writing something other than a "zero" to the device's configuration register. It is up to the host software to set the configuration to something that the device can actually use. As you'll see later, the device keeps a list of valid configurations from which the host can choose.

Setting a device to either its default configuration or one of the valid alternative configurations essentially causes the configuration of the device (and everything within the device) to revert to default values. This is important, because the host software must contain enough intelligence to "know" that it must reset whatever values it was using at the time it decided to change the state of the device.

▌ Suspended State

As we've mentioned before, there is a limited amount of power on the bus. The host has to decide who's using it and who can wait a while before using bus power. In addition, on a portable computer, the user may wish to suspend devices to conserve battery life. A device may also decide on its own, based upon certain criteria, that it wants to be a "friendly neighbor" to other devices it's sharing power with and suspend itself. Regardless of the mechanism that puts the device there, the **suspended state** is the state the device enters when it stops draining power from its power source.

If a device is compliant with the Universal Serial Bus specification, then it will suspend itself if it has not detected activity on the bus for some given length of time. A device in the *attached* state can be suspended at any time after it has been powered up, regardless of whether it has been configured or assigned an address. A device will also enter the suspended state when something causes the hub port to which the device is attached to become disabled; this is a condition referred to as **selective suspend**. The host can also suspend itself after some period of no bus activity. This is certainly a valid way to put the all of the hub and devices on the bus to sleep.

To wake up a device (i.e., take it out of suspend mode), there simply needs to be bus activity to the device. Optionally—and we're not going to explore this other than to say the capability exists—the device can send signaling over the Universal Serial Bus to request that the host exit the suspend mode. This capability is known as **remote wakeup**. It's optional for developers of a USB device to provide for remote wakeup. Note, though, that if a USB device supports remote wakeup, then it must also provide configuration options to the host of disabling it.

Bus Enumeration

Bus enumeration is the process that the host uses to "map" the devices and topology of its Universal Serial Bus. This is not done just one time when the host is first powered on, as you might think. Rather, bus enumeration occurs each time that a USB device is either attached to or removed from the bus. This dynamic bus enumeration is called "hot plug." The process is not really all that complicated and will be explained here.

First, let's talk about what happens when a USB device is initially plugged into a Universal Serial Bus. Before the host can configure the device, it first has to know that a device has been attached. This detection happens when the hub that the device was plugged into tells the host that it has a new device. The hub is informed by means of some electrical signaling that occurs between the device and the hub (see the previous chapter for discussion on this).

It's important to note that even if you plug a device directly into your computer, your computer has as a part of its hardware a *root hub*, which behaves just as any other hub. Likewise, hubs can be plugged into other hubs, in which case the host configures them just as any other device. We're keeping our description here strictly generic in terms of USB devices. Hub-specific behavior is talked about in the previous chapter.

The hub tells the host that the USB device is attached by sending a message on a special pipe called the *status-change pipe*. At this point, the USB device is put into the attached state, and the port that it is plugged into on the hub is disabled. The host then consults its internal data structures and by talking to the hub determines exactly what changed. The hub tells the host that there is a new device, and tells the host the port number of the hub the device is living at.

Once the host knows where the new device lives on the bus, it tells the hub to enable the port that the device is attached to. The hub sends a "reset" command to that port, thus causing the newly attached device to reset itself to default values. At this point, the hub is also sending bus power to the USB device, causing the device to transition to the powered state. Since the device just experienced a reset, it answers only to the default address.

The host next asks the device about its capabilities (e.g., what's the maximum amount of data it can send at a time). Once the host knows all of this information, it assigns a unique and currently unused address to the device. This causes the device to enter the addressed state.

The host next spends several bus transactions querying the newly attached device about its supported configurations. The client software on the host that is actually controlling how the device will be used decides which of the valid configuration options is best suited for this system. The host then assigns a valid configuration to the device. This, of course, causes the device to transition into the configured state.

Now that the device is in the configured state, its endpoints are available and ready to use. Also, the device can now begin drawing as much power from its power source as its configuration claimed it would draw. As far as the device is concerned, it is ready to use.

Device removal, in contrast with device attachment, is a relatively trivial operation. The hub, again, is the component responsible for telling the host that the device is gone from the bus. The host disables the port that the device was attached to. The host then updates its internal map of the bus to reflect the missing device. At this point, the unique address that the device was using is no longer valid and may be recycled and given to another newly attached device. Whether the host software actually reuses this address is completely up to that software and is not covered in either this book or the Universal Serial Bus specification.

USB Device Operations

The Universal Serial Bus supports a core set of operations for devices. These operations are common across USB implementations and must be supported by all devices. Before we can successfully delve into the form and function of the basic primitive operations that, in aggregate, make up higher-level operations, we should first address the functionality that we are attempting to achieve. We will delve into these high-level operations in this section.

■ Device Attachment and Removal

Devices on the Universal Serial Bus (and we include hubs among them) can be attached and removed from the bus at any time at the whim of the user. The hub that the device was plugged into, or is being plugged into, owns the responsibility of telling the host about the change. The host can then reconfigure its view of the bus—which is the only view that really matters.

Since the section on "Bus Enumeration" covered most of the specifics dealing with device insertion and detachment from the bus, we won't spend a great amount of time and space discussing it here. There are a few points to make, however, before we leave this topic for another.

When a device is attached to a hub, the host enables the port on the hub where the device was detected. This has the intentional side effect of resetting the device. A USB device that has been reset conforms to the following set of characteristics:

- The device responds to its *default address* (and only its default address).
- The device is essentially unconfigured.
- The device is not suspended.

The host software works under these assumptions when performing whatever tasks it must in order to make the newly attached device a well-behaving citizen of the bus that it is attaching to.

When the host detects that a device has disappeared from the bus, it handles it in essentially the opposite manner—it disables the hub port where the device was attached. The host also cleans up the host software that was relying on the device. Whether the client software that was using the device cleans up nicely is entirely up to that software, and that behavior is not addressed by the Universal Serial Bus specification.

Again, the detail of events involved in the dynamic attachment and detachment of devices on the USB is described in the "Bus Enumeration" section of this chapter.

■ Address Assignment

Another of the primary high-level functions that the host must perform on a device is that of **address assignment**. When a USB device is first powered up and attached to the Universal Serial Bus, it responds only to the default address. It isn't until the host assigns a unique address to the device that it can be used. The host performs this function as part of the bus-enumeration process. The address assignment occurs after the hub port where the device has been attached is enabled, or after a reset.

▌ Configuration

Before a USB device can be used, it must be configured. It is entirely up to the host software (often in conjunction with the controlling client software) to configure the device. The host must first find out which configuration options the device supports before it can attempt to set any. This all seems like common sense, but you might be surprised to find out how many other computer buses don't make this clear, and how many device-driver writers mess this up.

As you might well imagine, there are a quite a number of options that a device must be configured to support. We have already (in our discussion on device states) talked about bus-powered versus self-powered devices. This option is set by the host's device-configuration process. The maximum data-packet size (the amount of data the device can send or receive at a time) for each of the device's endpoints must also be configured.

A device might support multiple interfaces within a single configuration. A device **interface** is defined by the USB specification as "a related set of endpoints that present a single feature or function of the device to the host." There may be a different protocol used to talk to each of these endpoints within an interface. These may be specified by the device class and set as a part of the host's configuration of the device. At the very least, a device will have one interface.

Each device may be capable of handling more than one configuration for a given interface (although not at the same time!). These **alternate configurations** can be chosen by the host at any point in the device's existence on the USB. It is entirely up to the designer of the device as to whether or not multiple configurations can be supported. If alternate configurations are allowed, then extra effort must be made in designing the device (e.g., the "Get Interface" and "Set Interface" commands must be supported).

Every configuration on a device that supports alternate configurations has with it an associated *interface descriptor*. The interface descriptor associates an interface number with the alternate settings. The configuration setting that is in place when a device is initially configured is "alternate setting zero."

Some device drivers are capable of managing a group of related USB devices. These are called *adaptive device drivers*. A single adaptive device driver might manage, for example, a dozen connected USB modem devices. In order to support these adaptive device drivers, each device and interface descriptor contains data fields for the device's class, subclass, and supported protocol. These fields are used by the device driver to figure out what functions are provided by the attached device and which protocol should be used to communicate with those functions. The whole idea of class codes is discussed elsewhere in this book.

Device Requests

The host communicates with an attached USB device by issuing **device requests** to a pipe on the device. These requests are made using a mechanism called a **control transfer**. Each request is composed of both the actual request and the parameters that the request needs to complete. For example, a device request to change a device's configuration must be made with a control transfer containing the request to change and the configuration to change to (the parameter). It is the duty of the host to establish the values of whatever parameters are transferred.

A control transfer on the Universal Serial Bus has a very specific format. While we will cover the formats of the bus traffic in the next chapter, we will delve here just a bit into what the packet involved in a control transfer looks like. It is known as a **setup packet**. It looks as shown in Figure 5–2.

The host software initializes each of the data fields within the setup packet. Every setup packet is eight bytes long. The setup packet contains the following fields:

- The request type
- The actual request
- The parameter value(s) and index
- Data length

The **request-type** field is a bit-mapped field that identifies the characteristics of a given request. Bit-mapped means simply that each bit within the byte takes on a specific meaning; the meaning is not in the value of the byte as a whole. Specifically, the request-type field is used to set the direction for the data transfer that happens in the second part (or second *phase*) of the control transfer.

Following the request-type field is the actual **request**. Devices on the Universal Serial Bus respond to a standard set of device requests, and this

8 bits	8 bits	16 bits	16 bits	16 bits
Request type	Request	Value	Index	Length

Figure 5–2 Anatomy of a SETUP Packet

occurs whether the device is configured or not. The valid standard requests are, quite simply:

- CLEAR_FEATURE
- GET_CONFIGURATION
- GET_DESCRIPTOR
- GET_INTERFACE
- GET_STATUS
- SET_ADDRESS
- SET_CONFIGURATION
- SET_DESCRIPTOR
- SET_FEATURE
- SET_INTERFACE
- SYNCH_FRAME

These requests will be elaborated on further along in this text. They are listed here to give you an idea of what is valid in the request field of the setup packet.

After the request field comes the nebulous **value and index** field. These values vary according to the request and are used to pass a parameter to the device. This parameter is entirely dependent upon the request.

The very last thing that you will find in a setup packet is the **length**. This is not the length of the setup packet but rather the number of bytes that are going to be transferred when the request is satisfied in the next transfer (or transfer phase).

While most of the requests seem self-explanatory, we want to say a few words about some that need comment.

▌ GET_DESCRIPTOR

The **GET_DESCRIPTOR** request passed to a device supports three types of descriptors (keeping in mind that we'll discuss descriptors at length in Chapter 7): *device, configuration,* and *string*. A request for a configuration descriptor causes the device to return the active configuration descriptor for the device, all interface descriptors, and all endpoint descriptors for each interface.

These descriptors are sent across the wire in groups associated by device interface. For instance, after the configuration descriptor is passed, the first interface descriptor is sent across the USB. Immediately following that, the first interface's endpoint descriptors are sent. If there are additional interfaces in the device, then the sequence occurs again for each interface that is present in the device. All devices will provide at minimum a device descriptor and one configuration descriptor.

■ GET_INTERFACE

The **GET_INTERFACE** request exists in order to get the currently selected alternate setting for a given interface. This is because many devices have interface configurations with mutually exclusive settings. The host has a very real need to understand the configuration for a given interface in this context.

■ GET_STATUS

The **GET_STATUS** request offers up a great amount of information about a given device. It returns information detailing whether a bus is currently self-powered or bus powered. It indicates whether a device is currently configured to allow remote wakeup requests (the default is not remote wakeup).

For each of the status items that a host can query, it can also set with a SET_CONFIGURATION request.

■ SET_ADDRESS

When the host wants to change the default address of a USB device to an address unique to that device, it issues a **SET_ADDRESS** request to the device. It can take up to three stages to set the device's address. The first thing that happens is that a setup packet is sent to the device. The second stage is optional. In this stage, data may be transferred between the host and the device. The final, and not optional, stage is the transfer of status between the host and the device.

Status is sent to indicate the success or failure of the data stage. This means that status is always sent in the opposite direction of the data transfer. If there was no data transferred, then status is sent from the device to the host in acknowledgement of the SET_ADDRESS request.

It should be noted that the device does not actually change its address until after all three stages of the SET_ADDRESS request have completed. What this means is that all of the transactions making up the SET_ADDRESS request are directed to the same address (usually the default address); the data and status stages do not use the new address. This is different from other requests, where the request must be completely carried out before status is returned.

▮ SYNC_FRAME

When an endpoint in a USB device supports isochronous transfers, the data that's being sent may require that nonstandard frame sizes be sent (we'll talk about this in much more detail in Chapter 7). These varying frame sizes will vary according to a specific pattern. The **SYNC_FRAME** request defines this pattern, as the host and the device must agree upon which frame begins the repeating pattern.

The SYNC_FRAME request causes the endpoint to begin watching the start-of-frame frame numbers to decide where the frame is in the pattern it is transmitting. Once the device decides which frame the pattern began in, that frame number is returned to the host. This is done only when the device is sending data patterns isochronously and the data is synchronized with the client software on the host (using pattern matching). If the device endpont is not isochronous, then this request is not supported and will be ignored by the device. Like other configuration options, this procedure will need to be repeated after a device reset.

Descriptors

Throughout this book we have been talking about descriptors without explaining exactly what they are. This section will explain descriptors in probably far more detail than you need. Follow it, though, and you'll understand what descriptors are and why they are used.

Simply stated, a descriptor is nothing more than a well-defined data structure associated with some attributes on a device. The USB device reports its attributes using these descriptors.

Four basic types of descriptors are maintained by the USB device. These will all be explained a little later, but for reference they are:

- Device descriptors
- Endpoint descriptors
- Configuration descriptors
- Interface descriptors

Descriptors allow device attributes to be stored in data structures that look like something like database records. In this sense, different configurations within a device may reuse descriptors, or portions of descriptors, from configurations within the device that share characteristics.

Sometimes, descriptors need to convey string data (or human-readable text). Rather than storing this textual information on the device, a descriptor will *reference* text strings using an index number. This string reference is used by the client software to decide what the string text actually says. A USB device doesn't have to support strings, but it does have to support the fields that reference them. If a device does not support strings, then the string reference is simply set to zero. The software on the host understands that a zero string reference means that there is no string available.

One thing common to all descriptors is that they start out with the length of the descriptor. If a descriptor returns with a value in its length field that is less than it should be, then the host will reject the descriptor as invalid. If the value in the length field of the descriptor is greater than what it should be, then the extra bytes are simply ignored.

▌ Device Descriptor

Global information within a device, and used by all of the device's configurations, is described in the **device descriptor**. Each USB device only has one device descriptor.

As we've discussed before, each USB device has an endpoint zero, and it's used by the default pipe. The device provides the host with the maximum packet size that this endpoint will support. Other endpoints and interfaces are described in the configuration descriptor. There is no configuration descriptor for endpoint zero, and the maximum packet size is the only thing that a device can vary for a USB device. All other characteristics of endpoint zero are defined by the USB specification and are the same for all USB devices.

The device descriptor contains the following fields:

- Descriptor length
- Descriptor type
- Device-class code for the device
- Device-subclass code for the device
- Device protocol
- Maximum supported packet size
- Vendor ID
- Product ID
- Manufacturer string
- Product string
- Serial number
- Number of supported configurations

▌Configuration Descriptor

The **configuration descriptor** describes a device's specific configuration. A field within the configuration descriptor, the *configuration value*, describes which of the available configurations is currently active on the device. The host sets the configuration value when it issues a SET_CON-FIGURATION request to the device. This causes the device to assume the requested configuration.

The configuration descriptor also provides the number of interfaces provided by the selected configuration. As we've mentioned before, each interface may operate independently of any other. When the host asks for the device's configuration descriptor, all of the related interface and endpoint descriptors are returned. For example, a combination stereo speaker and microphone may contain separate and independent interfaces for each speaker and the microphone.

A device can maintain multiple configuration descriptors, one for each interface and interface endpoint. Endpoints are not shared between the various interfaces within a single configuration. They may be shared, however, among interfaces that use different configurations.

Very little can be changed within a configuration once a device is put into it. Alternate configurations can be selected, essentially causing the device to be "reconfigured." Beyond that, only the maximum packet size of an endpoint can be adjusted.

The fields of a configuration descriptor are as follows:

- Descriptor length
- Descriptor type (configuration descriptor)
- Total length of the data returned for this configuration (including all of the interface and endpoint descriptors)
- Number of interfaces
- Selected configuration value
- Configuration index (indexing a string describing this configuration)
- Device attributes (e.g., bus- or self-powered, remote wake-up enabled)
- Maximum power consumption

▌Interface Descriptor

The **interface descriptor** describes each interface within a given device on the Universal Serial Bus within the currently selected configuration. The interface descriptor for an interface is returned only when a device is satisfying a GET_CONFIGURATION request. Strange as it may seem, the interface descriptor cannot be accessed directly with a SET_DESCRIPTOR or GET_DESCRIPTOR request.

A configuration can contain one or more interfaces, each with its own set of endpoints. If this is the case, then each interface maintains a set of endpoint descriptors. If the active configuration supports multiple endpoints, then the endpoints for each interface are sent to the host immediately after the interface descriptor is sent when the device is satisfying a GET_CONFIGURATION request.

A device interface may allow its associated endpoint characteristics to be changed to alternate settings after the device has been initially configured. The default setting for an interface is *alternate setting zero*. These alternate settings can be put into place with SET_INTERFACE and GET_INTERFACE requests to the device. If an interface uses only endpoint zero, then it will not send any endpoint descriptors to the host. An interface descriptor *never* includes endpoint zero when it considers and tells the host the number of endpoints available.

The fields contained within an interface descriptor are:

- Descriptor length
- Descriptor type (interface descriptor)
- Interface number
- Alternate setting
- Number of endpoints
- Interface class
- Interface subclass
- Interface protocol
- Interface string (rather, a string index describing the interface)

▌ Endpoint Descriptor

Finally, we come to our last descriptor type: the **endpoint descriptor**. The endpoint descriptor provides information and configuration for each endpoint used in each interface. In fact, each endpoint used in an interface has its own descriptor. This descriptor contains all of the information that the host will need to calculate the bandwidth requirements of the endpoint.

Like the interface descriptor we just talked about, an endpoint descriptor cannot be directly manipulated or accessed with GET_DESCRIPTOR or SET_DESCRIPTOR requests from the host. Rather, it is returned as part of the configuration descriptor. Further, its capabilities can be adjusted only through a SET_CONFIGURATION request. As we've seen before, there is never an endpoint descriptor for endpoint zero.

The endpoint descriptor contains the following fields of information:

- Descriptor length
- Descriptor type (endpoint descriptor)
- Endpoint address (including the direction in which the endpoint transmits data)
- Endpoint attributes (i.e., control transfer, isochronous transfer, bulk transfer, interrupt transfer)
- Maximum packet size for the Endpont
- Polling interval (i.e., when should the host "poll" for information)

■ Device Communication

Having talked about device states, descriptors, and requests, we now discuss communication as a whole. Figure 5–3 illustrates how devices and the host communicate. In this section we focus on USB communication from the perspective of the device.

The bottommost "layer" of a device on the Universal Serial Bus is the USB bus interface. This bus interface provides the entire interaction between a device and the bus at an electrical and protocol layer. Above the bus-interface layer is the device-interface layer. The device-interface layer provides the interface between the device and the host. It is the layer that we will be talking about in this section. After all, the device's function layer only uses capabilities provided by the device layer (combined as interfaces) to support the needs of the host client software.

In Chapter 3 we talked about what happens within the Universal Serial Bus host system. To refresh quickly, the host system contains a hardware controller called the host bus controller. The host controller drives all of the actual traffic on the Universal Serial Bus. Above the host controller lives the host controller driver (or HCD). The Universal Serial Bus driver handles all of the bus-specific functions in the USB system. The USBD has an interface that it exports to client programs. This interface is called the USBDI. Controlling each device, ultimately, is the client software on the host. That is a lot of different layers of hardware and software on the host. As you can see from Figure 5–3, each layer communicates with a corresponding layer on the device.

There are a number of layers on a USB device, but the relationships between them are implementation specific. While communication between the host and the device must occur across the USB physical wire, the *logi-*

DEVICE

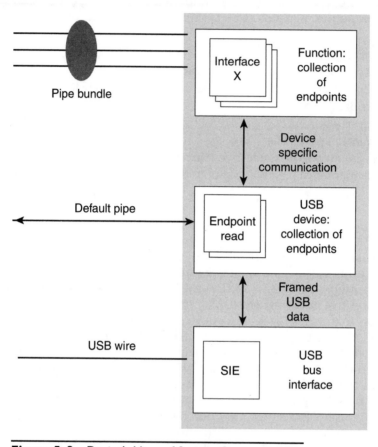

Figure 5–3 Device's View of System Communication

cal source and destinations of communication happen between the various layers on the host and USB device. It is the host client software that is the ultimate consumer of the function provided by the device. The relationship between the client software and the device function drives all other interaction between the device and the host.

At its most base level, a device on the Universal Serial Bus is nothing more than a collection of endpoints. Each endpoint supports a given pipe. Finally, each pipe supports a type of transfer. If you recall, there are four types of transfers, but a pipe can provide support for only one type. What type of transfer a pipe can effect is decided at configuration time. The Universal Serial Bus transfer types are described in great detail in Chapter 6, and they are as follows:

- Control transfers
- Isochronous transfers
- Interrupt transfers
- Bulk transfers

An endpoint must behave in a certain fashion for each of these transfer types. While a pipe can support only one transfer type, an endpoint may support a variety of transfer types. That flexibility goes away, however, once an association is made between a pipe and an endpoint. After all, if the pipe that an endpoint is attached to can support only control transfers, then there is little chance that the endpoint will ever see traffic other than control transfers. We will assume, for the purposes of this discussion, that an endpoint that is being used for communication is associated with a pipe.

Four basic communication primitives, or *mechanisms*, are used in communicating with endpoints. These are:

- Pipe mode, either stream or message mode
- Start-of-frame (SOF) synchronization, used to synchronize the device's internal clock
- Handshaking, used to implement error detection
- Data toggle, used to implement flow control in isochronous applications

We'll cover these various communication mechanisms in depth in the sections that follow.

▌ Pipe Mode

There are two modes that a pipe can support at any given time: **stream mode** and **message mode**. In stream mode, a pipe is considered to be a stream of data that flows in one direction. Message mode provides a bidirectional flow of bytes between the host and the device.

Stream-mode pipes always flow in one direction (i.e., are unidirectional). The receiving end of a stream pipe waits for a *token* indicating that data will be sent to it. The sending end of a stream-mode pipe, on the other hand, waits for a token asking it to send data. Data is always sent in chunks less than or equal to the maximum packet size specified in the pipe descriptor.

The host always initiates message-mode transfers. The host sends a command to the device, and then the device will send data to the host, or the host will send data to the device, or the command might require that no data change hands. In the case where no data packet is sent, a NULL data packet will be sent instead. It is the responsibility of the endpoint on the device to keep track of where it is in the context of the transmission sequence defined by the mode.

The first transaction in a message-mode transfer is a *setup* for subsequent communication. After the setup information is received by the endpoint on the device, the host will send to the endpoint a *token* indicating the direction of the transfer. If the device is to send data, it receives an IN token. If it is to receive data, it receives an OUT token. The setup command will determine the direction of subsequent transactions, even though some setup transactions do not require additional transactions to or from an endpoint.

■ Synchronization

Before the host and the device can communicate effectively, they must be synchronized with one another. To provide for this synchronization, the host sends out a *start-of-frame* (or SOF) token at a regularly timed periodic interval. This interval is 1 ms. Endpoints synchronize their internal clocks to this token. This enables each endpoint on a device to match its data transmission speed to that of the host. It also keeps both the host and the device from losing track of what data is being sent, since they both "look" for the data at the same point in time.

Not all endpoints in a USB device allow SOF synchronization, but they need to be synchronized nonetheless. These endpoints can force the entire Universal Serial Bus to synchronize to their internal clock, or they can attempt to adjust their transfer rate to compensate for the difference between the bus clock and their own clock.

The problem with attempting to have the bus adjust to the internal clock rate of an attached device is that there can be only one clock source on a given bus. If there is more than one device on the USB that cannot synchronize to the SOF packet, then something has to give. What happens in this case is that one of the devices becomes the "master clock" on the USB, and the other attempts to "adjust" to that clock rate. This is spelled out in the USB specification, but in the course of writing this book, the authors have not run across any devices that actually exhibit this restriction.

It is important to note that any device that cannot synchronize with the SOF packet **must** support both cases of either becoming the clock or adjusting. This is because there is no guarantee that it will be picked to provide the clock signal on the bus.

So, to sum up: three possible types of synchronization can occur for an endpoint with regard to the SOF synchronization. An endpoint can synchronize its clock with the USB clock, it can become the USB clock, or it can synchronize with the host by attempting to adjust its data flow.

▌ Handshakes

Error and data-flow information is sent by the endpoints to the host by using **handshakes**. The host also may send handshakes to the device endpoint to inform the endpoint of an error condition. Handshakes are transfer-type dependent, and as such vary with the transport type used by the endpoint. This subject is covered extensively in Chapter 7.

▌ Data Toggles

Sometimes when pipes are communicating, one or the other gets lost. This can occur because of an error on the bus or a simple flow-control problem. Some pipes are tolerant of this and are allowed to skip the frame that the error occurred in and resend the information during the next frame. In some cases, though, it is possible that the intended receiver thinks he received the data okay, but the sender knows better. In this case, the sender will attempt to retransmit the "lost" data. Unless the receiver knows that he is receiving the same data again, confusion can break out. Fortunately for us, the designers of the Universal Serial Bus considered this scenario.

The USB provides **data toggles**, which are packet IDs (PIDS) for the data phase of each transaction. Depending on the transfer type the endpoints are using, each endpoint needs to understand data toggles and handle the PIDs accordingly. Be patient, and refer to Chapter 7 for a complete discussion in the proper context of data toggles.

Wrapping It Up

This chapter has spent a lot of time talking about what happens *inside* a Universal Serial Bus device. Between this chapter and the two before it, you should be getting a pretty good feel for how the USB works. The only piece of the puzzle missing, from a Universal Serial Bus standpoint, is what

	Control	**Isochronous**	**Interrupt**	**Bulk**
Pipe Mode	Message	Stream	Stream	Stream
Synchronization	None	Bus, external, or software	None	None
Handshake	Yes	Not used	Yes	Yes
Data Toggles	Yes	Ignored	Yes	Yes
Error and Status Handling	Guaranteed delivery reports fatal errors only	Reports missing or corrupt data, no retries	Guaranteed deliverys reports fatal errors only	Guaranteed delivery reports fatal errors only

happens "on the wire" with the USB protocols and transactions. We cover that in the next chapter.

For your reference, the accompanying table summarizes the different modes and transfer types supported by USB devices.

On the Wire

The USB Protocol

It is all well and good to string USB devices and hosts and hubs together, but without a coherent communication scheme they aren't really much good. Fortunately, the designers of the Universal Serial Bus understood this fundamental limitation and gave us the Universal Serial Bus **protocol**.

The USB protocol allows the devices to all talk to and understand each other. It defines how a device should interpret a stream of bits flowing down the wire. Where does a frame start and end? What kind of data are we looking at? All of these questions, and many more, are answered for the device if it understands the USB bus protocol. We'll talk about the USB protocol in depth in this chapter.

We're going to look at things from the "bottom up," since so much of the high-level protocol definition relies on your understanding of what a frame and packet actually are. We'll talk a bit about *field* definitions within the actual packets that get sent across the Universal Serial Bus. We'll then discuss the different transaction types and the types of packets you will see associated with those transmission types. We will talk a little about *link-layer* flow control and error handling. The chapter will finish out with a brief discussion of babble, loss of activity (LOA) recovery, and retry synchronization. Heady words, but we'll define them all at the appropriate time.

▮ Bits on the Bus

The Universal Serial Bus sends data across the wire in a *serial* fashion. This means that one bit of information follows the next. Contrast this with something like the PCI bus within a PC, where upwards of 64 bits of information can flow across the bus at any given time.

Bits alone don't constitute communication between USB devices. The bits need to be segmented into "chunks" of information that the devices (and the host) can all understand. These segments of bits are called *fields*. Fields are the basic building block of the USB protocol, and we'll talk in depth about them as we move along. This can all be visualized in Figure 6–1, where you can clearly see bits, broken into fields, moving across the wire

If fields are the building blocks, then packets are what is constructed from these blocks. A packet of information on the Universal Serial Bus tells the devices what kind of communication is going on, and it what direction. There are packets for tokens, data, and handshaking. Since, as we now understand, every packet is broken into fields, then it should be logical to understand that the fields identify each packet as a specific type and provide other attributes to keep the device synchronized on what the sender of the packet is trying to say.

Before we get into the actual packet and transfer types, we're going to talk about the various fields that comprise packets. Then we'll talk about packets and the things that devices can do with them. We're going to simplify the discussion and not talk about the manipulations that the link-level hardware may perform on the bits (things like bit stuffing and NRZI coding).

▮ SYNC Field

Every packet has to be easy for the device to recognize. Each device also needs to be able to know when it has seen the end of the packet. For this reason, each packet has a distinct starting and ending bit pattern on the bus. This pattern is recognized by the bus-interface hardware on each device and is used by the input logic in the interface to synchronize the incoming packet with the clock within the device. This is called the **SYNC field**.

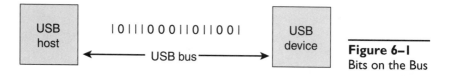

Figure 6–1
Bits on the Bus

The bit pattern for the SYNC field was chosen to maximize the number of times the bits "flip" from high to low (from 1 to 0) on the bus. This makes it an easier job for the hardware to detect it. The pattern is the binary representation of the letters "KJKJKJKK". Also note that the last two bits of the SYNC field are used to identify the first bit of the PID. All of the bits in the packets are offset from this point.

▍ Packet Identifier Field (PID)

The **packet identifier**, or **PID**, is the field that tells the device what to do with the packet. It comes immediately after the SYNC field and is the first really usable piece of information transmitted for each packet. As you can see in Figure 6–2, a PID is made up of a packet-type field (4 bits) and a *check field* (also 4 bits).

The check field is used to ensure that this is a valid packet. If there is an error on the bus that causes one of the PID bits to be wrong, then the check field is designed to catch that. The check field is a *one's complement* of the PID bits. What this means is that the check field should be bit for bit *opposite* the PID field. Again, you can see this demonstrated in Figure 6–2. If a packet is received and the check field isn't correct, then the rest of the packet is ignored by the device.

There are four broad groups of packets. Each group includes several possible types of packets. The first two bits in each PID tell the device what the packet group is, and the remaining two indicate the actual type of packet. We'll get into specifics in the next section, being satisfied for now with a listing. The packet groups are:

- Token, which is of type OUT, IN, SOF, or SETUP.
- Data, which is of type DATA0 or DATA1.
- Handshake, which is of type DATA0 or DATA1.
- Special, which can be used to enable downstream traffic to be low speed.

PID 0	PID 1	PID 2	PID 3
pcheck 0	pcheck 1	pcheck 2	pcheck 3

Figure 6–2
Format of a PID

■ Address Fields

As you are by now aware, each USB device is made up of a collection of *functions* which actually do something useful for the user (or so we hope). Each function within the device has an assigned address, which is transmitted in the **address field**. This address is different from the endpoint and is used in conjunction with it to completely identify the function. A packet that does not have both valid address and endpoint fields is ignored (as will accesses to endpoints which haven't been initialized yet).

The address field is 7 bits wide. This means that there can be at most 128 individual addresses on the Universal Serial Bus at any given time (128 is the highest number that can be represented by 7 bits). The address field is used only by IN, OUT, and SETUP tokens.

The address for each function is defined by the host during the *bus-enumeration* process on reset, or when the device is attached. When the device is first reset or powered on, the address defaults to zero—it remains this default address until the host configures it. It should be noted that a device could not be assigned the value of zero by the host because it is reserved for the default address.

■ Endpoint Field

It is the combination of the address and endpoint number that uniquely identifies a function within a USB device. That brings us to the **endpoint field**. The endpoint field is a 4-bit field that allows a single address to be used by multiple endpoints. This concept is called *subchanneling*. As with the address field, only the token packets IN, OUT, and SETUP use it.

Remember, all functions support the endpoint zero as a special control endpoint through which the host configures the device. Low-speed devices can support only two endpoints, while a full-speed device can support up to 16.

■ Frame-Number Field

Every frame has a unique number. This frame number is stored, naturally, in the **frame-number field**. It is an 11-bit number that is incremented by the host every time a new frame is transmitted. When the maximum frame number (hex 7ff) is reached, the number "rolls over" to zero again. The frame number is sent only in start-of-frame tokens at the start of the frame.

▌ Data Field

The **data field** is the part of the packet that holds, of course, the data for the packet. The contents of the data field will vary, based upon what is being done on the bus at the time, and is completely application and device dependent. The field can be between zero to 1023 bytes long, depending on the transfer type.

▌ Cyclic Redundancy Check Field

To provide error detection on token and data packets, the Universal Serial Bus uses a checksum called a cyclic redundancy check (CRC). This is stored in the **CRC field** of these packets. A checksum is, simply stated, the total value of all bytes in the packet added together. The host calculates the CRC when a packet is transmitted and stores it in the CRC field. When the device receives the packet, it calculates the CRC and checks what it thinks the CRC should be with what is actually in the CRC field. If the values match, then the packet is valid and is used. If the values do not match, however, then there is a problem and the packet is ignored. This provides complete and total coverage for all single- and double-bit errors.

It should be noted that the CRC calculations ignore the PID field in each packet, because the PID has a built-in check. See the previous discussion on the PID field for a refresher on how that works.

Checksums on token packets provide coverage of the address and endpoint fields of the IN, SETUP, and OUT tokens. They also cover the timestamp field of a start-of-frame (SOF) token. CRCs on data packets cover all of the data.

Packet Formats

Now that we understand the various fields that comprise packets on the Universal Serial Bus, it's time to talk about the actual packets. Just as fields are building blocks for packets, packets are building blocks for transactions (which we'll talk about next).

This section will talk about the formats for token, data, and handshake packets. We'll show diagrams of each packet and identify the relevant fields. You will walk away from this section knowing what each packet looks like on the Universal Serial Bus.

Token Packets

Token packets are used to indicate the type and direction of the transaction that is about to happen on the bus. As you can see in Figure 6–3, a token packet is made up of a PID field (which tells us whether it's an IN, OUT, or SETUP packet) and address and endpoint fields. If the transaction is either a SETUP or an OUT transaction, then the address and endpoint fields provide detail about which endpoint will receive the data that will invariably follow the token packet.

Now might be a good time to explain that the OUT and SETUP packet types describe transactions from the host to a function on the device. IN packet types, on the other hand, describe a transaction from a device function to the host. Only the host can only generate a token packet.

Earlier we talked about CRC checksums to protect data against "lost" and "corrupted" bits in the data stream. The token packet is one of the packet types that are protected by the CRC field. The address and endpoint fields of this packet are protected by checksums. If the transmitted CRC field does not match the CRC calculation that the device computes on the received packet, then the packet is simply ignored.

▌ Start-of-Frame (SOF) Packets

Frames are a little different from most of the other packets that we've talked about so far. Frames are not really a part of a transaction or transfer but are a synchronization mechanism. Once every millisecond (one millionth of a second) the host generates a **Start-of-Frame (SOF) packet**. As you can see from Figure 6–4, a SOF packet is fairly barren, containing only a PID and a frame number.

The SOF packet is a one-way packet that is not meant to elicit a response from the device that receives it—and all full-speed devices do receive it. The SOF packet is not sent to low-speed devices. Because the packet does not require acknowledgements from the receiving devices, there can be no guarantee that a device has received the SOF packet. It is the responsibility of the device to detect and handle missed SOF packets.

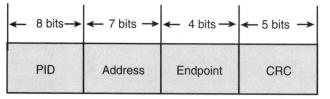

Figure 6–3
A TOKEN Packet

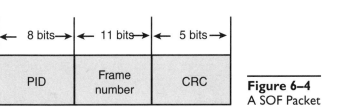

Figure 6–4
A SOF Packet

Data Packets

The **data packet** is the meat of any transaction. It is the packet that the actual values processed or generated by the devices are moved around in. The data packet is shown in Figure 6–5. Note that the entire data portion of the packet is protected by the CRC.

There can be two types of data packets, *Data0* and *Data1*. These two types are used in *data toggle synchronization*, which we will talk about later in this chapter. Basically stated, data toggle synchronization is used by the receiving side (either the device or the host) to keep track of which data packet is next, so that it can detect when a packet is lost (e.g., first the receiver expects DATA0, then DATA1).

Handshake Packets

Packets that are used to tell the status of a transaction are called **handshake packets**. A handshake packet provides the mechanism to report back to the host on a successful data transmission, provide flow control, and report stall conditions. Handshake packets are used only in transactions that support flow control and are always returned in either the handshake phase of the transaction or, in place of transmitted data, in the data phase of the transaction. The handshake packet, as you can see in Figure 6–6, consists of only a PID and is followed immediately by an end-of-packet (EOP) token.

Since a handshake packet is used for flow control, acknowledgement of data transactions, and reporting of stall conditions, it is only natural to assume that there are three types of handshake packets. These types are ACK, NAK, and STALL.

← 8 bits →	←0-1023 bytes→	←16 bits →
PID	Data	CRC

Figure 6–5
A DATA Packet

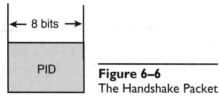

Figure 6–6
The Handshake Packet

An **ACK** handshake means that a data field in this transaction was received without any errors. This means that there were no bit-stuff or checksum (CRC) errors on the data field and that the data packet itself was received okay. The ACK handshake can also be issued when the sequence bits in the transaction mismatch, and the sender and receiver must resynchronize with one another. An ACK handshake packet is used only in transactions where data is transmitted and a handshake is expected. An ACK handshake packet is generated by the host for IN transactions (data sent by the USB device) and by a device function for OUT transactions (data sent by the USB host).

A **NAK** handshake, on the other hand, means either that the USB device wasn't able to accept data from the host (if the host was trying to send data at the time) or that the device function doesn't have any data to send to the host (when it's the device's "turn" to send data). The NAK handshake is returned in the data phase of a transaction by the USB device function when it isn't able to accept data, serving as a flow-control mechanism. The NAK means simply that the device cannot accept data and that it is a *temporary* condition. The device just needs time to catch up. The NAK handshake is also used by interrupt endpoints to tell the host that there is no interrupt pending.

Finally, there is the **STALL** handshake packet. This is returned by a USB device function to tell the host that the device cannot transmit or receive data and that the host must help the device rectify the situation. If host intervention were not required, then the device would return a NAK handshake packet instead. Once a device issues the STALL handshake, then it will remain in the STALL condition until the host does something about it (such as reset the device, etc.). A USB host can never issue a STALL handshake. After all, who would clear the STALL for the host?

Transaction Formats

Now that we have talked extensively about the different packet types and fields within the packets, it's time to talk about the different transaction types. Just as packets are made up of groupings of fields, transactions on the Universal Serial Bus are made up of groupings of packets.

The type of transaction, and the formats of the underlying packets, vary with each endpoint type. Remember, once an endpoint is established it can use only one transaction type. The four transaction types are bulk, control, interrupt, and isochronous transactions. We'll discuss each of these in turn.

■ Bulk Transactions

The first type of transaction we'll talk about is the **bulk transaction**. Bulk transactions are, as you might guess from the name, used to move data between devices and the host. Data moved around in bulk transactions is completely protected against error with the use of error detection and retry logic.

A bulk transaction occurs over three *phases*, illustrated in Figure 6–7. The first is the token phase, alerting the system that a bulk transaction is about to happen. Next is the data phase, in which the data is transmitted. Finally, there is a handshake phase. A handshake packet is sent from the receiving USB device to the transmitting device letting it know the outcome of the data phase. If there was a problem, the data is retransmitted. If not, then things move along.

For example, suppose that the host wants to send bulk audio data to a set of USB speakers. The first thing the host will do is issue an OUT token packet, telling the speaker that the next packet it receives will contain data that should be turned into sound. Next the host will send a data packet full of audio data to the speaker. If the data was received by the speaker without any errors being detected, then the speaker will send an ACK handshake packet indicating this fact. If, on the other hand, the speaker

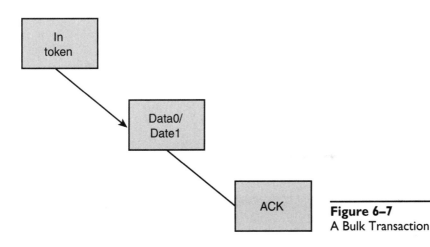

Figure 6–7
A Bulk Transaction

couldn't deal with the data for some reason, then it will send a NAK hand-shake packet to the host, asking it to resend the data. This might happen, for instance, if the input buffer on the speaker was full and it couldn't physically store the data that it was supposed to turn into sound.

■ Control Transfers

Control transfers are used for configuration and status reporting with Universal Serial Bus devices. Control transfers are a little different from other USB transactions in that each is made up of two control-transfer-specific transaction states: setup and status. There could also be a data transfer involved in a control transfer, but not necessarily.

The *setup stage* is used by the host to transmit information to the device's control endpoint. A setup transaction, as you can see in Figure 6–8, looks like an OUT token but uses the special SETUP token instead of the OUT. If there is data to be transferred during the setup, then the setup packet *always* uses a Data0 packet type for the data packet. (The significance of this will become clear in the section about data toggling.) The host expects the USB device that receives a setup transaction to respond with a handshake packet, indicating either ACK, NAK, or STALL.

If there is data to be transferred as part of the control transfer, then it happens after the setup stage. This *data stage* looks exactly like a bulk transfer (which we described in the last section). One caveat is that all of the transactions in the data stage must be in the same direction (e.g., all from the host to the device, or all from the device to the host, no mixing). During the setup phase, the host and device decide on the amount of data

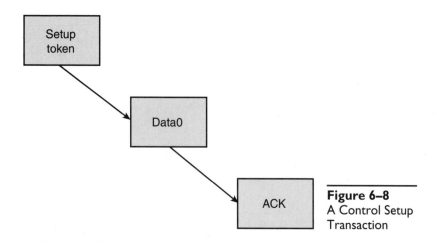

Figure 6–8
A Control Setup Transaction

to be sent and in which direction it will flow. If the data does not fit within a single packet, then it's spread over multiple packets.

After the setup and data transfers, a status is returned from the device to the host. This *status stage* is the last operation in the control-transfer sequence. The status is always reported in a data packet using the Data1 packet type. There are three possible statuses that a device might report back to the host: the command was handled without any errors, the command failed, or the device is still busy servicing the command.

Control transfers are one of the things that can cause a device to STALL. If the command endpoint on the device is sent more data, or if it asked for more data than it knows to expect, then the device will return a STALL handshake packet. If there is a stall, then, naturally, there will be no status stage for that control transfer. The device will have to be reset or reconfigured by the host at this point.

▌ Interrupt Transactions

When a device has data to send to the host that the host did not explicitly ask for, it comes in the form of an **interrupt transaction**. Actually, it's more accurate to say that the *client software* that's controlling the device hasn't asked for any data.

Remember that the Universal Serial Bus doesn't allow devices to take the initiative and transmit information whenever they have information to transmit. USB devices are all *slave devices* to the USB host. The USB host controller, without the explicit knowledge of the host software, *polls* each device in turn to ask if it has an interrupt to send. The host controller does this with an IN token, as you can see in Figure 6–9.

When a USB device receives this IN token, it decides if it has data it wants to send the host. If it does not have data to send (a condition where no interrupt is pending), then it responds to the IN token packet from the host with a NAK handshake packet.

If, on the other hand, the device does have new data to send to the host, then it returns a data packet to the host containing this new data. After the host receives the data and checks that it is error free, it sends an ACK handshake packet to the device. If there was an error in the data packet, then the host doesn't send any handshake packet. We'll talk next about why the host doesn't send a NAK.

When a device sends data to the host using the interrupt transfer mechanism, then it uses something called the *data toggle protocol* (which we discuss later in this chapter). The data toggle protocol allows the USB device to know whether or not data has been received by the host without explicit handshaking from the host. This allows the function to send in-

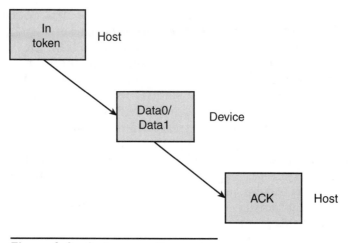

Figure 6–9   An Interrupt Transaction

terrupt information only until it has been successfully received by the host, rather than sending the same data time and again with each consecutive poll.

Earlier in the chapter we talked about the IN token packet. We discussed how it could have a PID specifying either Data0 or Data1. The data toggle protocol, simply stated, works by the host asking first for Data0 with an IN token, then asking for Data1. The device keeps track of what is being asked for. If the host asks for Data0, for example, twice in a row, then there was a problem the first time it was sent. The device will resend the data. This is more efficient than a NAK handshake from the host on a packet error and requires less bus traffic. The Data0/Data1 state on the device is toggled after each ACK handshake packet from the host.

▌ Isochronous Transactions

Isochronous transactions look just like bulk transactions, except that no error checking is done on the data, there is no handshake phase, and there is no retry capability. Only a token and a data phase are used in order to move data as quickly as possible between the host and a USB device. As you can see in Figure 6–10, the host issues either an IN token (if it's sending data to the device) or an OUT token (if it wants data from the device). After the IN or OUT token, data is transferred.

It's interesting to note that isochronous transactions do not support data toggling as interrupt transactions do. This is because devices (and soft-

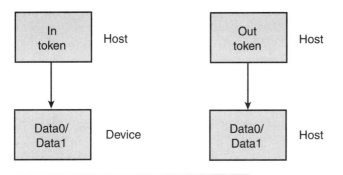

Figure 6–10 An Isochronous Transaction

ware) performing isochronous transactions do not care about data. It might seem strange that we would want to send guaranteed-bandwidth data across the bus without checking for errors, but keep in mind that error detection is expensive in terms of processor time in the computer—it simply slows things down. The kinds of devices that use isochronous data (e.g., multimedia devices) can usually tolerate the occasional "glitch" in the data that a bad packet or two would generate.

For example, a USB speaker might accept thousands of data points per second to reproduce the sound from a music CD. A couple of corrupted data points might not even be noticed in the output of the speakers.

Data Toggle Synchronization

In the discussion on interrupt transactions, we touched on the concept of **data toggle synchronization**. Simply stated, this means using Data0 and Data1 IN or OUT tokens to synchronize the data that's being moved between a USB device and host. There's more to it than that, of course, and that's what this section is about.

Data toggle synchronization gives us a mechanism that guarantees the handshake phase of a transaction was understood correctly by both the transmitter and receiver. If you remember from our discussion earlier on the PID field in the token packet, there are sequence bits that can be set to either Data0 or Data1. The receiver in a USB transaction toggles these sequence bits (from Data1 to Data0, for instance) when the receiver can accept data and has received a data packet with no detected errors. The transmitter in a transaction, on the other hand, toggles its sequence bits

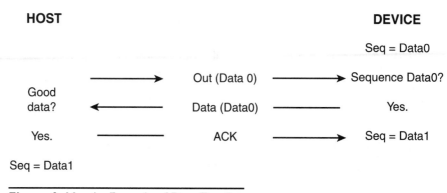

Figure 6–11   An Example of Data Toggling

only when it receives an ACK from the receiver. If this sounds confusing, then follow the example in Figure 6–11.

The example in Figure 6–11 shows what happens when data is successfully transferred from a device to a host. First the host issues an OUT token to the device with the sequence bits set to Data0. The device, since this is the first transaction, has its sequence bits set to Data0. When it receives the OUT (Data0) token, it compares the sequence bits in the token with the sequence bits it maintains. They are both Data0, so there is a match. The device sends the data.

If the host receives the packet and there is no error, then it sends an ACK packet to the device. When the device receives this ACK packet, it "toggles" its sequence bits to be Data1. The next time that the host asks for data, it will send an OUT token with the sequence bits set to Data1.

If, on the other hand, there had been an error when the host received the data packet, then it would not have sent an ACK to the device. The device would not have toggled its sequence bits. The next OUT token, then, would resend the Data0 token. This would continue until the host sent an ACK packet to the device.

▌ Initialization via the SETUP Token

Before the host and device can use data toggle synchronization, they must both agree upon an initial set of sequence bits (either Data0 or Data1). This is accomplished with a control transfer with a SETUP token. The host sends a SETUP token containing the initial sequence bits for the host and device. The device sends an ACK handshake to the host when it receives and processes the SETUP.

▌Corrupted ACK Handshake

We've talked about what happens when data is transmitted correctly, and when the receiver receives corrupt data. But what happens when the receiver receives good data, but the ACK handshake packet doesn't make it to the transmitter? This can lead to a temporary loss of consistency, as we'll see here.

The transmitter knows when good data was received when it receives an ACK handshake from the receiver. If that ACK handshake was lost or corrupted somewhere on the Universal Serial Bus, then there is a loss of synchronization between the transmitter and receiver.

After the first transaction, the device still has its sequence bits set to Data0, but the host has incremented its sequence bits to Data1. After all, the host has received valid data, but the device doesn't know it because the ACK was lost somewhere on the bus. During the next transaction, the transmitter will again send the data associated with the Data0 sequence. After all, as far as the device is concerned, this data was lost.

The host, though, is expecting a Data1 packet. When it receives the Data0 data from the device, it throws away the data and does not toggle its sequence bits. It does, however, issue an ACK for the data. Now the device knows that the host successfully received the data, and it toggles its sequence bits to Data1. The host and device are back in sync.

For this to work, the device must guarantee that the data packet being resent is the exact same length that was originally sent. If, for some reason, the transmitting device cannot do that (for example, there is a buffer underrun on the device), then it must report a bit-stuffing violation to the host and abort the transaction. This forces an error to occur that the receiving device can detect, and the host will not treat any partial packet as a good packet.

Low-Speed Signaling

The Universal Serial Bus handles transfers at both full speed (12 Mbps) and low speed (1.5 Mbps). As we discussed in Chapter 5, hubs disable bus traffic to downstream ports when full-speed transfers are happening. Hubs do this both to minimize the amount of electrical noise the devices have to deal with and to prevent any possibility of a low-speed device interpreting a full-speed packet as being addressed to it. Hubs, though, must be able to understand when low-speed communication is happening. To facilitate this, the designers of the Universal Serial Bus gave us **low-speed signaling**.

If a packet is being sent to a low-speed device, then it requires a *preamble*. This is series of tokens sent at full speed. A preamble is composed of a SYNC followed by a PID with the PRE bits set (refer back to our discussion earlier in this chapter on fields). All USB devices other than hubs ignore this combination of bits flowing across the bus.

After the host transmits this preamble, the host waits an extralong period of time (four full bit times) for the hub to process the preamble. It would be unreasonable for the host to expect the hub to handle this with normal full-speed timing. After all, the hub must reconfigure its repeater to accept low-speed signaling and drive its low-speed ports to the "idle" state.

Once the host sends the preamble to put the hub into low-speed mode, it is "safe" for the host to communicate with the low-speed device on the hub. This low-speed communication begins with the host issuing a SYNC packet at low speed. The rest of the packet then follows. After the low-speed packet is sent, the hub reconfigures itself to once again operate with full-speed devices.

If all of this sounds horribly inefficient, that's because it is. The USB designers understood the performance implications also and provided a number of restrictions on low-speed devices. These include:

■ The data is limited to 8 bytes at a time.
■ Only interrupt and control transfers are supported.
■ Low-speed devices do not handle the start-of-frame packet.

Error Detection and Recovery

A fundamental assumption in the USB world is that errors will be detected and handled. For the Universal Serial Bus to operate efficiently and reliably, it must handle a variety of error conditions that are occurring on an ongoing and transaction-type basis. Only isochronous transmissions are immune to error detection and correction by the USB.

The Universal Serial Bus provides for three distinct error-detection types: bit-stuff violations, PID field check bits, and checksums (or CRCs). A bit-stuff violation is an electrical condition having to do with data transmission across the bus. Since it is directly related to the physical-link level and is invisible to both the user and the software, we won't discuss it further in this book.

A PID field, as we described earlier in this chapter, is made up of four PID bits and four check bits. Each check bit in the PID field corresponds to a PID bit. For example, PID bit 1 corresponds to check bit 1. The check bit should be exactly the opposite value of the PID bit. So, for example, if PID bit 1 was a zero, then check bit 1 will be a one. If there is not a match, then there is a PID check mismatch and the PID is invalid.

Checksums we have also discussed extensively. Briefly restated, a CRC (cyclic redundancy check) is calculated on protected fields by adding the binary values of each byte in the field together. The resulting number is the CRC. Both the transmitting device and the receiving device calculate the CRC and compare. If there is a mismatch, then odds are that a transmission error occurred.

With the single exception of the SOF token, any packet that is received corrupted is ignored and any data that might have accompanied the packet is discarded. The accompanying table lists the error-detection types, the packets that the detection is valid for, and what the receiver does with the packet.

Field	Error	Action
PID	PID check, bit stuff	Ignore packet
Address	Bit stuff, address CRC	Ignore token
Frame Number	Bit stuff, frame-number CRC	Ignore frame-number field
Data	Bit stuff, data CRC	Discard data

▮ False EOPs

Sometimes, on the bus, a device might receive a false end-of-packet (or EOP) condition. This must be handled in such a way that the packet currently being transmitted completes before the host or another device attempts to transmit a new packet. If a new packet were to be transmitted when there was a false EOP, then there would be a *bus collision,* and up to two transactions could be corrupted. False EOPs are detected because any packet with a false EOP will appear as a truncated packet with a failed CRC to the device that is receiving it.

As you might expect, a USB device is going to handle a false EOP differently than the host will handle it. When a device receives a corrupted data packet, it simply ignores it and waits for the host to resend it. This happens because it ensures that the device won't be trying to send a handshake packet at the same time that the host may still be trying to get the initial packet out onto the bus. If there is a false EOP, for instance, the host will continue to send the packet. After all, the host doesn't know that the device thinks the packet has already ended. The device will be able to pick back up on the next token.

If, on the other hand, a packet from the device to the host is corrupted with a false EOP, then the host will ignore the packet and not issue a handshake, allowing the device to time out. The host assumes that a false EOP has occurred when it receives a corrupted data packet. It waits a period of time (16 bit times) to see if there is more traffic coming from the device. If it doesn't see any upstream traffic and the bus remains in the idle state, then it issues the next token. If it does, however, sense more data coming upstream, it waits for it to finish before moving on to the next packet.

■ Babble and Loss-of-Activity Recovery

The Universal Serial Bus must not ever be put into a condition where it is waiting forever for the end of a packet, or where it is in anything other than the idle state. If either of these conditions were ever allowed to happen, then the bus could lapse into a state where it could quickly become unusable. There are two conditions that must be detected that would put the bus in these states: *loss of activity* and *babble*.

Loss of activity (or simply **LOA**) is a condition that occurs when there is a start of packet (SOP) but no corresponding bus activity and no EOP at the end of the frame. If LOA isn't detected, then the devices on the bus spend all of their time waiting on the EOP that will never arrive. The bus is unusable.

Babble, on the other hand, is described simply as bus activity past the end of the frame. If babble isn't detected, then frames could be lost. Both babble and LOA are completely unacceptable and must be detected if the Universal Serial Bus is to be reliably used.

The most logical component to detect both babble and LOA is the hub. And, indeed, it is the hub that contains the logic that detects and corrects for these conditions. Any USB device that fails to complete its transmission at the end of a frame is stopped from transmitting further by having its ports turned off. A thorough discussion of these mechanisms can be found in Chapter 5 of this book.

Wrapping It Up

In this chapter we have talked at great length about what happens *between* the devices on the Universal Serial Bus. You learned about the four basic transaction types (bulk, control, interrupt, and isochronous) that make up USB communication. We discussed what happens when things go wrong on the wire, how these problems are detected, and which component is responsible for "fixing" the problem.

By this point you should understand how the Universal Serial Bus works. We've devoted a chapter to the host, the hub, the device, and now the protocol. Next we are going to delve into the issues you will encounter when setting up a USB system, and we'll see how such a system actually looks in the Microsoft Windows environment.

USB in the Windows World

Introduction

To show how new USB technology is, or maybe just how slowly the various implementations are going, consider that the original outline of this book had this chapter giving a survey and overview of the various USB implementations across the various operating systems. As this book leaves the author's word processor for the publisher, only Microsoft is providing operating-system support for the Universal Serial Bus. We know that others are working on it, it's just not available at the time of this writing. Perhaps we can give a thorough overview of all of the operating-system offerings in a subsequent edition of this book.

Microsoft has not disappointed us. They have jumped in with both feet and provided USB support in Windows 95 (when the OSR2 patches are applied), Windows 98, Windows/NT 4.0 (with a service packet applied), and Windows/NT 5.0. You will notice that Microsoft has not supported the Universal Serial Bus in any of the Windows 3.x products, and for good reason. Windows 3.x is years beyond being obsolete, and users should upgrade to Windows 95 or Windows 98 to get full advantage of progressing technology. What is surprising, though, is that Windows/CE is not yet supported. We're certain, though, that support will be forthcoming.

This chapter will give a high-level overview of how the Universal Serial Bus structure fits into the Windows world. For a detailed discussion of the underpinnings of USB support in Windows, we will point you to the Microsoft documentation included in the Device Driver Developer's Kit (the DDK) for the various operating systems. After all, this book is about understanding the Universal Serial Bus. It is not intended to be the sole reference for developers of USB software and hardware.

One quick note to help you understand this chapter a little better: we use the generic word *Windows* to signify all of Windows 95, Windows 98, and Windows/NT versions 4.0 and 5.0. This usage, while not really encouraged by Microsoft, will serve to keep the sentences and meanings clear. At the time of this writing, there are no differences worth mentioning between the various USB implementations.

USB Software Architecture

As you can see in Figure 7–1, Windows separates very distinctly the various software components that make up a USB host. There is the USB client software, consisting of nothing more than device drivers that control the various USB peripheral devices. The client software talks through a well-defined software interface to the root-hub driver. The root-hub driver talks to the Universal Serial Bus driver (the USBD) through the USBD interface (the USBDI). The USBD communicates with the underlying host-controller through a choice of two host-controller drivers. Finally, the host-controller drivers talk directly to the USB physical bus (through the PCI enumerator software, of all things!). So far, this all sounds like the discussion in Chapter 3 on the USB host architecture and, to be fair, it is. Beyond this, though, things become specific to Windows.

Like device drivers in the Windows NT environment, the various layers of the USB software stack communicate using a mechanism called *I/O Request Packets* (or *IRPs*). A device driver communicates with another device driver by populating the IRP structure with the request it wishes to make (such as "read a USB endpoint") and passes it to the next lower layer. When the lower layer has satisfied the request, it alerts the original caller. This procedure can be duplicated for as many layers of device drivers as necessary.

While the various layers communicate using IRPs, the actual USB requests are stored in something that Microsoft calls a **Universal Serial Bus Request** (or **URP**). The URP merely includes a structure containing fields that the underlying hardware needs in order to format a bus-level transaction to the USB device.

Understanding the inner working of IRPs, URPs, and NT device drivers is far from essential in following the discussions in this chapter. It is pointed out simply to show that there are mechanisms for *layered* device drivers to communicate between the layers, and that these mechanisms are common across Windows implementations of the USB software stack.

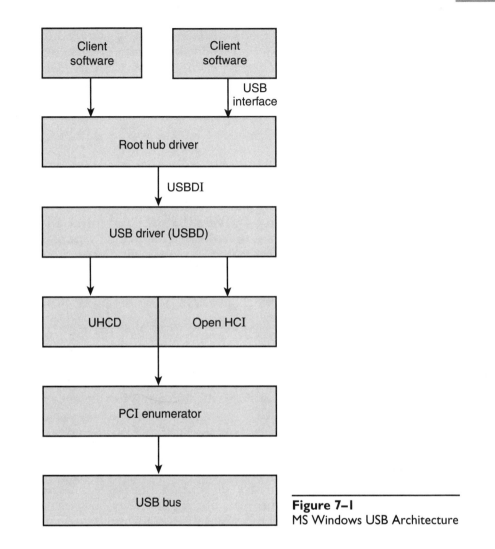

Figure 7–1
MS Windows USB Architecture

USBD

The **Universal Serial Bus Driver** (or **USBD**) is the component in a USB host that manages the "work" of the Universal Serial Bus. The USBD handles all of the protocol work and high-level interrupt handling. Windows defines the USBD in the context of a new device-driver model called the Windows Driver Model (or WDM).

The WDM was first brought to light by Microsoft in 1997 in order to provide a consistent and common device-driver model for certain classes of devices between the various Windows operating systems. Indeed, a WDM device driver written for a Windows 9x platform will run without change (or even recompilation) on a Win/NT 4.0 or 5.0 machine. It seems natural that the first device driver to take advantage of the portability provided by WDM is the USB software stack.

■ UHCD and OpenHCI

There are two interfaces that the various USB vendors are attempting to bring forward to control the USB host controller in a system and, surprisingly, Microsoft is not taking sides. Microsoft supports both host controller interfaces. These are the **Universal Host Controller Driver** (or **UHCD**) and the **Open Host Controller Interface** (or **OpenHCI**). The OpenHCI originated at, and is being supported by, Compaq Computer Corporation. Others are using the UHCD. One can only imagine that one of these interfaces will gain widespread acceptance and the other will fade from the scene. For now, though, the USB driver developer in the Windows world has her choice.

The host-controller driver (whichever is controlling the bus) communicates through the host controller to the physical bus. Or so it would seem. Windows places its *PCI Bus Enumerator* between the host-controller driver and the USB bus. It is the responsibility of the PCI Bus Enumerator to load the appropriate USB system software when it detects the presence of a Universal Serial Bus in the system.

■ Root-Hub Driver

While the host controller drivers sit beneath the USBD, the **root-hub driver** sits above it. Remember from our discussions of both the USB host and USB hubs that every host in a USB system contains an integrated, controlling hub called the USB root hub. By definition, every device on the USB bus is a *descendant* of this root hub. Microsoft finds it natural to have the client driver software for all attached devices communicate through a Windows-defined USB interface to this root hub's driver. Another way to do this would be to talk directly to the USBD through the USBDI.

■ USB Clients

The USB **client software**, in the form of device drivers, lives just above the root-hub driver. It communicates to the underlying USB software

Windows Programming Function	Purpose
UsbBuildFeatureRequest()	This function allows the client software to turn on and turn off individual features on a USB device.
UsbBuildGetDescriptorRequest()	This routine returns to the caller information about a given descriptor from the host controller.
UsbBuildGetStatusRequest()	This function provides a means for the client software to query the status of a given USB device, endpoint, pipe, or interface.
UsbBuildInterruptofBulkTransferRequest()	This routine formats a request for either a bulk transfer or an interrupt transfer between the host and a device.
UsbBuildSelectConfigurationRequest()	This function provides a mechanism to allow the configuration on a device to be set.
UsbBuildSelectInterfaceRequest()	This routine allows the host software to select an "alternate" endpoint to use on the USB device.
UsbBuildVendorRequest()	This "catch-all" function allows the user to send device-specific requests to pipes, endpoints, or interfaces on the USB device.
USBD_CreateConfigurationRequest()	This function allocates and formats an URB to configure (or reconfigure) an attached USB device.
USBD_GetInterfaceLength()	This routine returns to the caller the length of a given interface descriptor (including all endpoints).
USBD_GetUSBDIVersion()	This function returns the version of the USBD Interface that is running on the machine.
USBD_ParseConfigurationDescriptor()	This function scans all of the available configuration descriptors for one matching what the client software is looking for, and returns the first match.
USBD_ParseDescriptors()	This function searches all of the available descriptors for one matching the criteria specified by the user, and gives him the first match.
USBD_RegisterHcFilter()	This routine allows the programmer to insert his own code into the host controller path.

through a well-defined interface called the USB Interface. This is not to be confused with the USBDI is completely Windows specific. Don't expect your USB drivers for Windows to be portable to other systems. Of course, the same is true for just about every other Windows driver, so it should not be too much of a hardship.

The accompanying table provides a summary of the USB interface functions provided by the Windows USB Interface. A complete discussion of these functions can be found in the various Device Driver Development Kits (DDKs) for each Windows operating system. Additional information may be found on Microsoft's Web site.

USB Driver Loading

USB devices can contain multiple distinct interfaces, each with its own configuration. Each function contained within a device, and possibly each different configuration, requires its own device driver. This is a generalization, since it is more than possible for a device driver to be written to support multiple functions on a given USB device. You will usually see, however, a single device driver for any particular function. This is an important point to understand, because each device's configuration must be understood by the system at the time the bus is enumerated.

Each device driver can assist in determining what functions a particular device is supporting, but the device driver can be fully loaded. After all, the proper device driver cannot be loaded until the function of the device is fully understood and enumerated by the lower-layer host software. If it sounds like a "chicken and egg" problem, that's because it really is. The engineers at Microsoft provided mechanisms to make it all work, and that's described in their documentation.

The Windows USB software loads a client device driver not for each device as you might expect, but for each interface on a device. Remember that a device can have multiple interfaces that provide completely different functions. For example, a combination USB keyboard and mouse might have a separate interface for the mouse function and the keyboard function. It makes sense that different device drivers would exist for each.

If, during the bus-enumeration process, a device is found for which there is no device driver on the system, then the user is prompted to put one on the system. The user should load one, but if she doesn't have one (or just doesn't want to load it yet) then she will be warned that the device is there but is unusable.

USB Enumeration

Windows enumerates the Universal Serial Bus by building a list of objects called **physical-device objects** (or **PDOs** in Windows parlance). A PDO is nothing more than a data structure maintained by the operating system. The software operates on these PDOs, as they represent in software the attached USB device.

When the bus-enumeration process is first started, there is only one PDO—the root-hub PDO. The enumeration process then searches the Universal Serial Bus and creates a new PDO for each device it finds. It's important to note that a device is assigned a PDO in the order it is found; the actual physical layout does not make any difference to the software.

Just as there is a separate device driver for every interface on a device, there is a separate PDO for each device interface. This is illustrated in Figure 7–3, showing a configuration that has one device with three interfaces attached to the root hub.

Figure 7–4 further illustrates the concept of bus enumeration using PDOs. This clearly shows the physical layout of a bus with two hubs, each with two devices attached to the root hub. As the bus is enumerated, the PDOs are created in the order that the devices are scanned and not necessarily in the order that they actually exist. Figure 7–5 shows the PDO list for the physical USB topology shown in Figure 7–4.

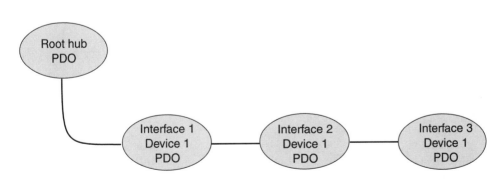

Figure 7–3   Root-Hub PDO

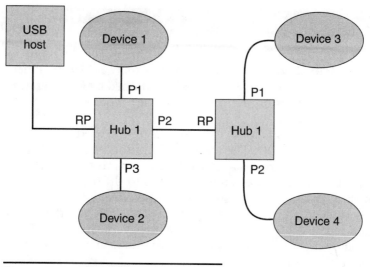

Figure 7–4   Example Physical Topology

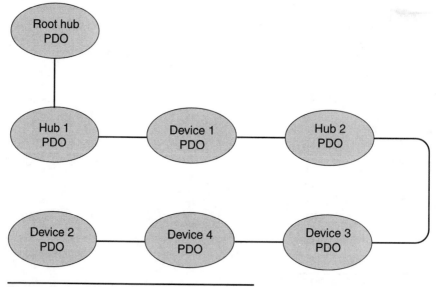

Figure 7–5   PDO List for Example Topology

User Interface

The Universal Serial Bus was designed to be a truly plug-and-play bus, and it is (at least in the Windows world). Devices are detected as they are plugged in, and the drivers configure themselves based upon the hardware they find. There is really no place for a user interface in a self-detecting, self-configuring environment. True to form, there is no user interface to the core USB components.

There may be, however, some device-driver-specific configuration screens. Such an interface is outside the scope of this book and should be well defined by the vendor that you bought the device from.

All of the bus- and device-configuration information is, however, stored in the systems registry. While you can use registry edit tools to modify these values, it is strongly discouraged. The values are not documented and will typically be implementation and device specific.

Wrapping It Up

In this chapter, we have talked briefly about what Microsoft has given us to "do" USB in the Windows world. They've made a very successful attempt at hiding the details of the implementation from all but people who write client software for USB devices. For the most part, in the Windows environment you simply have to plug a USB device in and the rest will be taken care of for you. The Universal Serial Bus is an early step toward true plug-and-play.

Frequently Asked Questions

What Do You Want to Know?

This chapter provides answers to frequently asked questions about the Universal Serial Bus.

What Is the Universal Serial Bus?

The USB is a specification developed by PC and telecommunications industry members for attaching peripheral devices to the PC. The USB allows computer peripherals to be attached to the outside of the computer, thus eliminating the need to install cards into dedicated computer slots and re-configure the system. The USB is designed to be plug-n-play—there are no dip switches or jumpers to configure. The Universal Serial Bus is a "hot-plug" bus, meaning devices can be attached to it without rebooting the computer. The USB allows up to 127 devices to run at the same time on the bus, with hubs connecting the devices to the bus. For more information about the history of the Universal Serial Bus, you can visit the home page of the USB Forum at http://www.usb.org.

What Kind of Devices Can I Plug Into the Universal Serial Bus?

Any kind of device that can talk to a computer can potentially become a USB device. This includes keyboards, monitors, joysticks, mice, tape drives, cameras, scanners, printers, telephones, and just about anything else you can imagine. The higher-than-normal transfer rates provided by the Universal Serial Bus also open the door to new devices that have traditionally been relegated to niche and specialty applications—items such as data gloves, digitizers, and streaming video devices.

What Do USB Plugs and Ports Look Like?

There is one "universal" plug for all USB connections between peripherals and PCs. This plug is illustrated in Figure 8–1.

Some USB ports on certain peripherals and PCs appear as shown in Figure 8–2.

Will I Need Special Software to Run USB?

You shouldn't, but that depends upon what operating system you are using. As this book is being written, some versions of UNIX do not support the Universal Serial Bus, though most desktop operating systems shipping

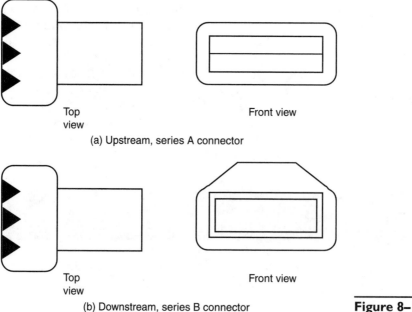

Top view

Front view

(a) Upstream, series A connector

Top view

Front view

(b) Downstream, series B connector

Figure 8–1   USB plug

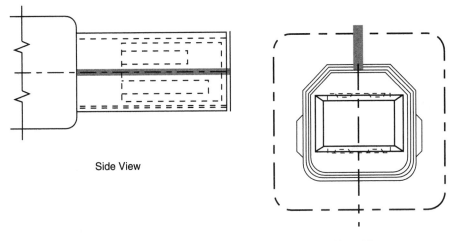

Side View

Front View

Figure 8–2 Alternative USB plug

do. Microsoft Windows 98 supports USB natively, while Windows 95 requires a special patch called OSR5 (see http://www.microsoft.com/windows95 for details). Windows NT also requires a special patch from Microsoft.

Is USB Available on Laptop Computers in Addition to Desktops?

Yes, the Universal Serial Bus is a key feature on many notebook computers from leading manufacturers. Very soon it will be standard issue on notebook computers. There are a number of advantages to using USB on portable computers, including the flexibility of adding peripherals in the slot-limiting space of a notebook computer.

What Are the Best Applications for USB?

USB plays a key role in the three fastest-growing areas: digital imaging, PC telephony, and multimedia games. The presence of USB means that PCs and peripherals will work together with a high degree of reliability in these exciting new application areas. USB opens the door to new levels of innovation and ease of use for input devices, such as the new generation of "force-feedback" digital joysticks.

Will Traditional PC Serial and Parallel Ports Disappear?

While USB will not replace traditional PC ports overnight, it is expected to rapidly become the preferred means of connecting I/O devices (such as digital joysticks, for example) as well as "medium-speed" peripherals such as phones, scanners, and digital cameras. Higher-speed devices, such as mass-storage devices, will require connectivity with higher data rates than USB currently provides. PCs will feature USB ports together with these higher-speed connections.

Does USB Affect the Cost of PCs and Peripheral Devices?

No, USB functionality is built into most modern PC chipsets as well as operating-system and other system software. It will not affect he price of your PC.

In addition, by eliminating add-in cards and separate power supplies, USB can help make PC peripheral devices more affordable than they otherwise would be. In addition, USB's "hot-swapping" capability allows the business user to easily attach and detach peripherals. Device sharing can reduce the cost of ownership of such equipment.

How Many USB Peripherals Can I Connect at Once?

Technically, you can connect up to 127 individual USB peripherals at one time. It's interesting to note that just one UB plug must be connected to the USB port on the PC. Other connections may be made on the desktop, using USB ports on hub peripherals.

How Can I Plug my RS-232 and Parallel-Port Devices Into My Computer's USB Port?

Many manufacturers sell devices called "bridges" or "converters" that provide a level of translation between the Universal Serial Bus and these other buses. The bridge device looks and behaves like a USB device. To the host computer, it looks like a traditional RS-232 or parallel-port device.

What Is Isochrony and Why Is It Important?

A key feature of the Universal Serial Bus is its support of *isochronous* transmission of device data. Isochrony means, simply, that a device is guaranteed bandwidth on the bus. If a device, such as a video camera, requires a certain amount of "room" on the bus, then it asks the system to reserve an amount of isochronous bandwidth. If there is bandwidth available, then the host computer guarantees that it is always available for that device. If there isn't bandwidth available, then it is up to the device (or, rather, the software controlling the device) whether to accept the nonguaranteed bandwidth.

What Does the USB Mean to Peripherals and Computer Vendors?

The compatibility of USB is built on the foundation of a technically solid and open specification that meets customer needs for affordable and easily expandable PCs. Universal Serial Bus compatibility in turn may enable both suppliers and resellers of PCs, peripherals, and software to profit from powerful new marketing methods:

- "Platform packaging" allows logically related hardware and software products to be marketed together.
- USB can reduce the incompatibility risk associated with bundling PCs, peripherals, and software to create specialized turnkey systems that meet the needs of specialized market niches.
- USB-compliant peripherals may result in offering corporate purchasers and home users more purchasing choices, without fear of system degradation.
- Resellers may have more flexibility to mix and match selected products and systems in order to stage seasonal promotions and to offer purchase incentives.
- USB may help suppliers to reduce their develement costs, which will allow them to establish highly competitive new price points.

Where Can I Get the Latest Revision of the USB Specification?

The latest revision of the USB specification, together with a number of useful white papers, is available for downloading from the USB Implementer's Forum at http://www.usb.org.

How Many USB-Compliant Computers Will Be Available to Buy?

Dataquest (5/96) has expressed the opinion that all PCs shipped in 1998 and later will feature USB technology. Indeed, USB functionality is included in all current processor "chipsets" that Intel ships for the current generation of processors. In addition, by the end of 1998 all popular PC operating systems will have native support for Universal Serial Bus hardware.

What IS the USB-IF?

The USB Implementers Forum is a support organization formed by the seven promoters of USB to help speed development of high-quality compatible devices using USB. The seven sponsors of the USB definition are: Compaq, Digital Equipment Corp (now a subsidiary of Compaq), IBM PC Co., Intel, Microsoft, NEC, and Northern Telecom.

USB Device and Tool Manufacturers

This appendix lists the manufacturers of equipment for use in a Universal Serial Bus system. It is current as this book goes to press. For an up-to-date listing, please visit the USB homepage at www.usb.org.

Audio/Speakers

DesTech

Address: No. 3, Alley 1, Lane 113
Ming-Teh Rd.
PeiTou, Taipei
Taiwan
Tel: +886-2-28202925
Fax: +886-2-28251282
Email: dtsi02@ms19.hinet.net
Web: www.destechinc.com

TC Data Security

Address: 8 Gables Road
Hicksville, NY 11801
USA
Tel: (516) 433-1441
Email: scifiman@erols.com

Telex Communications, Inc.

Address: 9600 Aldrich Avenue South
Minneapolis, MN 55420-4288
USA

Tel: (612) 887-9280
Fax: 612/884-0043
Email: computeraudio@telex.com
Email: deborah.haupert@haupert@telex.com
Web: www.computeraudio.telex.com

Tycoon Enterprises

Address: Dland Company
43126 Christy Street
Fremont, CA 94538-3168
USA
Email: tycoon@public.szonline.net
Web: www.opm.com.cn

ZMM

Address: Ishak Sade 2
Givatatim, 53467
Israel
Tel: +972-3-5731994
Email: nissim@usbphone.com
Email: powerphn@netvision.net.il
Web: www.usbphone.com

Cables

Belkin Components

Address: 501 W. Walnut St.
Compton, CA 90220
USA

Tel: (310) 898-1100xt.1760
Fax: (310) 898-1111
Web: www.belkin.com

Cable Systems International

Address: 505 North 51st Avenue
         Phoenix, AZ 85043-2701
         USA
Tel: (602) 233-5645
Fax: (602) 233-5850

DDK Electronics, Inc.

Address: 3001 Oakmead Village Drive
         Santa Clara, CA 95051
         USA
Tel: (408) 980-8344
Fax: (408) 980-9750
Web: www.ddkconnectors.com

Good Way Ind. Co., Ltd.

Address: 5F, No. 8, Alley 6
         Lane 45 Pao-Shin Rd.
         Taipei Hsien, Taiwan
         Taiwan
Tel: +886-2-2911 5756
Fax: +886-2-2911 5854
Email: info@goodway.com.tw
Web: www.goodway.com.tw

Harting

Address: 2155 Stonington Ave.
         Hoffman Estates, IL 60195-5211
         USA
Tel: (847) 519-7700
Fax: (847) 519-9771

LTK International Ltd.

Address: Unit 1314, Vanta Industrial Centre
         21-33 Tai Lin Pai Road
         Kwai Chung, N.T., Hong Kong
         China
Tel: +852 2425 4399
Fax: +852 2480 6327
Email: sales@ltkcable.com
Web: www.ltkcable.com

Longwell Electronics

Address: 510 W. Central Ave., #C
         Brea, CA 92821
         USA
Tel: (714) 255-9986
Fax: (714) 255-8559
Email: sales@longwell.com
Web: www.longwell.com

Newnex

Address: 1190 T Miraloma Way
         Sunnyvale, CA 94086
         USA
Tel: (408) 749-1480
Fax: (408) 749-1963
Email: info@newnex.com
Web: www.newnex.com

Northstar Systems

Address: 9400 Seventh Street
         Bldg. A2
         Rancho Cucamonga, CA 91730
         USA
Tel: (909) 483-9900
Fax: (909) 944-0464
Email: usbsales@northstar1.com
Web: www.northstar1.com

Technical Devices of North America, Inc.

Address: 9181 North Dixie Drive
         Dayton, OH 45414
         USA
Tel: (937) 890-6811
Fax: (937) 890-5136
Email: info@tdna.com
Email: sales@tdna.com
Web: www.tdna.com

Technical Writing Services

Address: 435 East 14th Street
         Suite 7F
         New York, NY
         USA
Tel: (212) 533-5406
Fax: (212) 533-5406

ing büro h doran

Address: beim Pfarrwäldle 7
St Johann Upfingen, D-72813
Germany
Tel: +49 7122 82243
Fax: +49 7122 82263
Email: usb@ibhdoran.com
Web: www.ibhdoran.com

Cameras

Aims Lab, Inc

Address: 46740 Lakeview Blvd
Fremont, CA 94538
USA
Tel: (510) 661-2525
Fax: (510) 252-1572
Web: www.aimslab.com

Belgacom

Address: Rue de Lombardie, 5
Saint-Vaast, Hainaut B-7100
Belgium
Tel: + 32 65 345487
Fax: + 32 65 346378
Web: www.belgacom.be

Compaq

Address: PO Box 692000
Houston, TX 77269-2000
USA
Tel: (713) 514-9542
Fax: (713) 514-0924
Web: www.compaq.com

ETEK Labs

Address: 1057 East Henrietta Road
Rochester, NY 14623
USA
Tel: (716) 292-6400
Fax: (716) 292-6273
Email: sales@eteklabs.com
Web: www.eteklabs.com

LG Electronics

Address: Yoido, YoungDungPo
Seoul, Seoul 140-111
Korea
Tel: +82-2-526-7343
Fax: +82-2-526-7346
Web: www.lge.co.kr

NetChip Technology

Address: 625 Clyde Ave
Mountain View, CA 94043
USA
Tel: (650) 526-1490
Fax: (650) 526-1494
Email: sales@netchip.com
Web: www.netchip.com

USBStuff.com

Address: 335 Kentucky Street
Petaluma, CA 94952
USA
Tel: (707) 778-6299
Fax: (707) 762-7672
Web: www.usbstuff.com

Zoran Corporation

Address: P.O.B 2495
Haifa, 31024
Israel
Tel: +972-4-854-5761
Fax: +972-4-855-1550
Web: www.zoran.com

Connectors

Astron-A.T. Corp.

Address: 774 Charcot Ave.
San Jose, CA 95131
USA
Tel: (408) 232-1100
Fax: (408) 232-1108
Email: info@astron-us.com
Email: sales@astron-us.com
Web: www.astron-us.com

CDSI

Address: 7028 Stanford Dr
        Alexandria, VA 22307-1521
        USA
Tel: (202) 685-2161
Fax: (202) 433-7322

DAU Components Ltd

Address: 70-74 Barnham Road
        Barnham
        West Sussex, PO22 0ES
        United Kingdom
Tel: +44 1243 553031
Fax: +44 1243 553860
Email: sales@dau-components.co.uk

DDK Electronics, Inc.

Address: 3001 Oakmead Village Drive
        Santa Clara, CA 95051
        USA
Tel: (408) 980-8344
Fax: (408) 980-9750
Web: www.ddkconnectors.com

ETEK Labs

Address: 1057 East Henrietta Road
        Rochester, NY 14623
        USA
Tel: (716) 292-6400
Fax: (716) 292-6273
Email: sales@eteklabs.com
Web: www.eteklabs.com

Longwell Electronics

Address: 510 W. Central Ave., #C
        Brea, CA 92821
        USA
Tel: (714) 255-9986
Fax: (714) 255-8559
Email: sales@longwell.com
Web: www.longwell.com

Newnex Technology Corp.

Address: 1190-T Miraloma Way
        Sunnyvale, CA 94086
        USA
Tel: (408) 749-1480
Fax: (408) 749-1963

Email: info@newnex.com
Web: www.newnex.com

ing büro h doran

Address: beim Pfarrwäldle 7
        St Johann Upfingen, D-72813
        Germany
Tel: + 49 7122 82243
Fax: + 49 7122 82263
Email: usb@ibhdoran.com
Web: www.ibhdoran.com

Telephone and CTI

Mitel

Address: 350 Legget Drive
        Kanata, ON
        Canada, K2K 1X3
Tel: (800) MITEL-SX
Fax: (613) 592-4784
Email: mpa@mitel.com
Web: www.mitel.com

ZMM

Address: Ishak Sade 2
        Givatatim, 53467
        Israel
Tel: +972-3-5731994
Email: nissim@usbphone.com
Email: powerphn@netvision.net.il
Web: www.usbphone.com

Gamepads and Joysticks

ANKO Electronic Co., Ltd.

Address: 189 Keelung Rd., Section 2, 9F
        Suite 6
        Taipei, 110
        Taiwan
Tel: +886 (2) 2378-8962
Fax: +886 (2) 2377-1992
Web: www.ankojoysticks.com

AVB

Address: 12155 Mora Drive, Suite 14
        Santa Fe Springs, CA 90670
        USA

Tel: (562) 903-7002
Fax: (562) 903-7003
Web: www.avbtech.com

Belkin Components

Address: 501 W. Walnut St.
 Compton, CA 90220
 USA
Tel: (310) 898-1100xt.1760
Fax: (310) 898-1111
Web: www.belkin.com

ETEK Labs

Address: 1057 East Henrietta Road
 Rochester, NY 14623
 USA
Tel: (716) 292-6400
Fax: (716) 292-6273
Email: sales@eteklabs.com
Web: www.eteklabs.com

Pacetec IMG

Address: The Boott Mills
 100 Foot of John St.
 Lowell, MA 01852
 USA
Tel: (508) 970-0330
Fax: (508) 970-0199
Web: www.spacetec.com

Thrustmaster

Address: 7175 NW Evergreen Pkwy. #400
 Hillsboro, OR 97124
 USA
Tel: (503) 615-3200
Fax: (503) 615-3300
Web: www.thrustmaster.com

Hubs

ADS Technologies, Inc

Address: 13909 Bettencourt Street
 Cerritos, CA 90703
 USA
Tel: (800) 888-5244
Fax: (562) 926-0518
Web: adstech.com

Belkin Components

Address: 501 W. Walnut St.
 Compton, CA 90220
 USA
Tel: (310) 898-1100xt.1760
Fax: (310) 898-1111
Web: www.belkin.com

Good Way Ind. Co., Ltd.

Address: 5F, No. 8, Alley 6
 Lane 45 Pao-Shin Rd.
 Taipei Hsien, Taiwan
 Taiwan
Tel: +886-2-2911 5756
Fax: +886-2-2911 5854
Email: info@goodway.com.tw
Web: www.goodway.com.tw

HCL Peripherals Limited

Address: 158, Arcot Road, Vadapalani
 Tamilnadu 600 026
 India
Tel: +91-44-427088
Fax: +91-44-4834563
Email: rbm@hclhppd.hclt.com

Macally Peripherals

Address: 5101 Commerce Dr.
 Baldwin Park, CA 91706
 USA
Tel: (626) 338-8787
Fax: (626) 338-3585
Email: info@macally.com
Email: sales@macally.com
Web: www.macally.com

Nichimen Data Systems Corporation

Address: 2-19 Yanagibashi
 Taito-ku, Tokyo 111
 Japan
Tel: +81-3-3864-7789
Fax: +81-3-3864-7566
Web: www.nichimen-nds.co.jp

Peracom

Address: 13000 Weston Parkway
Suite 105
Cary, NC 27513
USA
Tel: (919) 379-2700
Fax: (919) 379-9420
Email: sales@peracom.com
Web: www.peracom.com

Premiere Systems

Address: 12860 Beach Blvd., Suite G-219
Stanton, CA 90680
USA
Tel: (714) 901-7301
Fax: (714) 901-7319
Email: info@premieresys.net
Email: sales@premieresys.net
Web: www.premieresys.net

SIIG, Inc.

Address: 6078 Stewart Avenue
Fremont, CA 94538
USA
Tel: (510) 657-8688
Fax: (510) 657-3181
Web: www.siig.com

Simple Silicon Inc.

Address: 10430, South De Anza Blvd
Suite 195
Cupertino, CA 95051
USA
Tel: (408) 873-2260
Fax: (408) 873-2261
Email: sales@simplesi.com
Web: www.simplesi.com

Sunny Trading Construction

Address: Blk16 #03-2839
Eunos Crescent, - 400016
Singapore
Tel: +65-96803827
Fax: +65-8463117

Kpn Research

Address: st. Paulusstraat 4
2264 XZ Leidschendam
P.O. Box 421
2260 AK Leidschendam
Netherlands
Tel: +31 70 3326442
Fax: +31 70 3326477
Web: www.kpn.com/research/en

ISDN

AMB

Address: Travesera de Dalt 6
Barcelona, SPAIN 08024
Spain
Tel: +34932183932
Fax: +34932183932

AVM GmbH&KG

Address: Alt-Moabit 95
Berlin, 10559
Germany
Tel: +49-30-399 84 0
Fax: +49-30-399 84 299
Web: www.avm.de

DrayTek Corp.

Address: No-10, Lane 162
Science-Park Road
Hsin Chu 300
Taiwan, ROC.
Tel: +886 35 641 518
Fax: +886 35 641 519
Email: info@draytek.com.tw
Email: support@draytek.com.tw
Web: www.draytek.com.tw
Web: www.draycom.hinet.net

Lighthouse Cove Development Limited

Address: 21-24 Earl Drive
Chatham, Ontario
Canada N7M 6E7
Tel: (519) 354-5688
Fax: (519) 354-8530

Email: itsme@mnsi.net
Web: www.marineontario.com/radlins.htm

NetChip Technology

Address: 625 Clyde Ave
        Mountain View, CA 94043
        USA
Tel: (650) 526-1490
Fax: (650) 526-1494
Email: sales@netchip.com
Web: www.netchip.com

Keyboards and Mice

Alps

Address: 3553 N. First Street
        San Jose, CA 95134-1804
        USA
Tel: (408) 432-6000
Fax: (408) 321-8494
Web: www.alpsusa.com/kybdwin.html

Alps Interactive

Address: 3553 N. First Street
        San Jose, CA 95134-1804
        USA
Tel: (408) 432-6000
Fax: (408) 321-8494
Web: www.alps.com

Behavior Tech Computer

Address: 4180 Business Center Dr.
        Fremont, CA 94538
        USA
Tel: (510) 657-3956
Fax: (510) 657-1859

Belkin Components

Address: 501 W. Walnut St.
        Compton, CA 90220
        USA
Tel: (310) 898-1100xt.1760
Fax: (310) 898-1111
Web: www.belkin.com

Cherry Electrical Products

Address: 11200 88th Ave P.O. Box 913
        Pleasant Prairie, Wisconsin 53158
        USA
Tel: (800) 510-1689
Fax: (414) 942-6566
Web: www.cherrycorp.com

Chicony Electronics Co. Ltd.

Address: No. 25 Wu-Gong 6th Rd.
        Wu-Ku Industrial Park
        Taipei Hsien,
        Taiwan R.O.C.
Tel: +886 2 298-8120
Fax: +886 2 298-8442

ETEK Labs

Address: 1057 East Henrietta Road
        Rochester, NY 14623
        USA
Tel: (716) 292-6400
Fax: (716) 292-6273
Email: sales@eteklabs.com
Web: www.eteklabs.com

EzKey Corp.

Address: 11F No. 167 Fu Ho Rd.
        Yung Ho City
        Taipei Hsien,
        Taiwan R.O.C.
Tel: +886 2 232-5838
Fax: +886 2 232-5841
Web: www.ezkey.com.tw

HCL Peripherals Limited

Address, 158, Arcot Road, Vadapalani
        Tamilnadu 600 026
        India
Tel: +91-44-427088
Fax: +91-44-4834563
Email: rbm@hclhppd.hclt.com

Key Tronic Corporation

Address: P.O. 14687
        Spokane, WA 99214-0687
        USA
Tel: (509) 928-8000

Fax: (509) 927-5503
Email: info@keytronic.com
Web: www.keytronic.com

Sejin America Inc.

Address: 2004 Martin Ave.
Santa Clara, CA 95050
USA
Tel: (888) 373-3273
Fax: (408) 980-7562
Web: www.sejin.com

Sejin Electron Inc.

Address: 60-19 Kasan-Dong Keumchon-Ku
Seoul 153-023,
Korea
Tel: +02 866-3333
Fax: +02 864-3375
Email: sjkorea@nuri.net

Siemens Telecommunication Systems Limited

Address: 12f/1 90 Chien Kuo North Road
Sec. 1
Taipei
Taiwan
Tel: +886-2-25186117
Fax: +886-2-25053866
Email: mingwen@stsl.siemens.com.tw

Modems

3Com

Address: 3800 Golf Road
Rolling Meadows, IL 60008
USA
Tel: (847) 262-5000
Web: www.3com.com/client/pcd

ETEK Labs

Address: 1057 East Henrietta Road
Rochester, NY 14623
USA
Tel: (716) 292-6400
Fax: (716) 292-6273

Email: sales@eteklabs.com
Web: www.eteklabs.com

NetChip Technology

Address: 625 Clyde Ave
Mountain View, CA 94043
USA
Tel: (650) 526-1490
Fax: (650) 526-1494
Email: sales@netchip.com
Web: www.netchip.com

Philips Taiwan

Address: 23fb, No. 66, Chung-Hsiao W. Rd
Sec. 1
Taipei
Taiwan
Tel: +886-2-23824766
Fax: +886-2-23824777
Web: www.philips.com.tw

Monitors

ADI Corp.

Address: 14F, No. 1, Sec. 4, Nanking E. Road
Taipei, 105
Taiwan R.O.C.
Tel: 886-2-27133337
Fax: 886-2-27136555
Web: www.adi.com.tw

ETEK Labs

Address: 1057 East Henrietta Road
Rochester, NY 14623
USA
Tel: (716) 292-6400
Fax: (716) 292-6273
Email: sales@eteklabs.com
Web: www.eteklabs.com

LG Electronics Inc.

Address: 184 Kongdan-dong Kumi-city
Kyougbuck
Korea
Tel: +82-546-460-3266
Fax: +82-546-460-3272

Shamrock Technology Co. Ltd.

Address: 7F No. 108-4 Min-Chuan Rd. Hsin-
Tien City
Taipei Hsien,
Taiwan R.O.C.
Tel: +886 2 218-2155
Fax: +886 2 218-5154
Web: www.shamrock-tech.com

USB Systems Design

Address: 375 NW 95th Ave
Portland, OR 97229
USA
Tel: (503) 297-6519
Email: admin@usbsys.com
Web: www.usbsys.com

Networking

MCCI

Address: 3520 Krums Corners Road
Ithaca, NY 14850
USA
Tel: (607) 277-1029
Fax: (607) 277-6844
Web: www.mcci.com

Printers

Canon

Address: 3-30-2 Shimomaruko Ohta-ku
Tokyo 146
Japan
Tel: +81-3-3758-2111
Fax: +81-3-3756-6052
Web: www.canon.com

NetChip Technology

Address: 625 Clyde Ave
Mountain View, CA 94043
USA
Tel: (650) 526-1490
Fax: (650) 526-1494
Email: sales@netchip.com
Web: www.netchip.com

ScanLogic Co.

Address: 4 Preston Court
Bedford, MA 01730
USA
Tel: (781) 271-1750
Fax: (781) 271-1760
Email: Sales@scanlogic.com
Web: www.scanlogic.com

ing büro h doran

Address: beim Pfarrwäldle 7
St Johann Upfingen, D-72813
Germany
Tel: +49 7122 82243
Fax: +49 7122 82263
Email: usb@ibhdoran.com
Web: www.ibhdoran.com

Scanners

BASF Corp.

Address: 73 Jumping Branch Road
Stafford, VA 22554
USA
Tel: (800) 255-3212
Fax: (540) 657-9334

ETEK Labs

Address: 1057 East Henrietta Road
Rochester, NY 14623
USA
Tel: (716) 292-6400
Fax: (716) 292-6273
Email: sales@eteklabs.com
Web: www.eteklabs.com

NetChip Technology

Address: 625 Clyde Ave
Mountain View, CA 94043
USA
Tel: (650) 526-1490
Fax: (650) 526-1494
Email: sales@netchip.com
Email: dtu@netchip.com

Siemens ElectroCom GmbH

Address: Buecklestr. 1-5
Konstanz, D-78459
Germany
Tel: +49 7531/86-2439
Fax: +49 7531/86-3030

ScanLogic Co.

Address: 4 Preston Court
Bedford, MA 01730
USA
Tel: (781) 271-1750
Fax: (781) 271-1760
Email: Sales@scanlogic.com
Web: www.scanlogic.com

Mytec Technologies

Address: 1220 Sheppard Ave East
Suite 200
Toronto, Ontario
Canada M2K-2S5
Tel: (416) 467-3316
Fax: (416) 467-5368

Test and Measurement

Helsinki University of Technology/Applied Electronics Laboratory

Address: Otakaari 5 A
Espoo, 02150
Finland
Tel: +358 9 451 2305
Fax: +358 9 451 2307

IOtech

Address: 25971 Cannon Road
Cleveland, OH 44146
USA
Tel: (440) 439-4091
Fax: (440) 439-4093
Email: sales@iotech.com
Web: www.iotech.com

MCCI

Address: 3520 Krums Corners Road
Ithaca, NY 14850
USA
Tel: (607) 277-1029
Fax: (607) 277-6844
Web: www.mcci.com

USB Systems Design

Address: 375 NW 95th Ave
Portland, OR 97229
USA
Tel: (503) 297-6519
Email: admin@usbsys.com
Web: www.usbsys.com

Acromag Inc.

Address: PO Box 437
30765 S. Wixom Road
Wixom, MI 48393-7037
USA
Tel: (248) 624-1541
Fax: (248) 624-9234
Web: www.acromag.com

Tools

BlueWater Systems, Inc.

Address: P.O. Box 776
Edmonds, WA 98020
USA
Tel: (425) 771-3610
Fax: (425) 771-2742
Email: info@bluewatersystems.com
Email: sales@bluewatersystems.com
Web: www.bluewatersystems.com

Computer Access Technology Corporation

Address: 2403 Walsh Avenue
Santa Clara, CA 95051-1302
USA
Tel: (408) 727-6600
Fax: (408) 727-6622
Email: sales@catc.com
Web: www.catc.com

Decicon Inc.

Address: 1250 Oakmead Parkway Suite 316
Sunnyvale, CA 94086
USA
Tel: (408) 720-7690
Fax: (408) 720-7691

FTDI

Address: St. Georges Studios
93 / 97 St. Georges Road
Glasgow, na G3 6JA
United Kingdom
Tel: +44 141 353 2565
Fax: +44 141 353 2656
Email: ftdi@email.msn.com
Web: www.ftdi.co.uk

FuturePlus Systems

Address: 2790 N. Academy Blvd., Suite 307
Colorado Springs, CO 80917-5329
USA
Tel: (719) 380-7321
Fax: (719) 380-7362
Email: sales@futureplus.com
Web: www.futureplus.com

Genoa

Address: 5401 Tech Circle
Moorpark, CA 93021
USA
Tel: (805) 531-9030
Fax: (805) 531-9045
Web: www.gentech.com

Oki Semiconductor

Address: 785 North Mary Ave.
Sunnyvale, CA 94086-2909
USA
Tel: (408) 720-1900
Fax: (408) 720-1918

Sand Microelectronics Inc.

Address: 3350 Scott Blvd. #24
Santa Clara, CA 95054
USA
Tel: (408) 235-8600
Fax: (408) 235-8601
Web: www.sandmicro.com

Sapien Design

Address: 45335 Potawatami Dr.
Fremont, CA 94539
USA
Tel: (510) 668-0200
Fax: (510) 668-0200
Email: sapien@pacbell.net
Web: www.sapeindesign.com

Sycard Technology

Address: 1180-F Miraloma Way
Sunnyvale, CA 94086
USA
Tel: (408) 749-0130
Fax: (408) 749-1323
Email: sales@sycard.com
Web: www.sycard.com

USAR Systems

Address: 568 Broadway
New York, NY 10012
USA
Tel: (212) 226-2042
Fax: (212) 226-3215

Xyratex

Address: 4101 Westerly Place Suite 105
Newport Beach, CA 92660
USA
Tel: (714) 476-1016
Fax: (714) 476-1916
Web: www.xyrate.com

Glossary of
USB Terms

ACK: Handshake packet indicating a positive acknowledgement between d evices, or a host and device on the Universal Serial Bus.

Active Device: A device that is not in the suspended state and is powered on.

Asynchronous Data: Data that is sent across the Universal Serial Bus without regard to timing requirements; the opposite of *isochronous*.

Babble: Persistent data on the bus that is not expected by any device or the host.

Bandwidth: The amount of data that can be transmitted over the bus in a given amount of time; this is usually expressed in bits per second (bps).

Bit: A single element of data within the computer (or on the bus) that is either a 1 or a 0 (indicating high voltage or low). There are eight bits in a *byte* of information.

Buffer: Temporary storage area used by the computer (or USB devices) to put data when it cannot be immediately used. For example, if data is arriving faster than the application software can use it, then it is buffered by the underlying host software components.

Bulk Transfer: Movement of large blocks of data across the Universal Serial Bus that is **not** time critical (i.e., a large asynchronous transfer).

Bus Enumeration: The process of detecting and identifying USB devices.

Byte: A piece of data composed of eight bits.

Capabilities: The functional parameters of a device that can be controlled by the host software.

Characteristics: Functionality within a USB device that is not changeable by the host software.

Client: The software on the host that is the highest-level user of the USB device.

Control Pipe: A pipe used to send configuration and control information from the host computer to a device on the Universal Serial Bus.

Control Transfer: A transfer of data over the control pipe from the host computer to a device on the Universal Serial Bus to provide configuration and control information to a USB device.

CRC: Cyclic redundancy check; used to detect errors in the transmission of data across the bus. The CRC is transmitted along with the data packets for comparison with a CRC calculated by the receiving device.

Default Address: The address that a USB device responds to before the host software sets the desired address on the device.

Default Pipe: A message pipe created by the host-system software to exchange control and status information with USB device's endpoint zero.

Device: A logical or physical entity that performs a function. The actual entity described depends on the context of the reference. At the lowest level, device may refer to a single hardware component, as in a memory device. At a higher level, it may refer to a collect of hardware components that perform a particular function, such as a USB interface device. At an even higher level, device may refer to the function performed by an entity attached to the USB—e.g., a data/FAX modem device. Devices may be physical, electrical, addressable, and logical.

Device Address: The address of a device on the USB. The device address is the default address when the USB device is first powered or reset. Hubs and functions are assigned a unique device address by the USB host software.

Device Endpoint: A uniquely identifiable portion of a USB device that is the source or sink of information in a communication flow between the host and device.

Device: Resources provided by USB devices, such as buffer space and endpoints. See *Host Resources* and *USB Resources*.

Device Software: Software that is responsible for using a USB device. This software may or may not also be responsible for configuring the device for use.

Downstream: The direction of data flow from the host or away from the host. A downstream port is the port on a hub electrically further from the host that generates downstream traffic from the hub. Downstream ports receive upstream data traffic.

Driver: A program responsible for interfacing to a hardware device—that is, a device driver.

Endpoint: See *Device Endpoint*.

Endpoint Address: The combination of a device address and an endpoint number on a USB device.

Endpoint Number: A unique pipe endpoint on a USB device.

EOP: End of packet.

False EOP: A spurious, usually noise-induced, event that is interpreted by a packet receiver as an end of packet.

Frame: The time from the start of one SOF token to the start of the subsequent SOF token. Consists of a series of transactions.

Frame Pattern: A sequence of frames that exhibit a repeating pattern in the number of samples transmitted per frame.

Full Duplex: Computer data transmissions occurring in both directions simultaneously.

Function: A USB device that provides a capability to the host. For example, an ISDN connection, microphone, or speakers.

Handshake Packet: A packet that acknowledges or rejects a specific condition. See *ACK* or *NAK*.

Host: The host computer system where the USB host controller is installed. This includes the host hardware platform and the OS in use.

**Host
Controller:** The host's USB interface.

**Host-Controller
Driver (HCD):** The USB software layer that abstracts the host-controller
hardware. Host controller driver provides an SPI for interaction with a host controller. HCD hides the specifics of the
HC implementations.

Host Resources: Resources provided by the host, such as buffer space and
interrupts. See *Device Resources* and *USB Resources*.

Hub: A USB device that provides additional connections to the
USB.

Hub Tier: The level of connect within a USB network topology, given
as the number of hubs that the data has to flow through.

**Interrupt
Request:** A hardware signal that allows a device to request attention
from a host. The host typically invokes an interrupt service
routine to handle the condition which caused the request.

**Interrupt
Transfer:** One of four USB transfer types. Interrupt transfers are
small-data, nonperiodic, low-frequency, bounded-latency,
device-initiated communication typically used to notify the
host of device service needs.

IRQ: See *Interrupt Request*.

**Isochronous
Data:** A stream of data whose timing is implied by its delivery
rate.

**Isochronous
Device:** An entity with isochronous endpoints, as defined in the
USB specification, that sources or sinks sampled analog
streams or synchronous data streams.

**Isochronous
Sink Endpoint:** An endpoint that is capable of consuming an isochronous
data stream.

**Isochronous
Source Endpoint:** An endpoint that is capable of producing an isochronous
data stream.

Isochronous Transfer: One of four USB transfer types. Isochronous transfers are used when working with isochronous data. Isochronous transfers provide periodic, continuous communication between host and device.

Jitter: A tendency toward lack of synchronization caused by mechanical or electrical changes. More specifically, the phase shift of digital pulses over a transmission system.

LOA: Loss of bus activity characterized by a start of packet without a corresponding end of packet.

Message Pipe: A pipe that transfers data using a request/data/status paradigm. The data has an imposed structure which allows a request to be reliably identified and communicated.

NAK: Negative acknowledgement. Handshake packet indicating a negative.

Object: Host software or data structure representing a USB entity.

Packet: A bundle of data organized in a group for transmission. Packets typically contain three elements: control information (e.g., source, destination, and length), the data to be transferred, and error-detection and correction bits.

Packet Buffer: The logical buffer used by a USB device for sending or receiving a single packet. This determines the maximum packet size the device can send or receive.

Packet ID (PID): A field in a USB packet that indicates the type of packet, and by inference the format of the packet and the type of error detection applied to the packet.

Phase: A token, data, or handshake packet. A transaction has three phases.

Physical Device: A device that has a physical implemenation; e.g., speakers, microphone, and CD players.

PID: See *Packet ID*.

Pipe: A logical abstraction representing the association between an endpoint on a device and software on the host. A pipe has several attributes; e.g., a pipe may transfer data streams (stream pipe) or messages (message pipes).

Plug-n-Play (PNP): A technology for configuring I/O devices to use nonconflicting resources in a host. Resources managed by PNP include I/O address ranges, memory address ranges, IRQs, and DMA channels.

PNP: See *Plug-n-Play*.

Polling: Asking multiple devices, one at a time, if they have any data to transmit.

Port: Point of access to or from a system or circuit. The point where a USB device is attached.

Power-On Reset: Restoring a storage device, register, or memory to a pre-determined state when power is applied.

Protocol: A specific set of rules, procedures, or conventions relating to format and timing of data transmission between two devices.

Request: A request made to a USB device contained within the data portion of a SETUP packet.

Retire: The action of completing service for a transfer and notifying the appropriate software client of the completion.

Root Hub: A USB hub directly attached to the host controller. This hub is attached to the host, tier 0.

Root Port: The upstream port on a hub.

Sample: The smallest unit of data on which an endpoint operates; a property of an endpoint.

Sample Rate: The number of samples per second, expressed in hertz.

Service Interval: The period between consecutive requests to a USB endpoint to send or receive data.

Service Jitter: The deviation of service delivery from its scheduled delivery time.

Service Rate: The number of services to a given endpoint per unit time.

SOF: Acronym for start of frame. The SOF is the first transaction in each frame. SOF allows endpoints to identify the start of frame and synchronize internal endpoint clocks to the host.

Stage: One part of the sequence composing a control transfer; i.e., the setup stage, data stage, and status stage.

Stream Pipe: A pipe that transfers data as a stream of samples with no defined USB structure.

Synchronization Type: A classification that characterizes an isochronous end-point's capability to connect to other isochronous endpoints.

Termination: Passive component attached at the end of a cable to prevent signals from being reflected or echoed.

Time-out: The detection of a lack of bus activity for some predetermined interval.

Token Packet: A type of packet that identifies what transaction is to be performed on the bus.

Transaction: The deliver of service to an endpoint; consists of a token packet, optional data packet, and optional handshake packet. Based on transaction type.

Transfer: One or more bus transactions to move information between a software client and its function.

Transfer Type: Determines the characteristics of the data flow between a software client and its function. Four types are defined: control, interrupt, bulk, and isochronous.

Turnaround Time: The time a device needs to wait to begin transmitting a packet after a packet has been received to prevent collisions on USB. This time is based on the length and propagation-delay characteristics of the cables and the location of the transmitting device in relation to other devices on USB.

Universal Serial Bus: A collection of USB devices and the software and hardware that allow them to connect the capabilities provided by functions to the host.

USB Device: Includes hubs and functions. See *Device*.

USB Interface: The hardware interface between the USB cable and a USB device. This includes the protocol engine requred for all USB devices to be able to receive and send packets.

USB Resources: Resources provided by USB, such as bandwidth and power. See *Device Resources* and *Host Resources*.

USB Software: The host-based software responsible for managing the interactions between the host and the attached USB devices.

USB: See *Universal Serial Bus*.

Upstream: The direction of data flow toward the host. An upstream port is the port on a device electrically closest to the host that generates upstream data traffic from the hub. Upstream ports receive downstream data traffic.

USB Cables and Common Industry-Standard Cables

If industry-standard ports are provided on devices, cabling requirements can be often met by using industry-standard cables. With USB, industry-standard cables will be provided. This appendix features some industry-standard cables that are available to connect standard compliant ports. USB cables are included to connect computers and peripherals with USB ports. Other cables for standard PC ports, although not required for USB connection, are included for completeness.

Please don't infer from this information that bridging two buses is as simple as creating a cable with comparable signal names; it is much more complex than this. If you want to bridge different types of buses and you have never attempted building a bridge or converter device, then the reader is encouraged to buy one. Attempting to build your own bridge or converter is dangerous and can destroy or damage your computer and the attached peripherals.

USB Cables

Function	Pin #	Pin #	Function
VCC	1	1	Cable Power
Data–	2	2	Negative Data Path
Data+	3	3	Positive Data Path
GND	4	4	Cable Ground

Null Modem Cables

Standard Null-Modem Cable (DB-25 to DB-25)

Function	Pin #	Pin #	Function
Chassis Ground	1 ◀——▶ 1		Chassis Ground
Signal Ground	7 ◀——▶ 7		Signal Ground
Transmit Data (out)	2 ——▶ 3		Receive Data (in)
Receive Data (in)	3 ◀—— 2		Transmit Data (out)
Request to Send (out)	4 ——⏐——▶ 8		Data Carrier Detect (in)
Clear to Send (in)	5 ◀—⏐		
Data Carrier Detect (in)	8 ◀—⏐—— 4		Request to Send (out)
	⏐——▶ 5		Clear to Send (in)
Data Terminal Ready (out)	20 ——▶ 6		Data Set Ready (in)
Data Set Ready (in)	6 ◀—— 20		Data Terminal Ready (out)

Standard IBM PC and Compatibles Cables

Standard PS/2 and PC/XT to Modem Cable (DB-25S to DB-25P)

Function	Pin #	Pin #	Function
Transmit Data (out)	2 ——▶	2	Transmit Data (in)
Receive Data (in)	3 ◀——	3	Receive Data (out)
Request to Send (out)	4 ——▶	4	Request to Send (in)
Clear to Send (in)	5 ◀——	5	Clear to Send (out)
Data Set Ready (in)	6 ◀——	6	Data Set Ready (out)
Signal Ground	7 ——	7	Signal Ground
Data Carrier Detect (in)	8 ◀——	8	Data Carrier Detect (out)
Data Terminal Ready (out)	20 ——▶	20	Data Terminal Ready (in)
Ring Indicator (in)	22 ——▶	22	Ring Indicator (out)

Standard PC/AT to Hayes Smartmodem Cable (DB-9S to DB-25P)

Function	Pin #	Pin #	Function
Transmit Data (out)	3 ——▶	2	Transmit Data (in)
Receive Data (in)	2 ◀——	3	Receive Data (out)
Request to Send (out)	7 ——▶	4	Request to Send (in)
Clear to Send (in)	8 ◀——	5	Clear to Send (out)
Data Set Ready (in)	6 ◀——	6	Data Set Ready (out)
Signal Ground	5 ——	7	Signal Ground
Data Carrier Detect (in)	1 ◀——	8	Data Carrier Detect (out)
Data Terminal Ready (out)	4 ——▶	20	Data Terminal Ready (in)
Ring Indicator (in)	9 ◀——	22	Ring Indicator (out)

Standard PC/XT or PS/2 Null-Modem Cable (DB-25S to DB-25S)

Function	Pin #	Pin #	Function
Signal Ground	7 ←→	7	Signal Ground
Transmit Data (out)	2 ——→	3	Receive Data (in)
Receive Data (in)	3 ←——	2	Transmit Data (out)
Request to Send (out)	4 ——|→	8	Data Carrier Detect (in)
Clear to Send (in)	5 ←—|		
Data Carrier Detect (in)	8 ←|——	4	Request to Send (out)
		|→ 5	Clear to Send (in)
Data Terminal Ready (out)	20 ——→	6	Data Set Ready (in)
Data Set Ready (in)	6 ←——	20	Data Terminal Ready (out)

Standard Null-Modem Cable—PC/AT to PC/AT (DB-9S to DB-9S)

Function	Pin #	Pin #	Function
Signal Ground	5 ←→	5	Signal Ground
Transmit Data (out)	3 ——→	2	Receive Data (in)
Receive Data (in)	2 ←——	3	Transmit Data (out)
Request to Send (out)	7 ——|→	1	Data Carrier Detect (in)
Clear to Send (in)	8 ←—|		
Data Carrier Detect (in)	1 ←|——	7	Request to Send (out)
		|→ 8	Clear to Send (in)
Data Terminal Ready (out)	4 ——→	6	Data Set Ready (in)
Data Set Ready (in)	6 ←——	4	Data Terminal Ready (out)

Null-Modem Cable—PS/2 or PC/XT (DB-25S to DB-9S)

Function	Pin #	Pin #	Function
Signal Ground	7 ◄——► 5		Signal Ground
Transmit Data (out)	2 ——► 2		Receive Data (in)
Receive Data (in)	3 ◄—— 3		Transmit Data (out)
Request to Send (out)	4 ——|——► 1		Data Carrier Detect (in)
Clear to Send (in)	5 ◄—|		
Data Carrier Detect (in)	8 ◄—|—— 7		Request to Send (out)
	|——► 8		Clear to Send (in)
Data Terminal Ready (out)	20 ——► 6		Data Set Ready (in)
Data Set Ready (in)	6 ◄—— 4		Data Terminal Ready (out)

PC/AT and PS/2 or PC/XT to Printer Cable (using hardware flow control)

Function	DB-9SS Pin #	DB-25S Pin #	DB-25S/P Pin #	Function
Transmit Data (out)	3	2 ——►	3	Receive Data (in)
Receive Data (in)	2	3 ◄——	2	Transmit Data (out)
Clear to Send (in)	8	5 ◄—|—	20	Data Terminal Ready (out)
Data Set Ready (in)	6	6 ◄—|		
Data Carrier Detect (in)	1	8 ◄—|		
Signal Ground	5	7 ——	7	Signal Ground
Chassis Ground	n/a	1 ——	1	Chassis Ground

Notes: If your printer uses a different lead for hardware flow control, such as 4, 11, 19, or 25, substitute this lead for lead 20 of the above cable design. Also, printers may require that some input control leads be on, such as 5, 6, 8. If so, connect lead 20 from the PS/2 and PC connector or lead 4 from a PC/AT connector across to all these input control leads. The gender for the printer connector will vary based on the printer.

IBM Parallel Cable (DB-25P to Cinch-36 pin)

Function	Pin #	Pin #	Function
Data strobe (out)	1 ——— 1		Data strobe (in)
Data bit 0 (out)	2 ——▶ 2		Data bit 0 (in)
Data bit 1 (out)	3 ——▶ 3		Data bit 1 (in)
Data bit 2 (out)	4 ——▶ 4		Data bit 2 (in)
Data bit 3 (out)	5 ——▶ 5		Data bit 3 (in)
Data bit 4 (out)	6 ——▶ 6		Data bit 4 (in)
Data bit 5 (out)	7 ——▶ 7		Data bit 5 (in)
Data bit 6 (out)	8 ——▶ 8		Data bit 6 (in)
Data bit 7 (out)	9 ——▶ 9		Data bit 7 (in)
Acknowledge (in)	10 ◀—— 10		Acknowledge (out)
Busy (in)	11 ◀—— 11		Busy (out)
Paper end (in)	12 ◀—— 12		Paper end (out)
Select (in)	13 ◀—— 13		Select (out)
Auto feed (out)	14 ——▶ 14		Auto feed (in)
Error (in)	15 ◀—— 32		Fault (out)
Init (out)	16 ——▶ 31		Prime/Init/Reset (in)
Ground	18 –|—|– 19		Ground
Ground	19 –| |– 20		Ground
Ground	20 –| |– 21		Ground
Ground	21 –| |– 22		Ground
Ground	22 –| |– 23		Ground
Ground	23 –| |– 24		Ground
Ground	24 –| |– 25		Ground
Ground	25 –| |– 26		Ground
	– |– 27		Ground
	– |– 28		Ground
	– |– 29		Ground
	– |– 30		Ground

Note: Your cable may not need to include the leads for the Reset function and not all printers support it. Furthermore, the ground leads may need to be connected to lead 16 of the 36-pin connector.

Standard Macintosh and Compatibles Cables

Macintosh to Hayes Smartmodem 2400 Cable (Mini-DIN Male to DB–25P)

Mac Plus/SE/II	Mini-DIN	DB–25	Smartmodem 2400
Function	Pin #	Pin #	Function
Signal Ground	4 ←|→	7	Signal Ground
RxD+ (in)	8 ←|		
Chassis Ground	Shell ←→	1	Chassis Ground
TxD– (out)	3 ——→	2	Transmit Data (in)
RxD– (in)	5 ←——	3	Receive Data (out)
CTS (in)	2 ←|——	8	Data Carrier Detect (out)
DCD (in)	7 ←|		
DTR (out)	1 ——|→	20	Data Terminal Ready (in)
	|→	4	Request to Send (in)
TxD+ (out)	6 (no connection)		

Mac 128KB/512K/512KE DB-9, DB-25, Smartmodem 2400

Function	Pin #	Pin #	Function
Signal Ground	3 ←|→	7	Signal Ground
RxD+ (in)	8 ←|		
Chassis Ground	1 ←→	1	Chassis Ground
TxD– (out)	5 ——→	2	Transmit Data (in)
RxD– (in)	9 ←——	3	Receive Data (out)
CTS (in)	7 ←——	8	Data Carrier Detect (out)
+12V (out)	6 ——|→	20	Data Terminal Ready (in)
	|→	4	Request to Send (in)
TxD+ (out)	4 (no connection)		

Null-Modem Cable for Macintosh (Mini-DIN male
to Mini-DIN male) Cable for Connecting Two Mac Plus
RS-422 Ports Together

Function	Pin #	Pin #	Function
Signal Ground	4 ——— 4		Signal Ground
TxD+ (out)	6 ——→ 8		RxD+ (in)
TxD– (out)	3 ——→ 5		RxD– (in)
RxD+ (in)	8 ←—— 6		TxD+ (out)
RxD– (in)	5 ←—— 3		TxD– (out)
DTR (out)	1 ←—— 2		CTS (in)
CTS (in)	2 ——→ 1		DTR (out)

Null-Modem Cable for Mac Plus to a Mac 512K
(Mini-DIN male to DB-9P)

Function	Pin #	Pin #	Function
Signal Ground	4 ——— 3		Signal Ground
TxD+ (out)	6 ——→ 8		RxD+ (in)
TxD– (out)	3 ——→ 9		RxD– (in)
RxD+ (in)	8 ←—— 4		TxD+ (out)
RxD– (in)	5 ←—— 5		TxD– (out)
DTR (out)	1 ——→ 7		CTS (in)
CTS (in)	2 ←—— 2		+5V (out)

IBM Parallel Port Pinout

DB25 Pin #	Function
1	Strobe
2	Data bit 0
3	Data bit 1
4	Data bit 2
5	Data bit 3
6	Data bit 4
7	Data bit 5
8	Data bit 6
9	Data bit 7
10	Acknowledge
11	Busy
12	Paper end (out of paper)
13	Select
14	Auto feed
15	Error
16	Initialize printer (reset)
17	Select input
18–25	Ground

PC Parallel-to-Centronics Amphenol Cable Lead Layout

DB-25	Amphenol
1	1
2	2
3	3
4	4
5	5
6	6
7	7
8	8
9	9
10	10
11	11
12	12
13	13
14	14
15	32
16	31
17	36
18	33
19	19
20	21
22	25
23	27
24	29
25	30

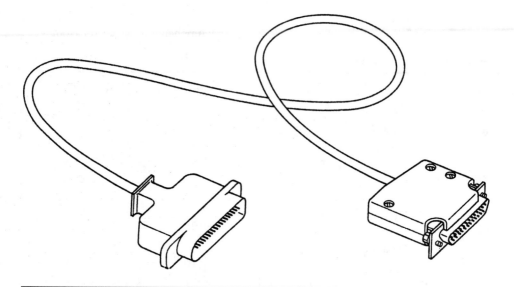

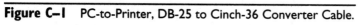

Figure C–1   PC-to-Printer, DB-25 to Cinch-36 Converter Cable.

Table C–1   Pinouts for a Typical
Modular Adapter

Signal Name	Pin #
Ring Indicator	1
Data Set Ready	2
Data Terminal Ready	3
Chassis Ground	4
Transmit Data	5
Received Data	6
Signal Ground	7
Clear to Send	8
Request to Send	9
Carrier Detect	10

Table C–2   RJ-45 Adapter and 2-, 3-, 4-, and 5-pair Cable Connections

Adapter Signal Name	Cable Conductors				
	Pin #	5-pair	4-pair	3-pair	2-pair
Ring Indicator	1	X			
Data Set Ready	2	X	X		
Data Terminal Ready	3	X	X	X	
Chassis Ground	4	X	X	X	X
Transmit Data	5	X	X	X	X
Received Data	6	X	X	X	X
Signal Ground	7	X	X	X	X
Clear to Send	8	X	X	X	
Request to Send	9	X	X		
Carrier Detect	10	X			

Table C–3   Modular Cable-pinning Diagrams

4-Pair Cable Straight-through	4-Pair Cable Crossed-conductors	2-Pair Cable Straight-through	2-Pair Cable Crossed-conductors
1 ——— 1	1 ——— 8	1 ——— 1	1 ——— 4
2 ——— 2	2 ——— 7	2 ——— 2	2 ——— 3
3 ——— 3	3 ——— 6	3 ——— 3	3 ——— 2
4 ——— 4	4 ——— 5	4 ——— 4	4 ——— 1
5 ——— 5	5 ——— 4		
6 ——— 6	6 ——— 3		
7 ——— 7	7 ——— 2		
8 ——— 8	8 ——— 1		

Table C–4 Back-to-back Cables with Crossed Conductors Using In-line Adapter

4-Pair Cable Crossed Pins	In-line Adapter	4-Pair Cable Crossed Pins
1 ——— 8	*	8 ——— 1
2 ——— 7	*	7 ——— 2
3 ——— 6	*	6 ——— 3
4 ——— 5	*	5 ——— 4
5 ——— 4	*	4 ——— 5
6 ——— 3	*	3 ——— 6
7 ——— 2	*	2 ——— 7
8 ——— 1	*	1 ——— 8

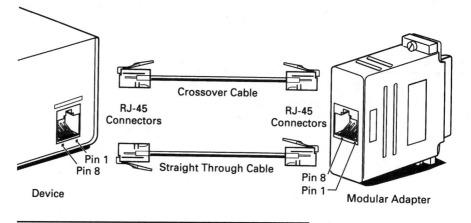

Figure C–2 Modular Cable and Modular/DB Adapter

Common Connectors, Pinouts, and Numbering Schemes for USB and Other Ports

This appendix contains tables and diagrams of common connectors. USB connectors are provided. Also, many other connectors are provided as reference for completeness. Many times the user needs to know how many conductors are provided within a cable. Furthermore, information about which leads are provided based on the number of conductors in a cable is very useful.

Table D–I   Typical RS-232 DB-25 Cable Conductors

# of Conductors	Pins Provided	Typical Use
4	2, 3, 7, 20	Interfacing with few or no input-control leads, generally considered a simplified EIA interface
7	2, 3, 4, 6, 7, 8, 20	Computer to computer (asynchronous) Computer to printer/plotter (asynchronous) Computer to terminal (asynchronous)
12	1–8, 15, 17, 20, 22	Same as 7-conductor: Computer to computer (synchronous) Computer to modem (asynchronous) Computer to modem (synchronous with DCE timing) Terminal to modem (asynchronous) Printer to modem
16	1–8, 15, 17, 20–25	Same as 7- and 12-conductor: Computer to modem (synchronous with DTE timing) Computer to modem with data-rate selection and signal-quality detection used
25	1–25	All uses; however if a ribbon cable is used, crossovers and jumpering are difficult

Table D–2   Typical USB Cable Connector

Pin	Name	Description
1	VCC	+5 VDC
2	D–	Data–
3	D+	Data+
4	Gnd	Ground

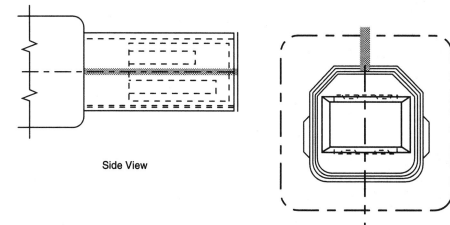

Side View

Front View

Figure D–1   USB Connector

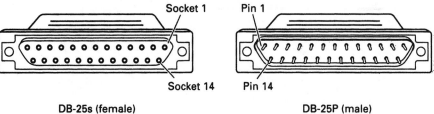

Socket 1   Pin 1

Socket 14   Pin 14

DB-25s (female)   DB-25P (male)

DB-25 Pin Numbering

Figure D–2   DB-25

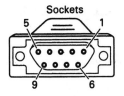

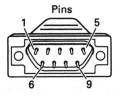

DB-9s (female)   DB-9P (male)

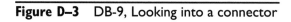

Figure D–3   DB-9, Looking into a connector

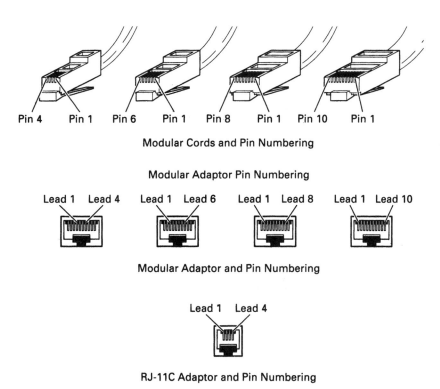

Pin 4   Pin 1   Pin 6   Pin 1   Pin 8   Pin 1   Pin 10   Pin 1

Modular Cords and Pin Numbering

Modular Adaptor Pin Numbering

Lead 1   Lead 4   Lead 1   Lead 6   Lead 1   Lead 8   Lead 1   Lead 10

Modular Adaptor and Pin Numbering

Lead 1   Lead 4

RJ-11C Adaptor and Pin Numbering

Figure D–4   Modular Adapters and Pin Numbering

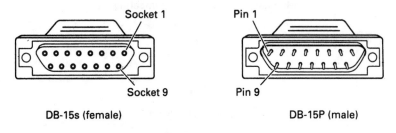

Figure D–5
DB25-to-Modular Adapters

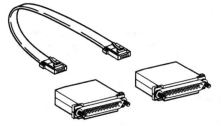

Socket 1   Pin 1

Socket 9   Pin 9

DB-15s (female)   DB-15P (male)

Figure D–6   DB-15, looking into a connector

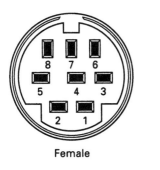

Female

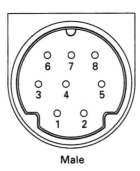

Male

Figure D–7
Mini-DIN for MAC, looking
into a connector

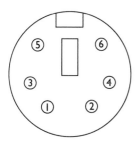

Figure D–8
PS/2 Mini-DIN, Looking into a Male Connector

D Connectors

The D specifies the shape (like a D, unsurprisingly). Then a letter after the D specifies the size of the shell, followed by the number of pins.

- DB-9: small serial ports
- DB-15: AUI ports (REAL IEE AUI)
- DB-25: bigger serial ports
- DC-37: used for some old floppy drives
- DD-50: used by Sun for SCSI, found on Sun-3's

Descriptions of Common Buses

This appendix contains information about common buses. Use this as a reference document as interfacing questions arise.

Much of the information is available online at http://www.gl.umbc. edu/~msokos1 and is printed with permission. The authors would like to thank Mark Sokos for his cooperation in compiling a large portion of this appendix. The reader is encouraged to visit his sites.

The PCI (Peripheral Component Interconnect) Bus

This section is not intended to be a thorough coverage of the PCI standard. It is for informational purposes only, and is intended to give designers and hobbyists an overview of the bus so that they might be able to design their own PCI cards. Thus, I/O operations are explained in the most detail, while memory operations, which will usually not be dealt with by an I/O card, are only briefly explained. Hobbyists are also warned that, due to the higher clock speeds involved, PCI cards are more difficult to design than ISA cards or cards for other slower busses. Many companies are now making PCI prototyping cards, and, for those fortunate enough to have access to FPGA programmers, companies like Xilinx are offering PCI-compliant designs which you can use as a starting point for your own projects.

For a copy of the full PCI standard, contact:

PCI Special Interest Group (SIG)
PO Box 14070
Portland, OR 97214
1–800–433–5177
1–503–797–4207

There is also a spec for CompactPCI, which uses the same timing and signals, but uses a eurocard connector and format. This is not presently covered in any detail within this document.

■ Pinout (5-volt and 3.3-volt boards)

–12V	01	*TRST
TCK		+12V
GND		TMS
TDO		TDI
+5V		+5V
+5V		*INTA
*INTB		*INTC
*INTD		+5V
*PRSNT1		reserved
reserved	10	+I/O V (+5 or +3.3)
*PRSNT2		reserved
GND	Key3.3	GND
GND	Key3.3	GND
reserved		reserved
GND		*RST
CLK		+I/O V (+5 or +3.3)
GND		*GNT
REQ		GND
+I/O V (+5 or +3.3)	20	reserved
AD31		AD30
AD29		+3.3V
GND		AD28
AD27		AD26
AD25		GND
+3.3V		AD24
C/BE3		IDSEL
AD23		+3.3V
GND		AD22
AD21		AD20
AD19	30	GND
+3.3V		AD18
AD17		AD16
C/BE2		+3.3V
GND		*FRAME
*IRDY		GND
+3.3V		*TRDY
*DEVSEL		GND
GND		*STOP

*LOCK		+3.3V
*PERR	40	SDONE
+3.3V		*SBO
*SERR		GND
+3.3V		PAR
C/BE1		AD15
AD14		+3.3V
GND		AD13
AD12		AD11
AD10	49	AD9
GND	Key5	GND
GND	Key5	GND
AD8	52	C/BE0
AD7		+3.3V
+3.3V		AD6
AD5		AD4
AD3		GND
GND		AD2
+I/O V (+5 or +3.3)		+I/O V (+5 or +3.3)
*ACK64	60	*REQ64
+5V		+5V
+5V	62	+5V

(Next section is for 64-Bit Bus Extension Only)

reserved	63	GND
GND		C/BE7
C/BE6		C/BE5
C/BE4		+I/O V (+5 or +3.3)
GND		PAR64
AD63		AD62
AD61		GND
+I/O V (+5 or +3.3)	70	AD60
AD59		AD58
AD57		GND
GND		AD56
AD55		AD54
AD53		+I/O V (+5 or +3.3)
GND		AD52
AD51		AD50
AD49		GND
+I/O V (+5 or +3.3)		AD48
AD47	80	AD46
AD45		GND
GND		AD44
AD43		AD42
AD41		+I/O V (+5 or +3.3)
GND		AD40

AD39		AD38
AD37		GND
+I/O V (+5 or +3.3)		AD36
AD35		AD34
AD33	90	GND
reserved		reserved
reserved		GND
GND	94	reserved

*Active Low

PCI slots are keyed so that a 3.3-volt card cannot be plugged into a 5-volt slot, and a 5.5-volt card cannot be plugged into a 3-volt card. Dual-voltage cards are possible.

Key3.3: At this location, a key is present on 3.3-volt boards. On 5-volt boards, these pins are GND.

Key5: At this location, a key is present on 5-volt boards. On 3.3-volt boards, these pins are GND.

▋ Signal Descriptions

AD(x):	Address/Data Lines.
CLK:	Clock. 33 MHz maximum.
C/BE(x):	Command, Byte Enable.
FRAME:	Used to indicate whether the cycle is an address phase or or a data phase.
DEVSEL:	Device Select.
IDSEL:	Initialization Device Select.
INT(x):	Interrupt.
IRDY:	Initiator Ready.
LOCK:	Used to manage resource locks on the PCI bus.
REQ:	Request. Requests a PCI transfer.
GNT:	Grant. indicates that permission to use PCI is granted.
PAR:	Parity. Used for AD0-31 and C/BE0-3.
PERR:	Parity Error.

RST:	Reset.
SBO:	Snoop Backoff.
SDONE:	Snoop Done.
SERR:	System Error. Indicates an address parity error for special cycles or a system error.
STOP:	Asserted by Target. Requests the master to stop the current transfer cycle.
TCK:	Test Clock.
TDI:	Test Data Input.
TDO:	Test Data Output.
TMS:	Test Mode Select.
TRDY:	Target Ready.
TRST:	Test Logic Reset.

The PCI bus treats all transfers as a burst operation. Each cycle begins with an address phase followed by one or more data phases. Data phases may repeat indefinitely but are limited by a timer that defines the maximum amount of time that the PCI device may control the bus. This timer is set by the CPU as part of the configuration space. Each device has its own timer (see the Latency Timer in the configuration space).

The same lines are used for address and data. The command lines are also used for byte enable lines. This is done to reduce the overall number of pins on the PCI connector.

The Command lines (C/BE3 to C/BE0) indicate the type of bus transfer during the address phase.

C/BE	Command Type
0000	Interrupt Acknowledge
0001	Special Cycle
0010	I/O Read
0011	I/O Write
0100	reserved
0101	reserved
0110	Memory Read
0111	Memory Write
1000	reserved
1001	reserved

1010	Configuration Read
1011	Configuration Write
1100	Multiple Memory Read
1101	Dual Address Cycle
1110	Memory-Read Line
1111	Memory Write and Invalidate

The three basic types of transfers are I/O, Memory, and Configuration.
PCI timing diagrams

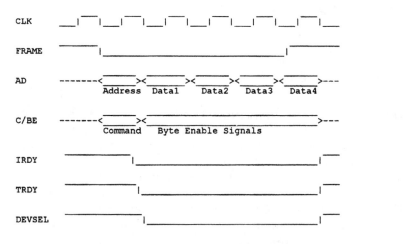

PCI transfer cycle, 4 data phases, no wait states.
Data is transferred on the rising edge of CLK.

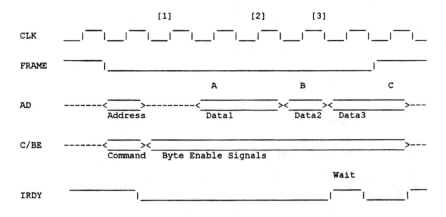

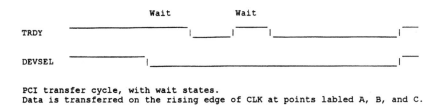

```
                       Wait            Wait
        _____     ____      ____
TRDY                    |___|    |    |    _____  __
                                 |____|                         |

        _____                                        __
DEVSEL                  |_____|
```

PCI transfer cycle, with wait states.
Data is transferred on the rising edge of CLK at points labled A, B, and C.

Bus Cycles

Interrupt Acknowledge (0000)

The interrupt controller automatically recognizes and reacts to the INTA (interrupt acknowledge) command. In the data phase, it transfers the interrupt vector to the AD lines.

Special Cycle (0001)

AD15-AD0

0x0000	Processor Shutdown
0x0001	Processor Halt
0x0002	x86 Specific Code
0x0003 to 0xFFFF	Reserved

I/O Read (0010) and I/O Write (0011)

Input/Output device read or write operation. The AD lines contain a byte address (AD0 and AD1 must be decoded).

PCI I/O ports may be 8 or 16-bits.

PCI allows 32-bits of address space. On IBM-compatible machines, the Intel CPU is limited to 16-bits of I/O space, which is further limited by some ISA cards that may also be installed in the machine (many ISA cards decode only the lower 10 bits of address space, and thus mirror themselves throughout the 16-bit I/O space). This limit assumes that the machine supports ISA or EISA slots in addition to PCI slots.

The PCI configuration space may also be accessed through I/O ports 0x0CF8 (Address) and 0x0CFC (Data). The address port must be written first.

Memory Read (0110) and Memory Write (0111)

A read or write to the system memory space. The AD lines contain a doubleword address. AD0 and AD1 do not need to be decoded. The Byte Enable lines (C/BE) indicate which bytes are valid.

Configuration Read (1010) and Configuration Write (1011)

A read or write to the PCI device configuration space, which is 256 bytes in length. It is accessed in doubleword units.

AD0 and AD1 contain 0, AD2–7 contain the doubleword address, AD8–10 are used for selecting the addressed unit as the malfunction unit, and the remaining AD lines are not used.

Address	Bit 32	16 | 15	0
00	Unit ID	| Manufacturer ID	
04	Status	| Command	
08	Class Code	| Revision	
0C	BIST | Header | Latency | CLS		
10–24	Base Address Register		
28	reserved		
2C	reserved		
30	Expansion ROM Base Address		
34	reserved		
38	reserved		
3C	MaxLat|MnGNT | INT-pin | INT-line		
40–FF	available for PCI unit		

Multiple Memory Read (1100)

This is an extension of the memory-read bus cycle. It is used to read large blocks of memory without caching, which is beneficial for long sequential memory accesses.

Dual Address Cycle (1101)

Two address cycles are necessary when a 64-Bit address is used, but only a 32-bit physical address exists. The least significant portion of the address is placed on the AD lines first, followed by the most significant 32-bits. The second address cycle also contains the command for the type of transfer (I/O, Memory, etc). The PCI bus supports a 64-Bit I/O address space, although this is not available on Intel-based PCs due to limitations of the CPU.

Memory-Read Line (1110)

This cycle is used to read in more than two 32-bit data blocks, typically up to the end of a cache line. It is more efficient than normal memory-read bursts for a long series of sequential memory accesses.

Memory Write and Invalidate (1111)

This indicates that a minimum of one cache line is to be transferred. This allows main memory to be updated, saving a cache write-back cycle.

The EISA Bus

This section is intended to provide a basic functional overview of the EISA bus, so that hobbyists and amateurs can design their own EISA-compatible cards. It is not intended to provide complete coverage of the EISA standard.

EISA is an acronym for Extended Industry Standard Architecture. It is an extension of the ISA architecture, which is a standardized version of the bus originally developed by IBM for their PC computers. EISA is upwardly compatible, which means that cards originally designed for the 8-bit IBM bus (often referred to as the XT bus) and cards designed for the 16-bit bus (referred to as the AT bus, and also as the ISA bus), will work in an EISA slot. EISA specific cards will not work in an AT or an XT slot.

The EISA connector uses multiple rows of connectors. The upper row is the same as a regular ISA slot, and the lower row contains the EISA extension. The slot is keyed so that ISA cards cannot be inserted to the point where they connet with the EISA signals.

■ Connector Signal Descriptions

Component Side

A1:	*CHKCHK	E1:	*CMD	F1:	GND	B1:	GND
A2:	SD7	E2:	*START	F2:	+5	B2:	*RESDRV
A3:	SD6	E3:	EXRDY	F3:	+5	B3:	+5
A4:	SD5	E4:	*EX32	F4:	reserved	B4:	IRQ2
A5:	SD4	E5:	GND	F5:	reserved	B5:	−5
A6:	SD3	E6:	(key)	F6:	(key)	B6:	DRQ2
A7:	SD2	E7:	*EX16	F7:	reserved	B7:	−12
A8:	SD1	E8:	*SLBURST	F8:	reserved	B8:	*NOWS

A9:	SD0	E9:	*MSBURST	F9:	+12	B9:	+12
A10:	CHRDY	E10:	W/R	F10:	M/IO	B10:	GND
A11:	AEN	E11:	GND	F11:	*LOCK	B11:	*SMWTC
A12:	SA19	E12:	reserved	F12:	reserved	B12:	*SMRDC
A13:	SA18	E13:	reserved	F13:	GND	B13:	*IOWC
A14:	SA17	E14:	reserved	F14:	reserved	B14:	*IORC
A15:	SA16	E15:	GND	F15:	*BE3	B15:	*DAK3
A16:	SA15	E16:	(key)	F16:	(key)	B16:	DRQ3
A17:	SA14	E17:	*BE1	F17:	*BE2	B17:	*DAK1
A18:	SA13	E18:	*LA31	F18:	*BE0	B18:	DRQ1
A19:	SA12	E19:	GND	F19:	GND	B19:	*REFRESH
A20:	SA11	E20:	*LA30	F20:	+5	B20:	BCLK
A21:	SA10	E21:	*LA28	F21:	*LA29	B21:	IRQ7
A22:	SA9	E22:	*LA27	F22:	GND	B22:	IRQ6
A23:	SA8	E23:	*LA25	F23:	*LA26	B23:	IRQ5
A24:	SA7	E24:	GND	F24:	*LA24	B24:	IRQ4
A25:	SA6	E25:	(key)	F25:	(key)	B25:	IRQ3
A26:	SA5	E26:	LA15	F26:	LA16	B26:	*DAK2
A27:	SA4	E27:	LA13	F27:	LA14	B27:	TC
A28:	SA3	E28:	LA12	F28:	+5	B28:	BALE
A29:	SA2	E29:	LA11	F29:	+5	B29:	+5
A30:	SA1	E30:	GND	F30:	GND	B30:	OSC
A31:	SA0	E31:	LA9	F31:	LA10	B31:	GND

G1:	LA7			H1:	LA8		
C1:	*SBHE	G2:	GND	H2:	LA6	D1:	*M16
C2:	LA23	G3:	LA4	H3:	LA5	D2:	*IO16
C3:	LA22	G4:	LA3	H4:	+4	D3:	IRQ10
C4:	LA21	G5:	GND	H5:	LA2	D4:	IRQ11
C5:	LA20	G6:	(key)	H6:	(key)	D5:	IRQ12
C6:	LA19	G7:	SD17	H7:	SD16	D6:	IRQ13
C7:	LA18	G8:	SD19	H8:	SD18	D7:	IRQ14
C8:	LA17	G9:	SD20	H9:	GND	D8:	*DAK0
C9:	*MRDC	G10:	SD22	H10:	SD21	D9:	DRQ0
C10:	*MWTC	G11:	GND	H11:	SD23	D10:	*DAK5
C11:	SD8	G12:	SD25	H12:	SD24	D11:	DRQ5
C12:	SD9	G13:	SD26	H13:	GND	D12:	*DAK6
C13:	SD10	G14:	SD28	H14:	SD27	D13:	DRQ65
C14:	SD11	G15:	(key)	H15:	(key)	D14:	*DAK7
C15:	SD12	G16:	GND	H16:	SD29	D15:	DRQ7
C16:	SD13	G17:	SD30	H17:	+5	D16:	+5
C17:	SD14	G18:	SD31	H18:	+5	D17:	*MASTER16
C18:	SD15	G19:	*MREQx	H19:	*MAKx	D18:	GND

* Active low.

+5, −5, +12, −12: Power supplies. −5 often is not implemented.

AEN: Address Enable. This is asserted when a DMAC has control of the bus. This prevents an I/O device from responding to the I/O command lines during a DMA transfer.

BALE: Bus Address Latch Enable. The address bus is latched on the rising edge of this signal. The address on the SA bus is valid from the falling edge of BALE to the end of the bus cycle. Memory devices should latch the LA bus on the falling edge of BALE.

BCLK: Bus Clock, 33% Duty Cycle. Frequency Varies. 8.33 MHz is specified as the maximum, but many systems allow this clock to be set to 10 MHz and higher.

BE(x):   Byte Enable. Indicates to the slave device which bytes on the data bus contain valid data. A 16-bit transfer would assert BE0 and BE1, for example, but not BE2 or BE3.

CHCHK: Channel Check. A low signal generates an NMI. The NMI signal can be masked on a PC, externally to the processor (of course). Bit 7 of port 70(hex) (enable NMI interrupts) and bit 3 of port 61 (hex) (recognition of channel check) must both be set to zero for an NMI to reach the CPU.

CHRDY: Channel Ready. Setting this low prevents the default ready timer from timing out. The slave device may then set it high again when it is ready to end the bus cycle. Holding this line low for too long can cause problems on some systems. CHRDY and NOWS should not be used simultaneously. This may cause problems with some bus controllers.

CMD: Command Phase. This signal indicates that the current bus cycle is in the command phase. After the start phase (see START), the data is transferred during the CMD phase. CMD remains asserted from the falling edge of START until the end of the bus cycle.

SD0-SD16:   System Data lines. They are bi-directional and tri-state.

DAKx: DMA Acknowledge.

DRQx: DMA Request.

EX16:   EISA Slave Size 16. This is used by the slave device to inform the bus master that it is capable of 16-bit transfers.

EX32:   EISA Slave Size 32. This is used by the slave device to inform the bus master that it is capable of 32-bit transfers.

EXRDY: EISA Ready. If this signal is asserted, the cycle will end on the next rising edge of BCLK. The slave device drives this signal low to insert wait states.

IO16: I/O size 16. Generated by a 16-bit slave when addressed by a bus master.

IORC: I/O Read Command line.

IOWC: I/O Write Command line.

IRQx: Interrupt Request. IRQ2 has the highest priority.

LAxx: Latchable Address lines.

LOCK: Asserting this signal prevents other bus masters from requesting control of the bus.

MAKx: Master Acknowledge for slot x: Indicates that the bus master Request (MREQx) has been granted.

MASTER16: 16-bit bus master. Generated by the ISA bus master when initiating a bus cycle.

M/IO: Memory/Input-Output. This is used to indicate whether the current bus cycle is a memory or an I/O operation.

M16: Memory Access, 16 bit

MRDC: Memory Read Command line.

MREQx: Master Request for Slot x:This is a slot-specific request for the device to become the bus master.

MSBURST: Master Burst. The bus master asserts this signal in response to SLBURST. This tells the slave device that the bus master is also capable of burst cycles.

MWTC: Memory Write Command line.

NOWS: No Wait State. Used to shorten the number of wait states generated by the default ready timer. This causes the bus cycle to end more quickly, since wait states will not be inserted. Most systems will ignore NOWS if CHRDY is active (low). However, this may cause problems with some bus controllers, and both signals should not be active simultaneously.

OSC: Oscillator, 14.318 MHz, 50% Duty Cycle. Frequency varies.

REFRESH: Refresh. Generated when the refresh logic is bus master.

RESDRV: This signal goes low when the machine is powered up. Driving it low will force a system reset.

SA0-SA19: System Address Lines, tri-state.

SBHE: System Bus High Enable, tri-state. Indicates a 16-bit data transfer.

SLBURST: Slave Burst. The slave device uses this to indicate that it is capable of burst cycles. The bus master will respond with MSBURST if it is also capable of burst cycles.

SMRDC: Standard Memory Read Command line. Indicates a memory read in the lower 1 MB area.

SMWTC: Standard Memory Write Command line. Indicates a memory write in the lower 1 MB area.

START: Start Phase. This signal is low when the current bus cycle is in the start phase. Address and M/IO signals are decoded during this phase. Data is transferred during the command phase (indicated by CMD).

TC: Terminal Count. Notifies the CPU that that the last DMA data transfer operation is complete.

W/R: Write or Read. Used to indicate if the current bus cycle is a read or a write operation.

The ISA and PC/104 Bus

IBM, IBM/XT, IBM PC, and IBM PC AT are registered trademarks of International Business Machines Corporation.

This section is designed to give a basic overview of the bus found in most IBM clone computers, often referred to as the XT or AT bus. The AT version of the bus is upwardly compatible, which means that cards designed to work on an XT bus will work on an AT bus. This bus was produced for many years without any formal standard. In recent years, a more formal standard called the ISA bus (Industry Standard Architecture) has been created, with an extension called the EISA (Extended ISA) bus also now as a standard. The EISA bus extensions will not be detailed here.

The PC/104 bus is an adaptation of the ISA bus for embedded computing use. It uses the same signals as ISA, but uses a smaller connector and cards that are stackable, which eliminates the need for a backplane. The name PC/104 comes from the fact that the bus was invented for the PC and has 104 pins.

This file is not intended to be a thorough coverage of the standard. It is for informational purposes only, and is intended to give designers and hobbyists sufficient information to design their own XT and AT compatible cards.

The IEEE P996 standard may be obtained from:

IEEE Standards Office
445 Hoes Lane
Piscataway, NJ 08854

The PC/104 standard may be obtained from:

The PC/104 Consortium
PO Box 4303
Mountain View, CA 94040

■ Connector Pinouts

ISA Connector

Component Side

A1:	*CHKCHK		B1:	GND
A2:	SD7		B2:	*RESDRV
A3:	SD6		B3:	+5
A4:	SD5		B4:	IRQ2
A5:	SD4		B5:	−5
A6:	SD3		B6:	DRQ2
A7:	SD2		B7:	−12
A8:	SD1		B8:	*NOWS [A]
A9:	SD0		B9:	+12
A10:	CHRDY		B10:	GND
A11:	AEN		B11:	*SMWTC
A12:	SA19		B12:	*SMRDC
A13:	SA18		B13:	*IOWC
A14:	SA17		B14:	*IORC
A15:	SA16		B15:	*DAK3
A16:	SA15		B16:	DRQ3
A17:	SA14		B17:	*DAK1
A18:	SA13		B18:	DRQ1
A19:	SA12		B19:	*REFRESH
A20:	SA11		B20:	BCLK

A21:	SA10	B21:	IRQ7
A22:	SA9	B22:	IRQ6
A23:	SA8	B23:	IRQ5
A24:	SA7	B24:	IRQ4
A25:	SA6	B25:	IRQ3
A26:	SA5	B26:	*DAK2
A27:	SA4	B27:	TC
A28:	SA3	B28:	BALE
A29:	SA2	B29:	+5
A30:	SA1	B30:	OSC
A31:	SA0	B31:	GND

AT Bus only

Component Side

C1:	*SBHE	D1:	*M16
C2:	LA23	D2:	*IO16
C3:	LA22	D3:	IRQ10
C4:	LA21	D4:	IRQ11
C5:	LA20	D5:	IRQ12
C6:	LA19	D6:	IRQ15 [B]
C7:	LA18	D7:	IRQ14
C8:	LA17	D8:	*DAK0
C9:	*MRDC	D9:	DRQ0
C10:	*MWTC	D10:	*DAK5
C11:	SD8	D11:	DRQ5
C12:	SD9	D12:	*DAK6
C13:	SD10	D13:	DRQ65
C14:	SD11	D14:	*DAK7
C15:	SD12	D15:	DRQ7
C16:	SD13	D16:	+5
C17:	SD14	D17:	*MASTER16
C18:	SD15	D18:	GND

*Active Low

[A] A signal called J8, or Card_Select, was used on this pin on the IBM XT. This signal was only active on the J8 slot on the motherboard (the slot closest to the keyboard connector).

[B] Many texts accidentally place IRQ13 on this pin. Note that IRQ13 (coprocessor) is not present on the ISA bus connector.

PC/104 Connector

PIN	ROW A (J1)	ROW B(J1)	ROW C (J2)	ROW D (J2)
0			GND	GND
1	*CHCHK	GND	*SBHE	*M16
2	SD7	RESDRV	LA23	*IO16
3	SD6	+5V	LA22	IRQ10
4	SD5	IRQ9	LA21	IRQ11
5	SD4	−5V	LA20	IRQ12
6	SD3	DRQ2	LA19	IRQ15
7	SD2	−12V	LA18	IRQ14
8	SD1	*ENDXFR	LA17	*DACK0
9	SD0	+12V	*MRDC	DRQ0
10	CHRDY	KEY	*MWTC	*DACK5
11	AEN	*SMWTC	SD8	DRQ5
12	SA19	*SMRDC	SD9	*DACK6
13	SA18	*IOWC	SD10	DRQ6
14	SA17	*IORC	SD11	*DACK7
15	SA16	*DACK3	SD12	DRQ7
16	SA15	DRQ3	SD13	+5V
17	SA14	*DACK1	SD14	*MASTER16
18	SA13	DRQ1	SD15	GND
19	SA12	*REFRESH	KEY	GND
20	SA11	CLK		
21	SA10	IRQ7		
22	SA9	IRQ6		
23	SA8	IRQ5		
24	SA7	IRQ4		
25	SA6	IRQ3		
26	SA5	*DACK2		
27	SA4	TC		
28	SA3	BALE		
29	SA2	+5V		
30	SA1	OSC		
31	SA0	GND		
32	GND	GND		

Rows C and D are used for 16-bit (AT) operation. Keys are missing pins, and holes are filled.

Electrical Characteristics

The actual drive capabilities of ISA motherboards can vary greatly. The IEEE P996 specs 1.0 offers these guidelines:

+12 V at 1.5 A
−12 V at 0.3 A
+5 V   at 4.5 A
−5 V   at 0.2 A

PC/104 specifies the following:

+12 V at 1.0 A
+5 V   at 2.0 A
−5 V   at 0.2 A
−12 V at 0.3 A

M16, IO16, MASTER16, and ENDXFR are 20 mA max. All other signals are 4 mA max.

Signal Descriptions

+5, −5,
+12, −12:   Power supplies. −5 is often not implemented. The PC/104 spec does not require unused voltages to be present on the bus.

AEN: Address Enable. This is asserted when a DMAC has control of the bus. This prevents an I/O device from responding to the I/O command lines during a DMA transfer.

BALE: Bus Address Latch Enable. The address bus is latched on the Rising edge of this signal. The address on the SA bus is valid from the falling edge of BALE to the end of the bus cycle. Memory devices should latch the LA bus on the falling edge of BALE. Some references refer to this signal as Buffered Address Latch Enable, or just Address Latch Enable (ALE).

BCLK: Bus Clock, 33% Duty Cycle. Frequency Varies. 4.77 to 8 MHz typical. 8.3 MHz is specified as the maximum, but many systems allow this clock to be set to 12 MHz and higher.

CHCHK: Channel Check. A low signal generates an NMI. The NMI signal can be masked on a PC, externally to the processor (of course). Bit 7 of port 70 (hex) (enable NMI interrupts) and bit 3 of port 61 (hex) (recognition of channel check) must both be set to zero for an NMI to reach the CPU.

CHRDY: Channel Ready. Setting this low prevents the default ready timer from timing out. The slave device may then set it high again when it is ready to end the bus cycle. Holding this line low for too long (15 microseconds, typically) can prevent RAM refresh cycles on some systems. This signal is called IOCHRDY (I/O Channel Ready) by some references. CHRDY and NOWS should not be used simultaneously. This may cause problems with some bus controllers.

DAKx: DMA Acknowledge.

DRQx: DMA Request.

ENDXFR
(PC/104
only): End Transfer.

GND: Ground (0 volts).

IO16: I/O size 16. Generated by a 16-bit slave when addressed by a bus master.

IORC: I/O Read Command line.

IOWC: I/O Write Command line.

IRQx: Interrupt Request. IRQ2 has the highest priority. IRQ 10–15 are available only on AT machines and are higher priority than IRQ 3–7.

LAxx: Latchable Address lines. Combine with the lower address lines to form a 24-bit address space (16 MB)

MASTER16: 16-bit bus master. Generated by the ISA bus master when initiating a bus cycle.

M16: Memory Access, 16 bit.

MRDC: Memory Read Command line.

MWTC: Memory Write Command line.

NOWS: No Wait State. Used to shorten the number of wait states generated by the default ready timer. This causes the bus cycle to end more quickly, since wait states will not be inserted. Most systems will ignore NOWS if CHRDY is active (low). However, this may cause problems with some bus controllers, and both signals should not be active simultaneously.

OSC: Oscillator, 14.318 MHz, 50% Duty Cycle. Frequency varies. This was originally divided by 3 to provide the 4.77-MHz CPU clock of early PCs, and divided by 12 to produce the 1.19 Mhz system clock. Some references have placed this signal as low as 1 MHz (possibly referencing the system clock), but most modern systems use 14.318 MHz. This frequency (14.318 MHz) is four times the television colorburst frequency. Refresh timing on many PCs is based on OSC/18, or approximately one refresh cycle every 15 microseconds. Many modern motherboards allow this rate to be changed, which frees up some bus cycles for use by software but also can cause memory errors if the system RAM cannot handle the slower refresh rates.

REFRESH: Refresh. Generated when the refresh logic is bus master. An ISA device acting as bus master may also use this signal to initiate a refresh cycle.

RESDRV: This signal goes low when the machine is powered up. Driving it low will force a system reset.

SA0-SA19: System Address Lines, tri-state.

SBHE: System Bus High Enable, tri-state. Indicates a 16-bit data transfer. This may also indicate an 8-bit transfer using the upper half of the data bus (if an odd address is present).

SD0-SD15: System Data lines, or Standard Data Lines. They are bidirectional and tri-state. On most systems, the data lines float high when not driven.

SMRDC: Standard Memory Read Command line. Indicates a memory read in the lower 1 MB area.

SMWTC: Standard Memory Write Commmand line. Indicates a memory write in the lower 1 MB area.

TC: Terminal Count. Notifies the CPU that that the last DMA data transfer operation is complete.

8-Bit Memory or I/O Transfer Timing Diagram (4 wait states shown)

Note: W1 through W4 indicate wait cycles.

BALE is placed high, and the address is latched on the SA bus. The slave device may safely sample the address during the falling edge of BALE, and the address on the SA bus remains valid until the end of the transfer cycle. Note that AEN remains low throughout the entire transfer cycle.

The command line is then pulled low (IORC or IOWC for I/O commands; SMRDSC or SMWTC for memory commands, read and write, respectively). For write operations, the data remains on the SD bus for the remainder of the transfer cycle. For read operations, the data must be valid on the falling edge of the last cycle.

NOWS is sampled at the midpoint of each wait cycle. If it is low, the transfer cycle terminates without further wait states.

CHRDY is sampled during the first half of the clock cycle. If it is low, further wait cycles will be inserted.

The default for 8-bit transfers is 4 wait states. Some computers allow the number of default wait states to be changed.

16-Bit Memory or I/O Transfer Timing Diagram (1 wait state shown)

```
SD0-SD15        -----------------------------<___>---------
(READ)                                         *


SD0-SD15        -----------------<_____>---------
(WRITE)
```

An asterisk (*) denotes the point where the signal is sampled.

[1] The portion of the address on the LA bus for the NEXT cycle may now be placed on the bus. This is used so cards may begin decoding the address early. Address pipelining must be active.

[2] AEN remains low throughout the entire transfer cycle, indicating that a normal (non-DMA) transfer is occurring.

[3] Some bus controllers sample this signal during the same clock cycle as M16, instead of during the first wait state, as shown above. In this case, IO16 needs to be pulled low as soon as the address is decoded, which is before the I/O command lines are active.

[4] M16 is sampled a second time, in case the adapter card did not activate the signal in time for the first sample (usually because the memory device is not monitoring the LA bus for early address information, or is waiting for the falling edge of BALE).

Sixteen-bit transfers follow the same basic timing as 8-bit transfers. A valid address may appear on the LA bus prior to the beginning of the transfer cycle. Unlike the SA bus, the LA bus is not latched, and it is not valid for the entire transfer cycle (on most computers). The LA bus should be latched on the falling edge of BALE. Note that on some systems the LA bus signals will follow the same timing as the SA bus. On either type of system a valid address is present on the falling edge of BALE.

I/O adapter cards do not need to monitor the LA bus or BALE, since I/O addresses are always within the address space of the SA bus.

SBHE will be pulled low by the system board, and the adapter card must respond with IO16 or M16 at the appropriate time, or else the transfer will be split into two separate 8-bit transfers. Many systems expect IO16 or M16 before the command lines are valid. This requires that IO16 or M16 be pulled low as soon as the address is decoded (before it is known whether the cycle is I/O or memory). If the system is starting a memory cycle, it will ignore IO16 (and vice versa for I/O cycles and M16).

For read operations, the data is sampled on the rising edge of the last clock cycle. For write operations, valid data appears on the bus before the end of the cycle, as shown in the timing diagram. While the timing diagram indicates that the data needs to be sampled on the rising clock, on most systems it remains valid for the entire clock cycle.

The default for 16-bit transfers is 1 wait state. This may be shortened or lengthened in the same manner as 8-bit transfers, via NOWS and CHRDY. Many systems allow only 16-bit memory devices (and not I/O devices) to transfer using 0 wait states (NOWS has no effect on 16-bit I/O cycles).

SMRDC/SMWTC follow the same timing as MRDC/MWTC, respectively, when the address is within the lower 1 MB. If the address is not within the lower 1 MB boundary, SMRDC/SMWTC will remain high during the entire cycle.

It is also possible for an 8-bit bus cycle to use the upper portion of the bus. In this case, the timing will be similar to a 16-bit cycle, but an odd address will be present on the bus. This means that the bus is transferring 8 bits using the upper data bits (SD8–SD15).

Shortening or Lengthening the Bus Cycle

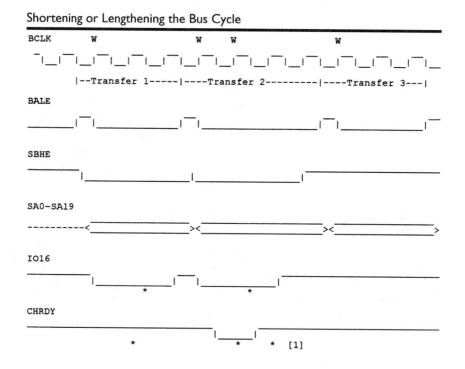

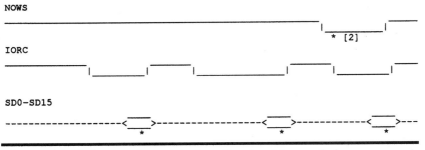

An asterisk (*) denotes the point where the signal is sampled.
W = Wait Cycle

This timing diagram shows three different transfer cycles. The first is a 16-bit standard I/O read. This is followed by an almost identical 16-bit I/O read, with one wait state inserted. The I/O device pulls CHRDY low to indicate that it is not ready to complete the transfer. This inserts a wait cycle, and CHRDY is again sampled. At this second sample the I/O device has completed its operation and released CHRDY, and the bus cycle now terminates. The third cycle is an 8-bit transfer, which is shortened to 1 wait state (the default is 4) by the use of NOWS.

▌ I/O Port Addresses

Note: Only the first 10 address lines are decoded for I/O operations. This limits the I/O address space to address 3FF (hex) and lower. Some systems allow for 16-bit I/O address space, but may be limited because some I/O cards decode only 10 of these 16 bits.

Port Address Assignments

Port (hex)

000–00F	DMA Controller
010–01F	DMA Controller (PS/2)
020–02F	Master Programmable Interrupt Controller (PIC)
030–03F	Slave PIC
040–05F	Programmable Interval Timer (PIT)
060–06F	Keyboard Controller
070–071	Real Time Clock
080–083	DMA Page Registers
090–097	Programmable Option Select (PS/2)

0A0–0AF	PIC #2
0C0–0CF	DMAC #2
0E0–0EF	reserved
0F0–0FF	Math coprocessor, PCJr Disk Controller
100–10F	Programmable Option Select (PS/2)
110–16F	available
170–17	Hard Drive 1 (AT)
180–1EF	available
1F0–1FF	Hard Drive 0 (AT)
200–20F	Game Adapter
210–217	Expansion Card Ports
220–26F	available
270–27F	Parallel Port 3
280–2A1	available
2A2–2A3	clock
2B0–2DF	EGA/Video
2E2–2E3	Data Acquisition Adapter (AT)
2E8–2EF	Serial Port COM4
2F0–2F7	Reserved
2F8–2FF	Serial Port COM2
300–31F	Prototype Adapter, Periscope Hardware Debugger
320–32F	available
330–33F	Reserved for XT/370
340–35F	available
360–36F	Network
370–377	Floppy Disk Controller
378–37F	Parallel Port 2
380–38F	SDLC Adapter
390–39F	Cluster Adapter
3A0–3AF	reserved
3B0–3BB	Monochome Adapter
3BC–3BF	Parallel Port 1
3C0–3CF	EGA/VGA
3D0–3DF	Color Graphics Adapter
3E0–3EF	Serial Port COM3
3F0–3F7	Floppy Disk Controller
3F8–3FF	Serial Port COM1

Soundblaster cards usually use I/O ports 220–22F.
Data acquisition cards frequently use 300–320.

■ DMA Read and Write

The ISA bus uses two DMA controllers (DMAC) cascaded together. The slave DMAC connects to the master DMAC via DMA channel 4 (channel 0 on the master DMAC). The slave therefore gains control of the bus through the master DMAC. On the ISA bus, the DMAC is programmed to use fixed priority (channel 0 always has the highest priority), which means that channels 0–4 from the slave have the highest priority (since they connect to the master channel 0), followed by channels 5–7 (which are channels 1–3 on the master).

The DMAC can be programmed for read transfers (data is read from memory and written to the I/O device), write transfers (data is read from the I/O device and written to memory), or verify transfers (neither a read nor a write—this was used by DMA CH0 for DRAM refresh on early PCs).

Before a DMA transfer can take place, the DMA Controller (DMAC) must be programmed. This is done by writing the start address and the number of bytes to transfer (called the transfer count) and the direction of the transfer to the DMAC.

After the DMAC has been programmed, the device may activate the appropriate DMA request (DRQx) line.

Slave DMA Controller

I/O Port

0000	DMA CH0 Memory Address Register
	Contains the lower 16-bits of the memory address, written as two consecutive bytes.
0001	DMA CH0 Transfer Count
	Contains the lower 16-bits of the transfer count, written as two consecutive bytes.
0002	DMA CH1 Memory Address Register
0003	DMA CH1 Transfer Count
0004	DMA CH2 Memory Address Register
0005	DMA CH2 Transfer Count
0006	DMA CH3 Memory Address Register
0007	DMA CH3 Transfer Count
0008	DMAC Status/Control Register
	Status (I/O read) bits 0–3: Terminal Count, CH 0–3; bits 4–7: Request CH 0–3
	Control (write)
	bit 0: Mem to mem enable (1 = enabled)
	bit 1: ch0 address hold enable (1 = enabled)
	bit 2: controller disable (1 = disabled)
	bit 3: timing (0 = normal, 1 = compressed)

bit 4: priority (0 = fixed, 1 = rotating)
bit 5: write selection (0 = late, 1 = extended)
bit 6: DRQx sense asserted (0 = high, 1 = low)
bit 7: DAKn sense asserted (0 = low, 1 = high)

0009	Software DRQn Request
	bits 0–1: channel select (CH 0–3)
	bit 2: request bit (0 = reset, 1 = set)
000A	DMA mask register
	bits 0–1: channel select (CH 0–3)
	bit 2: mask bit (0 = reset, 1 = set)
000B	DMA Mode Register
	bits 0–1: channel select (CH 0–3)
	bits 2–3: 00 = verify transfer, 01 = write transfer, 10 = read transfer, 11 = reserved
	bit 4: Auto init (0 = disabled, 1 = enabled)
	bit 5: Address (0 = increment, 1 = decrement)
	bits 6–7: 00 = demand transfer mode, 01 = single transfer mode, 10 = block transfer mode, 11 = cascade mode
000C	DMA Clear Byte Pointer—writing to this causes the DMAC to clear the pointer used to keep track of 16-bit data transfers into and out of the DMAC for hi/low byte sequencing.
000D	DMA Master Clear (Hardware Reset)
000E	DMA Reset Mask Register—clears the mask register
000F	DMA Mask Register
	bits 0–3: mask bits for CH 0–3 (0 = not masked, 1 = masked)
0081	DMA CH2 Page Register (address bits A16–A23)
0082	DMA CH3 Page Register
0083	DMA CH1 Page Register
0087	DMA CH0 Page Register
0089	DMA CH6 Page Register
008A	DMA CH7 Page Register
008B	DMA CH5 Page Register

Master DMA Controller

I/O Port	
00C0	DMA CH4 Memory Address Register
	Contains the lower 16-bits of the memory address, written as two consecutive bytes.
00C2	DMA CH4 Transfer Count
	Contains the lower 16-bits of the transfer count, written as two consecutive bytes.
00C4	DMA CH5 Memory Address Register
00C6	DMA CH5 Transfer Count

00C8	DMA CH6 Memory Address Register
00CA	DMA CH6 Transfer Count
00CC	DMA CH7 Memory Address Register
00CE	DMA CH7 Transfer Count
00D0	DMAC Status/Control Register

> Status (I/O read) bits 0–3: Terminal Count, CH 4–7
>> bits 4–7: Request CH 4–7
>
> Control (write)
>> bit 0: Mem to mem enable (1 = enabled)
>> bit 1: CH0 address hold enable (1 = enabled)
>> bit 2: controller disable (1 = disabled)
>> bit 3: timing (0 = normal, 1 = compressed)
>> bit 4: priority (0 = fixed, 1 = rotating)
>> bit 5: write selection (0 = late, 1 = extended)
>> bit 6: DRQx sense asserted (0 = high, 1 = low)
>> bit 7: DAKn sense asserted (0 = low, 1 = high)

00D2	Software DRQn Request

> bits 0–1: channel select (CH 4–7)
> bit 2: request bit (0 = reset, 1 = set)

00D4	DMA mask register

> bits 0–1: channel select (CH 4–7)
> bit 2: mask bit (0 = reset, 1 = set)

00D6	DMA Mode Register

> bits 0–1: channel select (CH 4–7)
> bits 2–3: 00 = verify transfer, 01 = write transfer, 10 = read
>> transfer, 11 = reserved
> bit 4: Auto init (0 = disabled, 1 = enabled)
> bit 5: Address (0 = increment, 1 = decrement)
> bits 6–7: 00 = demand transfer mode, 01 = single transfer
> mode, 10 = block transfer mode, 11 = cascade mode

00D8	DMA Clear Byte Pointer—writing to this causes the DMAC to clear the pointer used to keep track of 16-bit data transfers into and out of the DMAC for hi/low byte sequencing.
00DA	DMA Master Clear (Hardware Reset)
00DC	DMA Reset Mask Register—clears the mask register
00DE	DMA Mask Register

> bits 0–3: mask bits for CH 4–7 (0 = not masked, 1 = masked)

Single Transfer Mode

The DMAC is programmed for transfer.

The DMA device requests a transfer by driving the appropriate DRQ line high. The DMAC responds by asserting AEN and acknowledges the DMA request through the appropriate DAK line. The I/O and memory command lines are also asserted. When the DMA device sees the DAK signal, it drops the DRQ line.

The DMAC places the memory address on the SA bus (at the same time as the command lines are asserted), and the device either reads from or writes to memory, depending on the type of transfer. The transfer count is incrimented, and the address incrimented/decrimented. DAK is deasserted. The CPU now once again has control of the bus and continues execution until the I/O device is once again ready for transfer. The DMA device repeats the procedure, driving DRQ high and waiting for DAK, then transferring data. This continues for a number of cycles equal to the transfer count. When this has been completed, the DMAC signals the CPU that the DMA transfer is complete via the TC (terminal count) signal.

Timing for Transfer

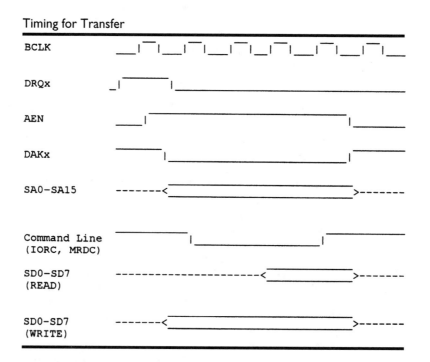

■ Block-Transfer Mode

The DMAC is programmed for transfer.

The device attempting DMA transfer drives the appropriate DRQ line high. The motherboard responds by driving AEN high and DAK low. This indicates that the DMA device is now the bus master.

In response to the DAK signal, the DMA device drops DRQ. The DMAC places the address for DMA transfer on the address bus. Both the memory and I/O command lines are asserted (since DMA involves both an I/O and a memory device). AEN prevents I/O devices from responding to the I/O command lines, which would not result in proper operation since the I/O lines are active, but a memory address is on the address bus.

The data transfer is now done (memory read or write), and the DMAC increments/decrements the address and begins another cycle. This continues for a number of cycles equal to the DMAC transfer count.

When this has been completed, the terminal count signal (TC) is generated by the DMAC to inform the CPU that the DMA transfer has been completed.

Note: Block transfer must be used carefully. The bus cannot be used for other things (like RAM refresh) while block mode transfers are being done.

▍Demand-Transfer Mode

The DMAC is programmed for transfer.

The device attempting DMA transfer drives the appropriate DRQ line high. The motherboard responds by driving AEN high and DAK low. This indicates that the DMA device is now the bus master.

Unlike single transfer and block transfer, the DMA device does not drop DRQ in response to DAK. The DMA device transfers data in the same manner as for block transfers. The DMAC will continue to generate DMA cycles as long as the I/O device asserts DRQ. When the I/O device is unable to continue the transfer (if it no longer had data ready to transfer, for example), it drops DRQ and the CPU once again has control of the bus. Control is returned to the DMAC by once again asserting DRQ. This continues until the terminal count has been reached, and the TC signal informs the CPU that the transfer has been completed.

Interrupts on the ISA Bus

	Interrupt (Hex)	
NMI	2	Parity Error, Mem Refresh
IRQ0	8	8253 Channel 0 (System Timer)
IRQ1	9	Keyboard
IRQ2	A	Cascade from slave PIC
IRQ3	B	COM2
IRQ4	C	COM1
IRQ5	D	LPT2
IRQ6	E	Floppy Drive Controller
IRQ7	F	LPT1

(continued)

	Interrupt (Hex)	
IRQ8	F	Real Time Clock
IRQ9	F	Redirection to IRQ2
IRQ10	F	reserved
IRQ11	F	reserved
IRQ12	F	Mouse Interface
IRQ13	F	Coprocessor
IRQ14	F	Hard Drive Controller
IRQ15	F	reserved

IRQ 0,1,2,8, and 13 are not available on the ISA bus.

The IBM PC and XT had only a single 8259 interrupt controller. The AT and later machines have a second interrupt controller, and the two are used in a master/slave combination. IRQ2 and IRQ9 are the same pin on most ISA systems.

Interrupts on most systems may be either edge triggered or level triggered. The default is usually edge triggered and active high (low to high transition).

The interrupt level must be held high until the first interrupt acknowledge cycle (two interrupt acknowledge bus cycles are generated in response to an interrupt request).

The software aspects of interrupts and interrupt handlers are intentionally omitted from this document, owing to the numerous syntactical differences in software tools and the fact that adequate documentation of this topic is usually provided with development software.

▌ Bus Mastering

An ISA device may take control of the bus, but this must be done with caution. There are no safety mechanisms involved, and so it is easily possible to crash the entire system by incorrectly taking control of the bus. For example, most systems require bus cycles for DRAM refresh. If the ISA bus master does not relinquish control of the bus or generate its own DRAM refresh cycles every 15 microseconds, the system RAM can become corrupted. The ISA adapter card can generate refresh cycles without relinquishing control of the bus by asserting REFRESH. MRDC can be then monitored to determine when the refresh cycle ends.

To take control of the bus, the device first asserts its DRQ line. The DMAC sends a hold request to the CPU, and when the DMAC receives a hold acknowledge, it asserts the appropriate DAK line corresponding to the DRQ line asserted. The device is now the bus master. AEN is asserted, so if the device wishes to access I/O devices, it must assert MASTER16 to release AEN. Control of the bus is returned to the system board by releasing DRQ.

VESA Local Bus (VLB)

This section is intended to provide a basic functional overview of the VESA Local Bus, so that hobbyists and amateurs can design their own VLB-compatible cards. It is not intended to provide complete coverage of the VLB standard.

VLB connectors are usually inline with ISA connectors, so that adapter cards may use both. However, the VLB is separate and does not need to connect to the ISA portion of the bus.

▌ Pinouts

64-Bit	Side B	Pin	Side A	64-Bit Signals
(Optional)	D0	01	D1	(Optional)
	D2		D3	
	D4		GND	
	D6		D5	
	D8		D7	
	GND		D9	
	D10		D11	
	D12		D13	
	VCC		D15	
	D14	10	GND	
	D16		D17	
	D18		VCC	
	D20		D19	
	GND		D21	
	D22		D23	
	D24		D25	
	D26		GND	
	D28		D27	
	D30		D29	
	VCC	20	D31	
D63	A31		A30	D62

(continued)

64-Bit	Side B	Pin	Side A	64-Bit Signals
	GND		A28	D60
D61	A29		A26	D58
D59	A27		GND	
D57	A25		A24	D56
D55	A23		A22	D54
D53	A21		VCC	
D51	A19		A20	D52
	GND	A18		D50
D49	A17	30	A16	D48
D47	A15		A14	D46
	VCC	A12		D44
D45	A13		A10	D42
D43	A11	A8	D40	
D41	A9	GND		
D39	A7	A6	D38	
D37	A5	A4	D36	
	GND	*WBACK		
D35	A3	*BEO	*BE4	
D34	A2	40	VCC	
*LBS64	n/c	*BE1	*BE5	
	*RESET	*BE2	*BE6	
	D/C	GND		
D33	M/IO		*BE3	*BE7
D32	W/R	45	*ADS	
	KEY	(46–47)		
	*RDYRTN	48	*LRDY	
	GND	*LDEV		
	IRQ9	50	*LREQ	
	*BRDY	GND		
	*BLAST	*LGNT		
	ID0	VCC		
	ID1	ID2		
	GND	ID3		
	LCLK	ID4		*ACK64
	VCC	*LKEN		
*LBS16	58	*LEADS		

*Indicates Active low.

The 64-bit expansion of the bus (optional) does not add additional pins or connectors. Instead, it multiplexes the existing pins. The 32-bit VLB bus does not use the 64-bit signals shown in the above pinouts.

A2–A31:   Address Bus.

*ADS: Address Strobe.

*BE0–*BE3: Byte Enable. Indicates that the eight data lines corresponding to each signal will deliver valid data.

*BLAST: Burst Last. Indicates a VLB burst cycle, which will complete with *BRDY. The VLB burst cycle consists of an address phase followed by four data phases.

*BRDY: Burst Ready. Indicates the end of the current burst transfer.

D0–D31: Data Bus. Valid bytes are indicated by *BE(x) signals.

D/C: Data/Command. Used with M/IO and W/R to indicate the type of cycle.

M/IO	D/C	W/R	
0	0	0	INTA sequence
0	0	1	Halt/Special (486)
0	1	0	I/O Read
0	1	1	I/O Write
1	0	0	Instruction Fetch
1	0	1	Halt/Shutdown (386)
1	1	0	Memory Read
1	1	1	Memory Write

ID0–ID4: Identification Signals.

ID0	ID1	ID4	CPU	Bus Width	Burst
0	0	0	(res)		
0	0	1	(res)		
0	1	0	486	16/32	Burst Possible
0	1	1	486	16/32	Read Burst
1	0	0	386	16/32	None
1	0	1	386	16/32	None
1	1	0	(res)		
1	1	1	486	16/32/64	Read/Write Burst

ID2 Indicates wait: 0 = 1 wait cycle (min), 1 = no wait.
ID3 Indicates bus speed: 0 = greater than 33.3 MHz,
1 = less than 33.3 MHz.

IRQ9: Interrupt Request. Connected to IRQ9 on ISA bus. This allows stand-alone VLB adapters (not connected to ISA portion of the bus) to have one IRQ.

*LEADS: Local Enable Address Strobe. Set low by VLB master (not CPU). Also used for cache invalidation signal.

*LBS16: Local Bus Size 16. Used by slave device to indicate that it has a transfer width of only 16-bits.

LCLK: Local Clock. Runs at the same frequency as the CPU, up to 50 Mhz. 66 MHz is allowed for on-board devices.

*LDEV: Local Device. When appropriate address and M/IO signals are present on the bus, the VLB device must pull this line low to indicate that it is a VLB device. The VLB controller will then use the VLB bus for the transfer.

*LRDY: Local Ready. Indicates that the VLB device has completed the cycle. This signal is only used for single-cycle transfers. *BRDY is used for burst transfers.

*LGNT: Local Grant. Indicates that an *LREQ signal has been granted, and control is being transferred to the new VLB master.

*LREQ: Local Request. Used by VLB Master to gain control of the bus.

M/IO: Memory/IO. See D/C for signal description.

*RDYRTN: Ready Return. Indicates VLB cycle has been completed. May precede LRDY by one cycle.

*RESET: Reset. Resets all VLB devices.

*WBACK: Write Back.

▌ 64-Bit Expansion Signals

*ACK64: Acknowledge 64-bit transfer. Indicates that the device can perform the requested 64-bit transfer cycle.

*BE4–*BE7: Byte Enable. Indicates which bytes are valid (similar to *BE0–*BE3).

D32–D63: Upper 32 bits of data bus. Multiplexed with address bus.

*LBS64: Local Bus Size 64 bits. Used by VLB Master to indicate that it desires a 64-bit transfer.

W/R: Write/Read. See D/C for signal description.

64-Bit Data-Transfer Timing Diagram

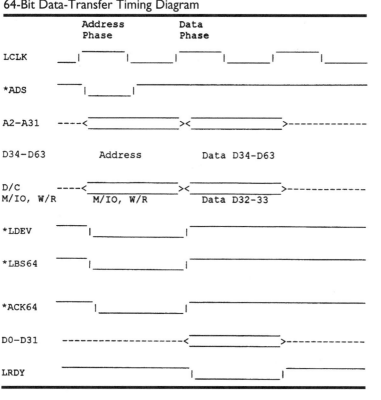

The Multibus standard was originally developed by Intel. It specified four buses, called the Multibus System Bus, the I/O Expansion Bus (iSBX), the Execution Bus (iLBX), and the Multichannel I/O Bus. The Multibus system bus was adopted as IEEE 796, and the iSBX bus was adopted as IEEE P959.

Multibus is popular in industrial systems, and while it is a fairly old bus, it is still in common use. The original design dates back to the early '70s. In the early '80s, Intel created Multibus II, which was later adopted as IEEE-STD 1296. Multibus II will not be covered in this article. Because of the existence of Multibus II, the original Multibus is often referred to as Multibus I.

This article is not intended to be a thorough coverage of the standard. It is designed to give hobbyists and designers a general overview of the bus and how it works, so that they may be able to design their own multibus cards. For a more information, the Intel "Multibus Handbook" is an excellent resource. The copy I have is dated 1983, and has an order number 210883-001. I have not contacted Intel to see if this book (or a later version) is still in print. The actual bus standards are also available from Intel. Contact Intel for more information (http://www.intel.com).

Multibus, Multichannel, iSBX, and iLBX are trademarks of Intel Corporation.

▌ Multibus Overview

The accompanying diagram shows a typical Multibus system. Note that many other combinations are possible. The diagram is given only to show how the various buses may all be used in a single system. The important concepts are the use of multiple bus masters, multiple data paths, and the use of dual-port RAM as a method of communication throughout the system (either CPU may access the RAM, making it an ideal method for transmitting data back and forth).

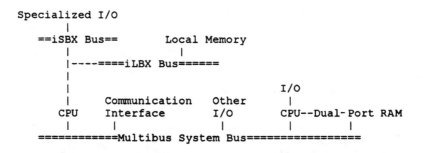

```
Specialized I/O
       |
   ==iSBX Bus==              Local Memory
       |                          |
       |----=====iLBX Bus======
       |
       |                                    I/O
       |        Communication    Other       |
      CPU       Interface         I/O      CPU--Dual-Port RAM
       |            |              |          |       |
   ===========Multibus System Bus=================
```

▌ Multibus System Bus

Multibus cards have two connectors. The larger is labeled P1 and is used for the Multibus system bus. P2 is used for the execution bus, although it also contains two address lines used by the system bus. I am using Intel's notation for the bus signals, with the exception of the address and data lines. Intel numbers these in hex and uses the designations ADR and DAT. I have numbered them in decimal and use the simpler A and D for address and data, respectively.

P1 connector pinouts

1	GND	2	GND
3	+5	4	+5
5	+5	6	+5

7	+12	8	+12
9	–5/Reserved [A]	10	–5/Reserverd [A]
11	GND	12	GND
13	*BCLK	14	*INIT
15	*BPRN	16	*BPRQ
17	*BUSY	18	*BREQ
19	*MRDC	20	*MWTC
21	*IORC	22	*IOWC
23	*XACK	24	*INH1
25	*LOCK	26	*INH2
27	*BHEN	28	*A16
29	*CBREQ	30	*A17
31	*CCLK	32	*A18
33	*INTA	34	*A19
35	*INT6	36	*INT7
37	*INT4	38	*INT5
39	*INT2	40	*INT3
41	*INT0	42	*INT1
43	*A14	44	*A15
45	*A12	46	*A13
47	*A10	48	*A11
49	*A8	50	*A9
51	*A6	52	*A7
53	*A4	54	*A5
55	*A2	56	*A3
57	*A0	58	*A1
59	*D14	60	*D15
61	*D12	62	*D13
63	*D10	64	*D11
65	*D8	66	*D9
67	*D6	68	*D7
69	*D4	70	*D5
71	*D2	72	*D3
73	*D0	74	*D1
75	GND	76	GND
77	Reserved	78	Reserved
79	–12	80	–12
81	+5	82	+5
83	+5	84	+5
85	GND	86	GND

The system bus also uses the following pins on the P2 connector:

55	*A22	56	*A23
57	*A20	58	*A21

* Indicates Active low.

[A] IEEE–796 reserves pins 9 and 10. Older systems may have –5 volts on both of these pins.

Signal Descriptions

+5, +12, −5, −12:	Voltage Supply Lines.
A0–A23:	Address Lines. Note that these lines are active low (a low voltage indicates a logic 1).
D0–D15:	Data Lines. Note that these lines are active low (a low voltage indicates a logic 1).
BCLK:	Bus Clock. 50% duty cycle. This clock is not constant. It may be stopped, single cycled, or used at a varying frequency. Any bus master in a system should be able to drive this clock. The maximum frequency is 10 MHz. This signal may be completely independent from CCLK, although in practical systems, both CCLK and BCLK will usually be derived from the same source.
CCLK:	Constant Clock. 50% duty cycle. Frequency varies but is fixed for a given system. 10 MHz is typical.
INIT:	Initialize. This causes all cards in the system to initialize. It is asserted on power-up. Bus masters may assert this signal. This signal may also be driven by a panel switch (debounced).
LOCK:	This signal prevents access to dual-port memory used as a shared resource between processors. Bus masters will drive this signal low between read and write operations during a Read-Modify-Write (RMW) cycle.
BREQ:	Bus Request. This is used by bus masters to request control of the bus. This signal is not shared between cards but instead goes to a parallel arbitration circuit on the motherboard.
BPRN:	Bus Priority In.
BPRO:	Bus Priority Out.
BUSY:	Bus Busy.
CBRQ:	Common Bus Request.
MRDC:	Memory Read Command. Used to indicate the type of bus transfer.
MWTC:	Memroy Write Command. Used to indicate the type of bus transfer.
IORC:	I/O Read Command. Used to indicate the type of bus transfer.
IOWC:	I/O Write Command. Used to indicate the type of bus transfer.
XACK:	Transfer Acknowledge. Asserted by the slave to acknowledge the transfer, so that the bus master knows to end the transfer cycle.

INH(x):   Inhibit.

BHEN: Byte High Enable. Indicates a 16-bit transfer.

INT(x):   Interrupt request.

  INTA: Interrupt Acknowledge.

■ Data Transfers

Data transfers may be 8 or 16 bits. The command lines are used to indicate the type of transfer. Eight-bit transfers use the lower 8 data lines for both even and odd byte transfers. Sixteen-bit transfers use all 16 data lines.

Multibus System Bus Read/Write Timing Diagram

```
A0-A23, BHEN [A]             ------<_____>----

Command Line                 _____                     _____
(MRDC, MWTC, IORC, IOWC)             |_____|

D0-D15 [B], Read             -------------------<_____>--------

D0-D15 [B], Write            ------<_____>----

XACK                         _____           _____
                                             |_____|

                    Address setup time        |---| 50 ns min
                    Data hold time (read)               |----| 60 ns min
                    XACK removed after command line removed  |----| 65 ns max
```

[A] BHEN will be inactive (high) for an 8-bit transfer and active (low) for a 16-bit transfer.
[B] D0–D7 only for 8-bit transfers

The bus master first drives the address lines. BHEN will be driven active for 16-bit transfers. For a write operation, the data lines are also driven using the same timing as the address lines. The command line is driven next, indicating the type of bus transfer (IORC for an I/O read, IOWC for an I/O write, MRDC for a memory read, MWTC for a memory write). For a read operation, the slave device places the data onto the bus and drives the acknowledge line (XACK). The master then reads the data from the bus. For a write operation, the slave device reads the data from the bus and drives the acknowledge signal to indicate that it has read the data and that the master no longer needs to drive the address and data lines.

A bus time out occurs when the slave device does not acknowledge the transfer. The time out mechanism prevents the master from waiting indefinitely for a response that it may never receive. The minimum time before the master is allowed to time out is 1 millisecond.

∎ Inhibit

The inhibit lines are used during memory operations (MRDC and MWTC). An inhibit line is asserted by a slave device to inhibit another slave device's bus activity during the memory operation. The inhibit system is based on priorities, and slave devices may be top-priority, middle priority, or bottom priority. A lower-priority device will be inhibited by a higher-priority device. A middle-priority device uses only INH1, which will inhibit activity by a bottom-priority device. A top-priority device would use INH2 to inhibit a middle-priority device, and also would use INH1 to inhibit a bottom-priority device at the same time.

Inhibit signals are ignored during I/O operations.

∎ Locking the Bus

The bus may be locked during a read-modify-write exchange. This prevents other processors from accessing the memory between the read and the write, which could cause problems in multiprocessor environments. To lock the bus, the current bus master must assert LOCK 100 ns before the read command line is removed and must hold this line active until at least 100 ns after the falling edge of the command line for the last locked cycle. LOCK must be released within 12 microseconds from its assertion (in other words, you can't lock the bus for more than 12 microseconds at a time).

∎ Interrupts

The interrupt request lines (INT0–INT7) are level triggered, active low. INT0 has the highest priority, and INT7 has the lowest.

Interrupts may be implemented on Multibus systems using either bus-vectored or non-bus-vectored interrupts. In a non-bus-vectored system, the bus master does not need to access the bus for the interrupt vector. It simply responds to the interrupt in the appropriate manner, then continues processing as normal (the exact function of interrupts depends on the particular system).

Bus-vectored interrupts transfer the interrupt vector over the bus during the interrupt-acknowledge process. In this case, the bus master generates two INTA signals.

Bus-Vectored Interrupt Timing

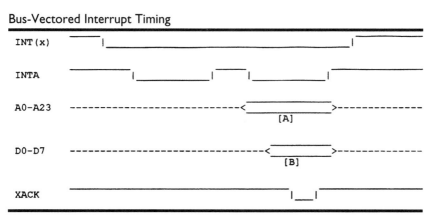

[A] The address lines contain the interrupt address while the second INTA signal is active.

[B] The data lines now contain the interrupt vector.

Some systems may use a third INTA pulse to transfer a second interrupt vector byte. Systems are permitted to use either a single byte interrupt vector, or a 2 byte interrupt vector, but not both in the same system.

It is possible to have both bus vectored and non-bus vectored interrupts on the same system.

I Bus Masters

I/O Expansion Bus (iSBX)

The iSBX bus was designed with small I/O cards in mind. It allows a small daughter board, like a serial I/O or parallel I/O port for example, to be attached to a multibus card.

iSBX Connector Pinouts

1	+12	2	−12
3	GND	4	+5
5	RESET	6	MCLK
7	MA2	8	MPST*
9	MA1	10	reserved
11	MA0	12	MINTR1
13	IOWRT*	14	MINTR0
15	IORD*	16	MWAIT*

17	GND	18	+5
19	MD7	20	MCS1*
21	MD6	22	MCS0*
23	MD5	24	reserved
25	MD4	26	TDMA
27	MD3	28	OPT1
29	MD2	30	OPT0
31	MD1	32	MDACK*
33	MD0	34	MDRQT
35	GND	36	+5
37	MD14	38	MD15
39	MD12	40	MD13
41	MD10	42	MD11
43	MD8	44	MD9

* - indicates an active low signal.

+5, +12, −12:	Voltage supply lines
GND:	Ground
IORD:	I/O Read Command line.
IOWRT:	I/O Write Command line.
MA0-MA2:	Module Address lines.
MCS0, MCS1:	Module Chip Select Lines. Note that these lines may be active when not required to be valid.
MD0-MD15:	Module Data Lines. MD8-MD15 are only used on 16-bit systems.
MDACK:	Module DMA Acknowledge.
MCLK:	Module Clock.
MDRQT:	Module DMA Request.
MINTRO, MINTR1:	Module Interrupt lines.
MPST:	Module Present.
MWAIT:	Module Wait.
OPT0, OPT1:	Option lines.
RESET:	Reset.
TDMA:	Terminate DMA.

Execution Bus (iLBX)

The iLBX bus uses the P2 (smaller) connector, and also may use an auxiliary connector (called the JX connector) located on the top right side of the board.

P2 Connector Pinouts

1	DB0	2	DB1
3	DB2	4	DB3
5	DB4	6	DB5
7	DB6	8	DB7
9	GND	10	DB8
11	DB9	12	DB10
13	DB11	14	DB12
15	DB13	16	DB14
17	DB15	18	GND
19	AB0	20	AB1
21	AB2	22	AB3
23	AB4	24	AB5
25	AB6	26	AB7
27	GND	28	AB8
29	AB9	30	AB10
31	AB11	32	AB12
33	AB13	34	AB14
35	AB15	36	GND
37	AB16	38	AB17
39	AB18	40	AB19
41	AB20	42	AB21
43	AB22	44	AB23
45	GND	46	*ACK
47	BHEN	48	R/W
49	*ASTB	50	*DSTB
51	*SMRQ	52	*SMACK
53	*LOCK	54	GND
55	A22 [A]	56	A23[A]
57	A20 [A]	58	A21[A]
59	reserved	60	TPAR

* Active low.

[A] These are the upper address lines
used by the system bus. They are not
used by the expansion bus.

Pinouts for Common Buses and Ports

This appendix contains pinout information for common buses and ports. Use this as a reference document as interfacing questions arise.

Note: DO NOT assume that USB is compatible with any of these interfaces merely because they are listed here. The information contained herein is provided as a reference only.

Much of the information is available online at http://ftp.sunet.se/pub/etext/hwb/menu_Connector.html.

The authors would like to thank the Swedish University Network (SUNET) for their cooperation in compiling a large portion of this appendix. The reader is encouraged to visit their sites.

Also the reader is encouraged to visit www.rs232.com for any assistance in designing RS-232 (EIA232) cables. Much of the pinout information for industry computers, printers, modems, and terminals is provided in that site. Furthermore, an online cable-designing capability is available free to the user.

Audio/Video

▌ 3.5-mm Mono Telephone Plug

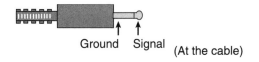

Ground   Signal   (At the cable)

3.5-mm MONO TELEPHONE MALE at the cable.

Name	Description
SIGNAL	Signal
GROUND	Ground

■ 3.5-mm Stereo Telephone Plug

Ground R L   (At the cable)

3.5-mm STEREO TELEPHONE MALE at the cable

Name	Description
L	Left Signal
R	Right Signal
GROUND	Ground

■ 6.25-mm Mono Telephone Plug

Ground   Signal   (At the cable)

6.25-mm MONO TELEPHONE MALE at the cable.

Name	Description
SIGNAL	Signal
GROUND	Ground

■ 6.25-mm Stereo Telephone Plug

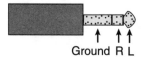

Ground R L   (At the cable)

6.25-mm STEREO TELEPHONE MALE at the cable.

Name	Description
L	Left Signal
R	Right Signal
GROUND	Ground

▌CGA

CGA = Color Graphics Adapter.
Videotype: TTL, 16 colors.
Also known as IBM RGBI.

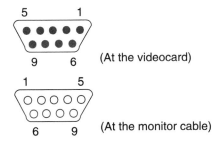

(At the videocard)

(At the monitor cable)

9-PIN D-SUB FEMALE at the videocard;
9-PIN D-SUB MALE at the monitor cable.

Pin	Name	Description
1	GND	Ground
2	GND	Ground
3	R	Red
4	G	Green
5	B	Blue
6	I	Intensity
7	RES	Reserved
8	HSYNC	Horizontal Sync
9	VSYNC	Vertical Sync

❚ Din Audio

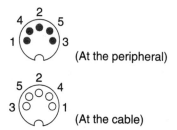

(At the peripheral)

(At the cable)

5-PIN DIN 180° (DIN41524) FEMALE at the peripheral;
5-PIN DIN 180° (DIN41524) MALE at the cable.

Peripheral	Connected	In L	In R	Out L	Out R	Ground
Amplifier	Pickup, tuner	3	5			2
Amplifier	Tape recorder	3	5	1	4	2
Tuner	Amplifier			3	5	2
Tuner	Tape recorder			1	4	2
Record player	Amplifier			3	5	2
Tape recorder	Amplifier	1	4	3	5	2
Tape recorder	Receiver	1	4	3	5	2
Tape recorder	Microphone	1	4			2

▌EGA

EGA = Enhanced Graphics Adapter.
Videotype: TTL, 16/64 colors.

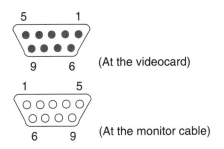

(At the videocard)

(At the monitor cable)

9 PIN D-SUB FEMALE at the videocard;
9 PIN D-SUB MALE at the monitor cable.

Pin	Name	Description
1	GND	Ground
2	SR	Secondary Red
3	PR	Primary Red
4	PG	Primary Green
5	PB	Primary Blue
6	SG/I	Secondary Green / Intensity
7	SB	Secondary Blue
8	H	Horizontal Sync
9	V	Vertical Sync

❚ MIDI In

MIDI = Musical Instrument Digital Interface.

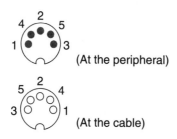

(At the peripheral)

(At the cable)

5-PIN DIN 180° (DIN41524) FEMALE at the peripheral;
5-PIN DIN 180° (DIN41524) MALE at the cable.

Pin	Name	Description
1	n/c	Not connected
2	n/c	Not connected
3	n/c	Not connected
4	CSRC	Current Source
5	CSINK	Current Sink

■ MIDI Out

MIDI = Musical Instrument Digital Interface.

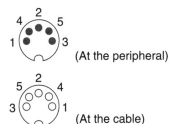

(At the peripheral)

(At the cable)

5-PIN DIN 180° (DIN41524) FEMALE at the peripheral;
5-PIN DIN 180° (DIN41524) MALE at the cable.

Pin	Name	Description
1	n/c	Not connected
2	GND	Ground
3	n/c	Not connected
4	CSINK	Current Sink
5	CSRC	Current Source

■ PC Speaker

UNKNOWN CONNECTOR at the computer.

Pin	Name	Description
1	–SP	–Speaker
2	key	Key
3	GND	Ground
4	+SP5V	+Speaker +5 V DC

▍PlayStation A/V

Available on the Sony PlayStation Videogame.

```
+------------------------+
¦ OOOOOOOOOOOO ¦
+------------------------+
 1                    12
```

12-PIN at the PlayStation.

Pin	Name	Description
1	GND	Ground
2	RT	Right Audio
3	GND	Ground
4	LT	Left Audio
5	Y	S-Video Y
6	SYNC	Composite Sync
7	C	S-Video C
8	VGND	Video Ground
9	B	Blue
10	+5V	+5 V DC
11	R	Red
12	G	Green

▌ SCART

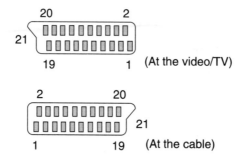

(At the video/TV)

(At the cable)

21-PIN SCART FEMALE at the video/TV;
21-PIN SCART MALE at the cable.

Pin	Name	Description	Signal Level	Impedance
1	AOR	Audio Out Right	0.5 V rms	< 1k ohm
2	AIR	Audio In Right	0.5 V rms	> 10k ohm
3	AOL	Audio Out Left + Mono	0.5 V rms	< 1k ohm
4	AGND	Audio Ground		
5	B GND	RGB Blue Ground		
6	AIL	Audio In Left + Mono	0.5 V rms	> 10k ohm
7	B	RGB Blue In	0.7 V	75 ohm
8	SWTCH	Audio/RGB switch / 16:9		
9	G GND	RGB Green Ground		
10	CLKOUT	Data 2: Clockpulse Out (Unavailable?)		
11	G	RGB Green In	0.7 V	75 ohm
12	DATA	Data 1: Data Out (Unavailable?)		
13	R GND	RGB Red Ground		
14	DATAGND	Data Ground		
15	R	RGB Red In / Chrominance	0.7 V (Crom.: 0.3 V burst)	75 ohm
16	BLNK	Blanking Signal	1–3 V = RGB, 0–0.4 V = Composite	75 ohm
17	VGND	Composite Video Ground		
18	BLNKGND	Blanking Signal Ground		
19	VOUT	Composite Video Out	1 V	75 ohm
20	VIN	Composite Video In / Luminance	1 V	75 ohm
21	SHIELD	Ground/Shield (Chassis)		

▮ S-Video

4-PIN MINI-DIN FEMALE at the peripheral.

Pin	Name	Description
1	GND	Ground (Y)
2	GND	Ground (C)
3	Y	Intensity (Luminance)
4	C	Color (Chrominance)

■ VESA Feature

```
2                        26
┌─────────────────────────┐
│ □□□□□□□□□□□□□ │
│ □□□□□□□□□□□□□ │
└─────────────────────────┘
1                        25
```

26-PIN IDC at the video card.

Pin	Name	Description
1	PD0	DAC Pixel Data Bit 0 (PB)
2	PD1	DAC Pixel Data Bit 1 (PG)
3	PD2	DAC Pixel Data Bit 2 (PR)
4	PD3	DAC Pixel Data Bit 3 (PI)
5	PD4	DAC Pixel Data Bit 4 (SB)
6	PD5	DAC Pixel Data Bit 5 (SG)
7	PD6	DAC Pixel Data Bit 6 (SR)
8	PD7	DAC Pixel Data Bit 7 (SI)
9	CLK	DAC Clock
10	BLK	DAC Blanking
11	HSYNC	Horizontal Sync
12	VSYNC	Vertical Sync
13	GND	Ground
14	GND	Ground
15	GND	Ground
16	GND	Ground
17		Select Internal Video
18		Select Internal Sync
19		Select Internal Dot Clock
20	n/c	Not used
21	GND	Ground
22	GND	Ground
23	GND	Ground
24	GND	Ground
25	n/c	Not used
26	n/c	Not used

▌ VGA (15)

VGA = Video Graphics Adapter or Video Graphics Array.
Videotype: Analog.

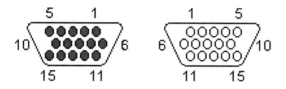

15-PIN HIGHDENSITY D-SUB FEMALE at the videocard;
15-PIN HIGHDENSITY D-SUB MALE at the monitor cable.

Pin	Name	Description
1	RED	Red Video (75 ohm, 0.7 V p-p)
2	GREEN	Green Video (75 ohm, 0.7 V p-p)
3	BLUE	Blue Video (75 ohm, 0.7 V p-p)
4	ID2	Monitor ID Bit 2
5	GND	Ground
6	RGND	Red Ground
7	GGND	Green Ground
8	BGND	Blue Ground
9	KEY	Key (No pin)
10	SGND	Sync Ground
11	ID0	Monitor ID Bit 0
12	ID1 or SDA	Monitor ID Bit 1
13	HSYNC or CSYNC	Horizontal Sync (or Composite Sync)
14	VSYNC	Vertical Sync
15	ID3 or SCL	Monitor ID Bit 3

Note: Direction is Computer relative to Monitor.

▌ VGA (VESA DDC)

VGA = Video Graphics Adapter or Video Graphics Array.
VESA = Video Electronics Standards Association.
DDC = Display Data Channel.

Videotype: Analog.

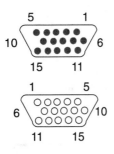

15-PIN HIGHDENSITY D-SUB FEMALE at the videocard;
15-PIN HIGHDENSITY D-SUB MALE at the monitor cable.

Pin	Name	Dir	Description
1	RED	→	Red Video (75 ohm, 0.7 V p-p)
2	GREEN	→	Green Video (75 ohm, 0.7 V p-p)
3	BLUE	→	Blue Video (75 ohm, 0.7 V p-p)
4	RES		Reserved
5	GND	—	Ground
6	RGND	—	Red Ground
7	GGND	—	Green Ground
8	BGND	—	Blue Ground
9	+5V	→	+5 VDC
10	SGND	—	Sync Ground
11	ID0	←	Monitor ID Bit 0 (optional)
12	SDA	←→	DDC Serial Data Line
13	HSYNC or CSYNC	→	Horizontal Sync (or Composite Sync)
14	VSYNC	→	Vertical Sync
15	SCL	←→	DDC Data Clock Line

Note: Direction is Computer relative Monitor.

Buses

▮ CompactPCI

PCI = Peripheral Component Interconnect.
CompactPCI is a version of PCI adapted for industrial and/or embedded applications.

7×47 PIN (IEC917 and IEC1076-4-101) CONNECTOR at the backplane;
7×47 PIN (IEC917 and IEC1076-4-101) CONNECTOR at the device (card).

Pin	Name	Description
Z1	GND	Ground
Z2	GND	Ground
Z3	GND	Ground
Z4	GND	Ground
Z5	GND	Ground
Z6	GND	Ground
Z7	GND	Ground
Z8	GND	Ground
Z9	GND	Ground
Z10	GND	Ground
Z11	GND	Ground
Z12	KEY	Keyed (no pin)
Z13	KEY	Keyed (no pin)
Z14	KEY	Keyed (no pin)
Z15	GND	Ground
Z16	GND	Ground
Z17	GND	Ground
Z18	GND	Ground
Z19	GND	Ground
Z20	GND	Ground
Z21	GND	Ground
Z22	GND	Ground
Z23	GND	Ground
Z24	GND	Ground

Pin	Name	Description
Z25	GND	Ground
Z26	GND	Ground
Z27	GND	Ground
Z28	GND	Ground
Z29	GND	Ground
Z30	GND	Ground
Z31	GND	Ground
Z32	GND	Ground
Z33	GND	Ground
Z34	GND	Ground
Z35	GND	Ground
Z36	GND	Ground
Z37	GND	Ground
Z38	GND	Ground
Z39	GND	Ground
Z40	GND	Ground
Z41	GND	Ground
Z42	GND	Ground
Z43	GND	Ground
Z44	GND	Ground
Z45	GND	Ground
Z46	GND	Ground
Z47	GND	Ground
A1	5V	+5 V DC
A2	TCK	Test Clock
A3	INTA#	Interrupt A
A4	BRSV	Bused Reserved (don't use)
A5	BRSV	Bused Reserved (don't use)
A6	REQ#	Request PCI transfer
A7	AD(30)	Address/Data 30
A8	AD(26)	Address/Data 26
A9	C/BE(3)#	Command: Byte Enable
A10	AD(21)	Address/Data 21

Pin	Name	Description
A11	AD(18)	Address/Data 18
A12	KEY	Keyed (no pin)
A13	KEY	Keyed (no pin)
A14	KEY	Keyed (no pin)
A15	3.3V	+3.3 V DC
A16	DEVSEL#	Device Select
A17	3.3V	+3.3 V DC
A18	SERR#	System Error
A19	3.3V	+3.3 V DC
A20	AD(12)	Address/Data 12
A21	3.3V	+3.3 V DC
A22	AD(7)	Address/Data 7)
A23	3.3V	+3.3 V DC
A24	AD(1)	Address/Data 1)
A25	5V	+5 V DC
A26	CLK1	Click (?) MHz
A27	CLK2	Click (?) MHz
A28	CLK4	Click (?) MHz
A29	V(I/O)	+3.3 V DC or +5 V DC
A30	C/BE(5)#	Command: Byte Enable
A31	AD(63)	Address/Data 63
A32	AD(59)	Address/Data 59
A33	AD(56)	Address/Data 56
A34	AD(52)	Address/Data 52
A35	AD(49)	Address/Data 49
A36	AD(45)	Address/Data 45
A37	AD(42)	Address/Data 42
A38	AD(38)	Address/Data 38
A39	AD(35)	Address/Data 35
A40	BRSV	Bused Reserved (don't use)
A41	BRSV	Bused Reserved (don't use)
A42	BRSV	Bused Reserved (don't use)
A43	USR	User Defined

Pin	Name	Description
A44	USR	User Defined
A45	USR	User Defined
A46	USR	User Defined
A47	USR	User Defined
B1	–12V	–12 V DC
B2	5V	+5 V DC
B3	INTB#	Interrupt B
B4	GND	Ground
B5	BRSV	Bused Reserved (don't use)
B6	GND	Ground
B7	AD(29)	Address/Data 29
B8	GND	Ground
B9	IDSEL	Initialization Device Select
B10	GND	Ground
B11	AD(17)	Address/Data 17
B12	KEY	Keyed (no pin)
B13	KEY	Keyed (no pin)
B14	KEY	Keyed (no pin)
B15	FRAME#	Address or Data phase
B16	GND	Ground
B17	SDONE	Snoop Done
B18	GND	Ground
B19	AD(15)	Address/Data 15
B20	GND	Ground
B21	AD(9)	Address/Data 9
B22	GND	Ground
B23	AD(4)	Address/Data 4
B24	5V	+5 V DC
B25	REQ64#	
B26	GND	Ground
B27	CLK3	Clock (?) MHz
B28	GND	Ground

Pin	Name	Description
B29	BRSV	Bused Reserved (don't use)
B30	GND	Ground
B31	AD(62)	Address/Data 62
B32	GND	Ground
B33	AD(55)	Address/Data 55
B34	GND	Ground
B35	AD(48)	Address/Data 48
B36	GND	Ground
B37	AD(41)	Address/Data 41
B38	GND	Ground
B39	AD(34)	Address/Data 34
B40	GND	Ground
B41	BRSV	Bused Reserved (don't use)
B42	GND	Ground
B43	USR	User Defined
B44	USR	User Defined
B45	USR	User Defined
B46	USR	User Defined
B47	USR	User Defined
C1	TRST#	Test Logic Reset
C2	TMS	Test Mode Select
C3	INTC#	Interrupt C
C4	V(I/O)	+3.3 V DC or +5 V DC
C5	RST	Reset
C6	3.3V	+3.3 V DC
C7	AD(28)	Address/Data 28
C8	V(I/O)	+3.3 V DC or +5 V DC
C9	AD(23)	Address/Data 23
C10	3.3V	+3.3 V DC
C11	AD(16)	Address/Data 16
C12	KEY	Keyed (no pin)
C13	KEY	Keyed (no pin)

Pin	Name	Description
C14	KEY	Keyed (no pin)
C15	IRDY#	Initiator Ready
C16	V(I/O)	+3.3 V DC or +5 V DC
C17	SBO#	Snoop Backoff
C18	3.3V	+3.3 V DC
C19	AD(14)	Address/Data 14
C20	V(I/O)	+3.3 V DC or +5 V DC
C21	AD(8)	Address/Data 8
C22	3.3V	+3.3 V DC
C23	AD(3)	Address/Data 3)
C24	V(I/O)	+3.3 V DC or +5 V DC
C25	BRSV	Bused Reserved (don't use)
C26	REQ1#	Request PCI transfer
C27	SYSEN#	
C28	GNT3#	Grant
C29	C/BE(7)	Command: Byte Enable
C30	V(I/O)	+3.3 V DC or +5 V DC
C31	AD(61)	Address/Data 61
C32	V(I/O)	+3.3 V DC or +5 V DC
C33	AD(54)	Address/Data 54
C34	V(I/O)	+3.3 V DC or +5 V DC
C35	AD(47)	Address/Data 47
C36	V(I/O)	+3.3 V DC or +5 V DC
C37	AD(40)	Address/Data 40
C38	V(I/O)	+3.3 V DC or +5 V DC
C39	AD(33)	Address/Data 33
C40	FAL#	Power Supply Status FAL (CompactPCI specific)
C41	DEG#	Power Supply Status DEG (CompactPCI specific
C42	PRST#	Push Button Reset (CompactPCI specific)
C43	USR	User Defined
C44	USR	User Defined
C45	USR	User Defined

Pin	Name	Description
C46	USR	User Defined
C47	USR	User Defined
D1	+12V	+12 V DC
D2	TDO	Test Data Output
D3	5V	+5 V DC
D4	INTP	
D5	GND	Ground
D6	CLK	
D7	GND	Ground
D8	AD(25)	Address/Data 25
D9	GND	Ground
D10	AD(20)	Address/Data 20
D11	GND	Ground
D12	KEY	Keyed (no pin)
D13	KEY	Keyed (no pin)
D14	KEY	Keyed (no pin)
D15	GND	Ground
D16	STOP#	Stop transfer cycle
D17	GND	Ground
D18	PAR	Parity for AD0-31 & C/BE0-3
D19	GND	Ground
D20	AD(11)	Address/Data 11
D21	M66EN	
D22	AD(6)	Address/Data 6)
D23	5V	+5 V DC
D24	AD(0)	Address/Data 0)
D25	3.3V	+3.3 V DC
D26	GNT1#	Grant
D27	GNT2#	Grant
D28	REQ4#	Request PCI transfer
D29	GND	Ground

Pin	Name	Description
D30	C/BE(4)#	Command: Byte Enable
D31	GND	Ground
D32	AD(58)	Address/Data 58
D33	GND	Ground
D34	AD(51)	Address/Data 51
D35	GND	Ground
D36	AD(44)	Address/Data 44
D37	GND	Ground
D38	AD(37)	Address/Data 37
D39	GND	Ground
D40	REQ5#	Request PCI transfer
D41	GND	Ground
D42	REQ6#	Request PCI transfer
D43	USR	User Defined
D44	USR	User Defined
D45	USR	User Defined
D46	USR	User Defined
D47	USR	User Defined
E1	5V	+5 V DC
E2	TDI	Test Data Input
E3	INTD#	Interrupt D
E4	INTS	
E5	GNT#	Grant
E6	AD(31)	Address/Data 31
E7	AD(27)	Address/Data 27
E8	AD(24)	Address/Data 24
E9	AD(22)	Address/Data 22
E10	AD(19)	Address/Data 19
E11	C/BE(2)#	Command: Byte Enable
E12	KEY	Keyed (no pin)
E13	KEY	Keyed (no pin)
E14	KEY	Keyed (no pin)

Pin	Name	Description
E15	TRDY#	Target Ready
E16	LOCK#	Lock Resource
E17	PERR#	Parity Error
E18	C/BE(1)#	Command: Byte Enable
E19	AD(13)	Address/Data 13
E20	AD(10)	Address/Data 10
E21	C/BE(0)#	Command: Byte Enable
E22	AD(5)	Address/Data 5)
E23	AD(2)	Address/Data 2)
E24	ACK64#	
E25	5V	+5 V DC
E26	REQ2#	Request PCI transfer
E27	REQ3#	Request PCI transfer
E28	GNT4#	Grant
E29	C/BE(6)#	Command: Byte Enable
E30	PAR64	
E31	AD(60)	Address/Data 60
E32	AD(57)	Address/Data 57
E33	AD(53)	Address/Data 53
E34	AD(50)	Address/Data 50
E35	AD(46)	Address/Data 46
E36	AD(43)	Address/Data 43
E37	AD(39)	Address/Data 39
E38	AD(36)	Address/Data 36
E39	AD(32)	Address/Data 32
E40	GNT5#	Grant
E41	BRSV	Bused Reserved (don't use)
E42	GNT6#	Grant
E43	USR	User Defined
E44	USR	User Defined
E45	USR	User Defined
E46	USR	User Defined
E47	USR	User Defined

Pin	Name	Description
F1	GND	Ground
F2	GND	Ground
F3	GND	Ground
F4	GND	Ground
F5	GND	Ground
F6	GND	Ground
F7	GND	Ground
F8	GND	Ground
F9	GND	Ground
F10	GND	Ground
F11	GND	Ground
F12	KEY	Keyed (no pin)
F13	KEY	Keyed (no pin)
F14	KEY	Keyed (no pin)
F15	GND	Ground
F16	GND	Ground
F17	GND	Ground
F18	GND	Ground
F19	GND	Ground
F20	GND	Ground
F21	GND	Ground
F22	GND	Ground
F23	GND	Ground
F24	GND	Ground
F25	GND	Ground
F26	GND	Ground
F27	GND	Ground
F28	GND	Ground
F29	GND	Ground
F30	GND	Ground
F31	GND	Ground
F32	GND	Ground
F33	GND	Ground

Pin	Name	Description
F34	GND	Ground
F35	GND	Ground
F36	GND	Ground
F37	GND	Ground
F38	GND	Ground
F39	GND	Ground
F40	GND	Ground
F41	GND	Ground
F42	GND	Ground
F43	GND	Ground
F44	GND	Ground
F45	GND	Ground
F46	GND	Ground
F47	GND	Ground

▌ ISA

ISA = Industry Standard Architecture.

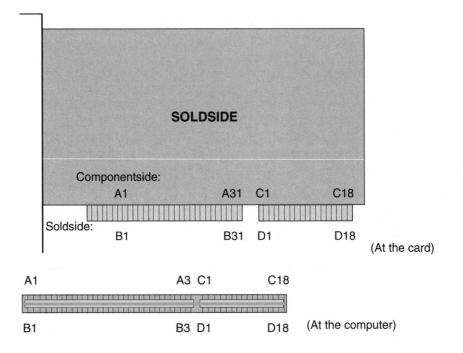

(At the card)

(At the computer)

62 + 36-PIN EDGE CONNECTOR MALE at the card;
62 + 36-PIN EDGE CONNECTOR FEMALE at the computer.

Pin	Name	Dir	Description
A1	/I/O CH CK	◄—	I/O channel check; active low = parity error
A2	D7	◄—►	Data bit 7
A3	D6	◄—►	Data bit 6
A4	D5	◄—►	Data bit 5
A5	D4	◄—►	Data bit 4
A6	D3	◄—►	Data bit 3
A7	D2	◄—►	Data bit 2
A8	D1	◄—►	Data bit 1
A9	D0	◄—►	Data bit 0
A10	I/O CH RDY	◄—	I/O Channel ready, pulled low to lengthen memory cycles

Pin	Name	Dir	Description
A11	AEN	→	Address enable; active high when DMA controls bus
A12	A19	→	Address bit 19
A13	A18	→	Address bit 18
A14	A17	→	Address bit 17
A15	A16	→	Address bit 16
A16	A15	→	Address bit 15
A17	A14	→	Address bit 14
A18	A13	→	Address bit 13
A19	A12	→	Address bit 12
A20	A11	→	Address bit 11
A21	A10	→	Address bit 10
A22	A9	→	Address bit 9
A23	A8	→	Address bit 8
A24	A7	→	Address bit 7
A25	A6	→	Address bit 6
A26	A5	→	Address bit 5
A27	A4	→	Address bit 4
A28	A3	→	Address bit 3
A29	A2	→	Address bit 2
A30	A1	→	Address bit 1
A31	A0	→	Address bit 0
B1	GND		Ground
B2	RESET	→	Active high to reset or initialize system logic
B3	+5V		+5 V DC
B4	IRQ2	←	Interrupt Request 2
B5	–5VDC		–5 V DC
B6	DRQ2	←	DMA Request 2
B7	–12VDC		–12 V DC
B8	/NOWS	←	No Wait State
B9	+12VDC		+12 V DC
B10	GND		Ground
B11	/SMEMW	→	System Memory Write
B12	/SMEMR	→	System Memory Read
B13	/IOW	→	I/O Write

Pin	Name	Dir	Description
B14	/IOR	→	I/O Read
B15	/DACK3	→	DMA Acknowledge 3
B16	DRQ3	←	DMA Request 3
B17	/DACK1	→	DMA Acknowledge 1
B18	DRQ1	←	DMA Request 1
B19	/REFRESH	←→	Refresh
B20	CLOCK	→	System Clock (67 ns, 8–8.33 MHz, 50% duty cycle)
B21	IRQ7	←	Interrupt Request 7
B22	IRQ6	←	Interrupt Request 6
B23	IRQ5	←	Interrupt Request 5
B24	IRQ4	←	Interrupt Request 4
B25	IRQ3	←	Interrupt Request 3
B26	/DACK2	→	DMA Acknowledge 2
B27	T/C	→	Terminal count; pulses high when DMA term. count reached
B28	ALE	→	Address Latch Enable
B29	+5V		+5 V DC
B30	OSC	→	High-speed Clock (70 ns, 14.31818 MHz, 50% duty cycle)
B31	GND		Ground
C1	SBHE	←→	System bus high enable (data available on SD8-15)
C2	LA23	←→	Address bit 23
C3	LA22	←→	Address bit 22
C4	LA21	←→	Address bit 21
C5	LA20	←→	Address bit 20
C6	LA18	←→	Address bit 19
C7	LA17	←→	Address bit 18
C8	LA16	←→	Address bit 17
C9	/MEMR	←→	Memory Read (active on all memory read cycles)
C10	/MEMW	←→	Memory Write (active on all memory write cycles)
C11	SD08	←→	Data bit 8
C12	SD09	←→	Data bit 9
C13	SD10	←→	Data bit 10
C14	SD11	←→	Data bit 11
C15	SD12	←→	Data bit 12
C16	SD13	←→	Data bit 13

Pin	Name	Dir	Description
C17	SD14	◄─►	Data bit 14
C18	SD15	◄─►	Data bit 15
D1	/MEMCS16	◄──	Memory 16-bit chip select (1 wait, 16-bit memory cycle)
D2	/IOCS16	◄──	I/O 16-bit chip select (1 wait, 16-bit I/O cycle)
D3	IRQ10	◄──	Interrupt Request 10
D4	IRQ11	◄──	Interrupt Request 11
D5	IRQ12	◄──	Interrupt Request 12
D6	IRQ15	◄──	Interrupt Request 15
D7	IRQ14	◄──	Interrupt Request 14
D8	/DACK0	──►	DMA Acknowledge 0
D9	DRQ0	◄──	DMA Request 0
D10	/DACK5	──►	DMA Acknowledge 5
D11	DRQ5	◄──	DMA Request 5
D12	/DACK6	──►	DMA Acknowledge 6
D13	DRQ6	◄──	DMA Request 6
D14	/DACK7	──►	DMA Acknowledge 7
D15	DRQ7	◄──	DMA Request 7
D16	+5 V		
D17	/MASTER	◄──	Used with DRQ to gain control of system
D18	GND		Ground

Note: Direction is Motherboard relative ISA-Cards. B8 was /CARD SLCDTD on the XT. Card selected, activated by cards in XT's slot J8.

▌ NuBus

Available on old Apple Macintosh computers and on NeXT computers.
Standard: IEEE 1196, "NuBus-A simple 32-bit backplane bus."
Texas Instruments owns the standard today.

UNKNOWN CONNECTOR at the card;
UNKNOWN CONNECTOR at the computer.

Row A

Pin	Name	Description
1	–12 V	–12 V DC
2	–	
3	/SPV	
4	/SP	
5	/TM1	
6	/AD1	Address/Data 1
7	/AD3	Address/Data 3
8	/AD5	Address/Data 5
9	/AD7	Address/Data 7
10	/AD9	Address/Data 9
11	/AD11	Address/Data 11
12	/AD13	Address/Data 13
13	/AD15	Address/Data 15
14	/AD17	Address/Data 17
15	/AD19	Address/Data 19
16	/AD21	Address/Data 21
17	/AD23	Address/Data 23
18	/AD25	Address/Data 25
19	/AD27	Address/Data 27
20	/AD29	Address/Data 29
21	/AD31	Address/Data 31
22	GND	Ground

Pin	Name	Description
23	GND	Ground
24	/ARB1	
25	/ARB3	
26	/ID1	
27	/ID3	
28	/ACK	
29	+5 V	+5 V DC
30	/RQST	
31	/NMRQ	
32	+12 V	+12 V DC

Row B

Pin	Name	Description
1	–12 V	–12 V DC
2	GND	Ground
3	GND	Ground
4	+5 V	+5 V DC
5	+5 V	+5 V DC
6	+5 V	+5 V DC
7	+5 V	+5 V DC
8	*	reserved (?)
9	*	reserved (?)
10	*	reserved (?)
11	*	reserved (?)
12	GND	Ground
13	GND	Ground
14	GND	Ground
15	GND	Ground

Pin	Name	Description
16	GND	Ground
17	GND	Ground
18	GND	Ground
19	GND	Ground
20	GND	Ground
21	GND	Ground
22	GND	Ground
23	GND	Ground
24	**	reserved (?)
25	**	reserved (?)
26	**	reserved (?)
27	**	reserved (?)
28	+5 V	+5 V DC
29	+5 V	+5 V DC
30	GND	Ground
31	GND	Ground
32	+12 V	

Row C

Pin	Name	Description
1	/RESET	Reset
2	–	
3	+5 V	+5 V DC
4	+5 V	+5 V DC
5	/TM0	
6	/AD0	Address/Data 0
7	/AD2	Address/Data 2
8	/AD4	Address/Data 4
9	/AD6	Address/Data 6

Pin	Name	Description
10	/AD8	Address/Data 8
11	/AD10	Address/Data 10
12	/AD12	Address/Data 12
13	/AD14	Address/Data 14
14	/AD16	Address/Data 16
15	/AD18	Address/Data 18
16	/AD20	Address/Data 20
17	/AD22	Address/Data 22
18	/AD24	Address/Data 24
19	/AD26	Address/Data 26
20	/AD28	Address/Data 28
21	/AD30	Address/Data 30
22	GND	Ground
23	/PFW	
24	/ARB0	
25	/ARB2	
26	/ID0	
27	/ID2	
28	/START	
29	+5 V	+5 V DC
30	+5 V	+5 V DC
31	GND	Ground
32	/CLK	Clock

▌ NuBus 90

Avaliable on old Apple Macintosh computers.

Row A

Pin	Name	Description
1	–12 V	–12 V DC
2	SB0	
3	/SPV	
4	/SP	
5	/TM1	
6	/AD1	Address/Data 1
7	/AD3	Address/Data 3
8	/AD5	Address/Data 5
9	/AD7	Address/Data 7
10	/AD9	Address/Data 9
11	/AD11	Address/Data 11
12	/AD13	Address/Data 13
13	/AD15	Address/Data 15
14	/AD17	Address/Data 17
15	/AD19	Address/Data 19
16	/AD21	Address/Data 21
17	/AD23	Address/Data 23
18	/AD25	Address/Data 25
19	/AD27	Address/Data 27
20	/AD29	Address/Data 29
21	/AD31	Address/Data 31
22	GND	Ground
23	GND	Ground
24	/ARB1	
25	/ARB3	
26	/ID1	
27	/ID3	
28	/ACK	

Pin	Name	Description
29	+5 V	+5 V DC
30	/RQST	
31	/NMRQ	
32	+12 V	+12 V DC

Row B

Pin	Name	Description
1	–12 V	–12 V DC
2	GND	Ground
3	GND	Ground
4	+5 V	+5 V DC
5	+5 V	+5 V DC
6	+5 V	+5 V DC
7	+5 V	+5 V DC
8	/TM2	
9	/CM0	
10	/CM1	
11	/CM2	
12	GND	Ground
13	GND	Ground
14	GND	Ground
15	GND	Ground
16	GND	Ground
17	GND	Ground
18	GND	Ground
19	GND	Ground
20	GND	Ground
21	GND	Ground

Pin	Name	Description
22	GND	Ground
23	GND	Ground
24	/CLK2X	
25	STDBYPWR	
26	/CLK2XEN	
27	/CBUSY	
28	+5 V	+5 V DC
29	+5 V	+5 V DC
30	GND	Ground
31	GND	Ground
32	+12 V	+12 V DC

Row C

Pin	Name	Description
1	/RESET	Reset
2	SB1	
3	+5 V	+5 V DC
4	+5 V	+5 V DC
5	/TM0	
6	/AD0	Address/Data 0
7	/AD2	Address/Data 2
8	/AD4	Address/Data 4
9	/AD6	Address/Data 6
10	/AD8	Address/Data 8
11	/AD10	Address/Data 10
12	/AD12	Address/Data 12
13	/AD14	Address/Data 14
14	/AD16	Address/Data 16

15	/AD18	Address/Data 18
16	/AD20	Address/Data 20
17	/AD22	Address/Data 22
18	/AD24	Address/Data 24
19	/AD26	Address/Data 26
20	/AD28	Address/Data 28
21	/AD30	Address/Data 30
22	GND	Ground
23	/PFW	
24	/ARB0	
25	/ARB2	
26	/ID0	
27	/ID2	
28	/START	
29	+5 V	+5 V DC
30	+5 V	+5 V DC
31	GND	Ground
32	/CLK	Clock

■ PCI

PCI = Peripheral Component Interconnect.

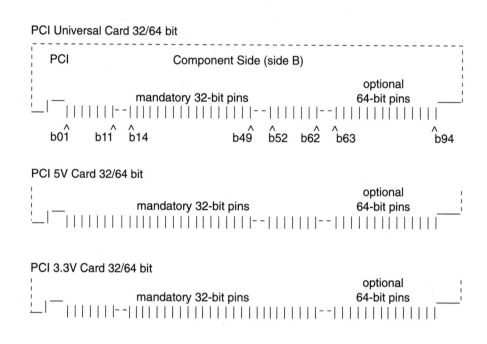

PCI Universal Card 32/64 bit

PCI 5V Card 32/64 bit

PCI 3.3V Card 32/64 bit

98 + 22-PIN EDGE CONNECTOR at the computer

Pin	+5V	+3.3V	Universal	Description
A1	TRST			Test Logic Reset
A2	+12V			+12 V DC
A3	TMS			Test Mde Select
A4	TDI			Test Data Input
A5	+5V			+5 V DC
A6	INTA			Interrupt A
A7	INTC			Interrupt C
A8	+5V			+5 V DC

Pin	+5V	+3.3V	Universal	Description
A9	RESV01			reserved V DC
A10	+5V	+3.3V	Signal Rail	+V I/O (+5 V or +3.3 V)
A11	RESV03			reserved V DC
A12	GND03	(OPEN)	(OPEN)	Ground or Open (Key)
A13	GND05	(OPEN)	(OPEN)	Ground or Open (Key)
A14	RESV05			reserved V DC
A15	RESET			Reset
A16	+5V	+3.3V	Signal Rail	+V I/O (+5 V or +3.3 V)
A17	GNT			Grant PCI use
A18	GND08			Ground
A19	RESV06			reserved V DC
A20	AD30			Address/Data 30
A21	+3.3V01			+3.3 V DC
A22	AD28			Address/Data 28
A23	AD26			Address/Data 26
A24	GND10			Ground
A25	AD24			Address/Data 24
A26	IDSEL			Initialization Device Select
A27	+3.3V03			+3.3 V DC
A28	AD22			Address/Data 22
A29	AD20			Address/Data 20
A30	GND12			Ground
A31	AD18			Address/Data 18
A32	AD16			Address/Data 16
A33	+3.3V05			+3.3 V DC
A34	FRAME			Address or Data phase
A35	GND14			Ground
A36	TRDY			Target Ready
A37	GND15			Ground
A38	STOP			Stop Transfer Cycle
A39	+3.3V07			+3.3 V DC
A40	SDONE			Snoop Done
A41	SBO			Snoop Backoff

Pin	+5V	+3.3V	Universal	Description
A42	GND17			Ground
A43	PAR			Parity
A44	AD15			Address/Data 15
A45	+3.3V10			+3.3 V DC
A46	AD13			Address/Data 13
A47	AD11			Address/Data 11
A48	GND19			Ground
A49	AD9			Address/Data 9
A52	C/BE0			Command, Byte Enable 0
A53	+3.3V11			+3.3 V DC
A54	AD6			Address/Data 6
A55	AD4			Address/Data 4
A56	GND21			Ground
A57	AD2			Address/Data 2
A58	AD0			Address/Data 0
A59	+5V	+3.3V	Signal Rail	+V I/O (+5 V or +3.3 V)
A60	REQ64			Request 64 bit ???
A61	VCC11			+5 V DC
A62	VCC13			+5 V DC
A63	GND			Ground
A64	C/BE[7]#			Command, Byte Enable 7
A65	C/BE[5]#			Command, Byte Enable 5
A66	+5V	+3.3V	Signal Rail	+V I/O (+5 V or +3.3 V)
A67	PAR64			Parity 64 ???
A68	AD62			Address/Data 62
A69	GND			Ground
A70	AD60			Address/Data 60
A71	AD58			Address/Data 58
A72	GND			Ground
A73	AD56			Address/Data 56
A74	AD54			Address/Data 54
A75	+5V	+3.3V	Signal Rail	+V I/O (+5 V or +3.3 V)
A76	AD52			Address/Data 52

Pin	+5V	+3.3V	Universal	Description
A77	AD50			Address/Data 50
A78	GND			Ground
A79	AD48			Address/Data 48
A80	AD46			Address/Data 46
A81	GND			Ground
A82	AD44			Address/Data 44
A83	AD42			Address/Data 42
A84	+5V	+3.3V	Signal Rail	+V I/O (+5 V or +3.3 V)
A85	AD40			Address/Data 40
A86	AD38			Address/Data 38
A87	GND			Ground
A88	AD36			Address/Data 36
A89	AD34			Address/Data 34
A90	GND			Ground
A91	AD32			Address/Data 32
A92	RES			reserved
A93	GND			Ground
A94	RES			reserved
B1	−12V			−12 V DC
B2	TCK			Test Clock
B3	GND			Ground
B4	TDO			Test Data Output
B5	+5V			+5 V DC
B6	+5V			+5 V DC
B7	INTB			Interrupt B
B8	INTD			Interrupt D
B9	PRSNT1			reserved
B10	RES			+V I/O (+5 V or +3.3 V)
B11	PRSNT2			??
B12	GND	(OPEN)	(OPEN)	Ground or Open (Key)
B13	GND	(OPEN)	(OPEN)	Ground or Open (Key)
B14	RES			reserved V DC

Pin	+5V	+3.3V	Universal	Description
B15	GND			Reset
B16	CLK			Clock
B17	GND			Ground
B18	REQ			Request
B19	+5V	+3.3V	Signal Rail	+V I/O (+5 V or +3.3 V)
B20	AD31			Address/Data 31
B21	AD29			Address/Data 29
B22	GND			Ground
B23	AD27			Address/Data 27
B24	AD25			Address/Data 25
B25	+3.3V			+3.3 V DC
B26	C/BE3			Command, Byte Enable 3
B27	AD23			Address/Data 23
B28	GND			Ground
B29	AD21			Address/Data 21
B30	AD19			Address/Data 19
B31	+3.3V			+3.3 V DC
B32	AD17			Address/Data 17
B33	C/BE2			Command, Byte Enable 2
B34	GND13			Ground
B35	IRDY			Initiator Ready
B36	+3.3V06			+3.3 V DC
B37	DEVSEL			Device Select
B38	GND16			Ground
B39	LOCK			Lock bus
B40	PERR			Parity Error
B41	+3.3V08			+3.3 V DC
B42	SERR			System Error
B43	+3.3V09			+3.3 V DC
B44	C/BE1			Command, Byte Enable 1
B45	AD14			Address/Data 14
B46	GND18			Ground
B47	AD12			Address/Data 12

Pin	+5V	+3.3V	Universal	Description
B48	AD10			Address/Data 10
B49	GND20			Ground
B50	(OPEN)	GND	(OPEN)	Ground or Open (Key)
B51	(OPEN)	GND	(OPEN)	Ground or Open (Key)
B52	AD8			Address/Data 8
B53	AD7			Address/Data 7
B54	+3.3V12			+3.3 V DC
B55	AD5			Address/Data 5
B56	AD3			Address/Data 3
B57	GND22			Ground
B58	AD1			Address/Data 1
B59	VCC08			+5 V DC
B60	ACK64			Acknowledge 64 bit ???
B61	VCC10			+5 V DC
B62	VCC12			+5 V DC
B63	RES			Reserved
B64	GND			Ground
B65	C/BE[6]#			Command, Byte Enable 6
B66	C/BE[4]#			Command, Byte Enable 4
B67	GND			Ground
B68	AD63			Address/Data 63
B69	AD61			Address/Data 61
B70	+5V	+3.3V	Signal Rail	+V I/O (+5 V or +3.3 V)
B71	AD59			Address/Data 59
B72	AD57			Address/Data 57
B73	GND			Ground
B74	AD55			Address/Data 55
B75	AD53			Address/Data 53
B76	GND			Ground
B77	AD51			Address/Data 51
B78	AD49			Address/Data 49
B79	+5V	+3.3V	Signal Rail	+V I/O (+5 V or +3.3 V)

Pin	+5V	+3.3V	Universal	Description
B80	AD47			Address/Data 47
B81	AD45			Address/Data 45
B82	GND			Ground
B83	AD43			Address/Data 43
B84	AD41			Address/Data 41
B85	GND			Ground
B86	AD39			Address/Data 39
B87	AD37			Address/Data 37
B88	+5V	+3.3V	Signal Rail	+V I/O (+5 V or +3.3 V)
B89	AD35			Address/Data 35
B90	AD33			Address/Data 33
B91	GND			Ground
B92	RES			reserved
B93	RES			reserved
B94	GND			Ground

Notes: Pin 63-94 exists only on 64-bit PCI implementations. +V I/O is 3.3 V on 3.3-V boards, 5 V on 5-V boards, and defines signal rails on the Universal board.

▌ PCMCIA

PCMCIA = Personal Computer Memory Card International Association.

68 PIN (?) MALE at the controller;
68 PIN (?) FEMALE at the peripherals.

Pin	Name	Dir	Description
1	GND	——	Ground
2	D3	◄─►	Data 3
3	D4	◄─►	Data 4
4	D5	◄─►	Data 5
5	D6	◄─►	Data 6
6	D7	◄─►	Data 7
7	/CE1	──►	Card Enable 1
8	A10	──►	Address 10
9	/OE	──►	Output Enable
10	A11	──►	Address 11
11	A9	──►	Address 9
12	A8	──►	Address 8
13	A13	──►	Address 13
14	A14	──►	Address 14
15	/WE:/P	──►	Write Enable : Program
16	/READY:/IREQ	◄──	Ready : Busy (IREQ)
17	VCC	──►	+5 V
18	VPP1	──►	Programming Voltage (EPROM)
19	A16	──►	Address 16
20	A15	──►	Address 15
21	A12	──►	Address 12
22	A7	──►	Address 7
23	A6	──►	Address 6
24	A5	──►	Address 5
25	A4	──►	Address 4
26	A3	──►	Address 3
27	A2	──►	Address 2

Pin	Name	Dir	Description
28	A1	→	Address 1
29	A0	→	Address 0
30	D0	←→	Data 0
31	D1	←→	Data 1
32	D2	←→	Data 2
33	/WP:/IOIS16	←	Write Protect: IOIS16
34	GND	——	Ground
35	GND	——	Ground
36	/CD1	←	Card Detect 1
37	D11	←→	Data 11
38	D12	←→	Data 12
39	D13	←→	Data 13
40	D14	←→	Data 14
41	D15	←→	Data 15
42	/CE2	→	Card Enable 2
43	/VS1	→	Refresh
44	/IORD	?	I/O Read
45	/IOWR	?	I/O Write
46	A17	→	Address 17
47	A18	→	Address 18
48	A19	→	Address 19
49	A20	→	Address 20
50	A21	→	Address 21
51	VCC	→	+5V
52	VPP2	→	Programming Voltage 2 (EPROM)
53	A22	→	Address 22
54	A23	→	Address 23
55	A24	→	Address 24
56	A25	→	Address 25
57	/VS2	?	RFU
58	RESET	?	RESET
59	/WAIT	?	WAIT
60	/INPACK	?	
61	/REG	→	Register Select

Pin	Name	Dir	Description
62	/BVD2:SPKR	←	Battery Voltage Detect 2: SPKR
63	/BVD1:STSCHG	←	Battery Voltage Detect 1: STSCHG
64	D8	←→	Data 8
65	D9	←→	Data 9
66	D10	←→	Data 10
67	/CD2	←	Card Detect 2
68	GND	—	Ground

Note: Direction is Controller (computer) relative PCMCIA-card.

▮ SCSI External Centronics 50 (Single-Ended)

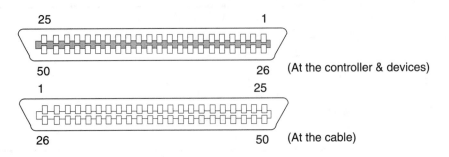

50-PIN CENTRONICS FEMALE at the controller & devices;
50-PIN CENTRONICS MALE at the cable.

Pin	Name	Dir	Description
1–25	GND	———	Ground
26	DB0	◄─►	Data Bus 0
27	DB1	◄─►	Data Bus 1
28	DB2	◄─►	Data Bus 2
29	DB3	◄─►	Data Bus 3
30	DB4	◄─►	Data Bus 4
31	DB5	◄─►	Data Bus 5
32	DB6	◄─►	Data Bus 6
33	DB7	◄─►	Data Bus 7
34	PARITY	◄─►	Data Parity (odd parity)
35	GND	———	Ground
36	GND	———	Ground
37	GND	———	Ground
38	TMPWR	◄─►	Termination Power
39	GND	———	Ground
40	GND	———	Ground
41	/ATN	◄───	Attention
42	n/c	—	Not connected
43	/BSY	◄─►	Busy
44	/ACK	◄───	Acknowledge

Pin	Name	Dir	Description
45	/RST	←→	Reset
46	/MSG	→	Message
47	/SEL	←→	Select
48	/C/D	→	Control/Data
49	/REQ	→	Request
50	/I/O	→	Input/Output

■ SCSI External Centronics 50 (Differential)

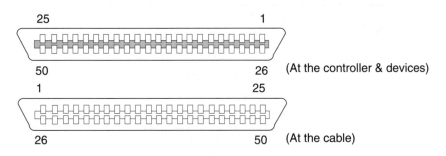

25   1

50   26   (At the controller & devices)
1   25

26   50   (At the cable)

50-PIN CENTRONICS FEMALE at the controller and devices;
50-PIN CENTRONICS MALE at the cable.

Pin	Name	Dir	Description
01	GND	———	Ground
02	+DB0	◄─►	+Data Bus 0
03	+DB1	◄─►	+Data Bus 1
04	+DB2	◄─►	+Data Bus 2
05	+DB3	◄─►	+Data Bus 3
06	+DB4	◄─►	+Data Bus 4
07	+DB5	◄─►	+Data Bus 5
08	+DB6	◄─►	+Data Bus 6
09	+DB7	◄─►	+Data Bus 7
10	+DBP	◄─►	+Data Bus Parity (odd parity)
11	DIFFSENS	?	?
12	res	—	reserved
13	TERMPWR	◄─►	Termination Power
14	res	—	Reserved
15	+ATN	◄──	+Attention
16	GND	———	Ground
17	+BSY	◄─►	+Bus is busy
18	+ACK	◄──	+Acknowledge
19	+RST	◄─►	+Reset
20	+MSG	──►	+Message

Pin	Name	Dir	Description
21	+SEL	◄►	+Select
22	+C/D	──►	+Control or Data
23	+REQ	──►	+Request
24	+I/O	──►	+In/Out
25	GND	──	Ground
26	GND	──	Ground
27	–DB0	◄►	–Data Bus 0
28	–DB1	◄►	–Data Bus 1
29	–DB2	◄►	–Data Bus 2
30	–DB3	◄►	–Data Bus 3
31	–DB4	◄►	–Data Bus 4
32	–DB5	◄►	–Data Bus 5
33	–DB6	◄►	–Data Bus 6
34	–DB7	◄►	–Data Bus Parity 7
35	–DBP	◄►	–Data Bus Parity (odd parity)
36	GND	──	Ground
37	res	–	reserved
38	TERMPWR	◄►	Termination Power
39	res	–	Reserved
40	–ATN	◄──	–Attention
41	GND	──	Ground
42	–BSY	◄►	–Bus is busy
43	–ACK	◄──	–Acknowledge
44	–RST	◄►	–Reset
45	–MSG	──►	–Message
46	–SEL	◄►	–Select
47	–C/D	──►	–Control or Data
48	–REQ	──►	–Request
49	–I/O	──►	–In/Out
50	GND	──	Ground

Note: Direction is Device relative Bus (other Devices).

▌ SCSI External D-Sub (PC/Amiga/Mac)

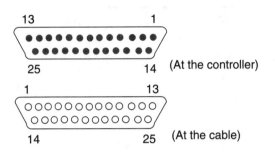

13   1

25   14   (At the controller)

1   13

14   25   (At the cable)

25-PIN D-SUB FEMALE at the controller;
25-PIN D-SUB MALE at the cable.

Pin	Name	Dir	Description
1	/REQ	→	Request
2	/MSG	→	Message
3	I/O	→	Input/Output
4	/RST	←→	Reset
5	/ACK	←	Acknowledge
6	BSY	←→	Busy
7	GND	—	Ground
8	DB0	←→	Data Bus 0
9	GND	—	Ground
10	DB3	←→	Data Bus 3
11	DB5	←→	Data Bus 5
12	DB6	←→	Data Bus 6
13	DB7	←→	Data Bus 7
14	GND	—	Ground
15	C/D	→	Control/Data
16	GND	—	Ground
17	/ATN	←	Attention
18	GND	—	Ground
19	/SEL	←→	Select
20	PARITY	←→	Data Parity

Pin	Name	Dir	Description
21	DB1	←→	Data Bus 1
22	DB2	←→	Data Bus 2
23	DB4	←→	Data Bus 4
24	GND	———	Ground
25	TMPWR	←→	Termination Power

Note: Direction is Device relative Bus (other Devices).

■ SCSI-II External Hi D-Sub (Single-Ended)

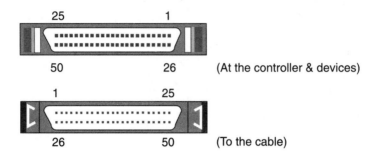

(At the controller & devices)

(To the cable)

50-PIN HI-DENSITY D-SUB FEMALE at the controller and devices;
50-PIN HI-DENSITY D-SUB MALE at the cable.

Pin	Name	Dir	Description
1–25	GND	————	Ground
26	DB0	◄—►	Data Bus 0
27	DB1	◄—►	Data Bus 1
28	DB2	◄—►	Data Bus 2
29	DB3	◄—►	Data Bus 3
30	DB4	◄—►	Data Bus 4
31	DB5	◄—►	Data Bus 5
32	DB6	◄—►	Data Bus 6
33	DB7	◄—►	Data Bus 7
34	PARITY	◄—►	Data Parity (odd parity)
35	GND	————	Ground
36	GND	————	Ground
37	GND	————	Ground
38	TMPWR	◄—►	Termination Power
39	GND	————	Ground
40	GND	————	Ground
41	/ATN	◄—	Attention
42	n/c		Not connected
43	/BSY	◄—►	Busy
44	/ACK	◄—	Acknowledge

Pin	Name	Dir	Description
45	/RST	←→	Reset
46	/MSG	→	Message
47	/SEL	←→	Select
48	/C/D	→	Control/Data
49	/REQ	→	Request
50	/I/O	→	Input/Output

Note: Direction is Device relative Bus (other Devices).

▌ SCSI-II External Hi D-Sub (Differential)

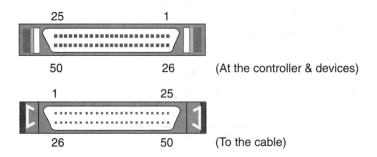

(At the controller & devices)

(To the cable)

50-PIN HI-DENSITY D-SUB FEMALE at the controller and devices;
50-PIN HI-DENSITY D-SUB MALE at the cable.

Pin	Name	Dir	Description
01	GND	———	Ground
02	+DB0	◄►	+Data Bus 0
03	+DB1	◄►	+Data Bus 1
04	+DB2	◄►	+Data Bus 2
05	+DB3	◄►	+Data Bus 3
06	+DB4	◄►	+Data Bus 4
07	+DB5	◄►	+Data Bus 5
08	+DB6	◄►	+Data Bus 6
09	+DB7	◄►	+Data Bus 7
10	+DBP	◄►	+Data Bus Parity (odd Parity)
11	DIFFSENS	?	?
12	res	—	reserved
13	TERMPWR	◄►	Termination Power
14	res	—	reserved
15	+ATN	◄—	+Attention
16	GND	———	Ground
17	+BSY	◄►	+Bus is busy
18	+ACK	◄—	+Acknowledge
19	+RST	◄►	+Reset
20	+MSG	—►	+Message

Pin	Name	Dir	Description
21	+SEL	◀▶	+Select
22	+C/D	▶	+Control or Data
23	+REQ	▶	+Request
24	+I/O	▶	+In/Out
25	GND	—	Ground
26	GND	—	Ground
27	–DB0	◀▶	–Data Bus 0
28	–DB1	◀▶	–Data Bus 1
29	–DB2	◀▶	–Data Bus 2
30	–DB3	◀▶	–Data Bus 3
31	–DB4	◀▶	–Data Bus 4
32	–DB5	◀▶	–Data Bus 5
33	–DB6	◀▶	–Data Bus 6
34	–DB7	◀▶	–Data Bus Parity 7
35	–DBP	◀▶	–Data Bus Parity (odd Parity)
36	GND	—	Ground
37	res		reserved
38	TERMPWR	◀▶	Termination Power
39	res		reserved
40	–ATN	◀	–Attention
41	GND	—	Ground
42	–BSY	◀▶	–Bus is busy
43	–ACK	◀	–Acknowledge
44	–RST	◀▶	–Reset
45	–MSG	▶	–Message
46	–SEL	◀▶	–Select
47	–C/D	▶	–Control or Data
48	–REQ	▶	–Request
49	–I/O	▶	–In/Out
50	GND	—	Ground

Note: Direction is Device relative Bus (other Devices)

▌ SCSI Internal (Single-Ended)

SCSI = Small Computer System Interface.
Based on an original design by Shugart Associates. SCSI was ratified in
1986.

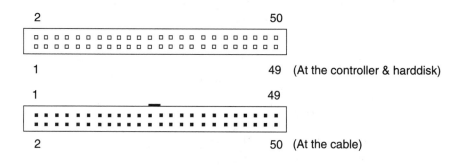

50-PIN IDC MALE at the controller and hard disk;
50-PIN IDC FEMALE at the cable.

Pin	Name	Dir	Description
2	DB0	←→	Data Bus 0
4	DB1	←→	Data Bus 1
6	DB2	←→	Data Bus 2
8	DB3	←→	Data Bus 3
10	DB4	←→	Data Bus 4
12	DB5	←→	Data Bus 5
14	DB6	←→	Data Bus 6
16	DB7	←→	Data Bus 7
18	PARITY	←→	Data Parity (odd Parity)
20	GND	——	Ground
22	GND	——	Ground
24	GND	——	Ground
26	TMPWR	←→	Termination Power
28	GND	——	Ground
30	GND	——	Ground
32	/ATN	←	Attention
34	GND	——	Ground

Pin	Name	Dir	Description
36	/BSY	◄─►	Busy
38	/ACK	◄───	Acknowledge
40	/RST	◄─►	Reset
42	/MSG	──►	Message
44	/SEL	◄─►	Select
46	/C/D	──►	Control/Data
48	/REQ	──►	Request
50	/I/O	──►	Input/Output

Notes: Direction is Device relative Bus (other Devices). All odd-numbered pins, except pin 25, are connected to ground. Pin 25 is left open.

■ SCSI Internal (Differential)

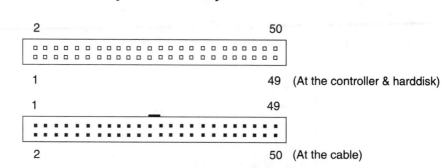

2   50

1   49   (At the controller & harddisk)

1   49

2   50   (At the cable)

50-PIN IDC MALE at the controller and hard disk;
50-PIN IDC FEMALE at the cable.

Pin	Name	Dir	Description
01	GND	———	Ground
02	GND	———	Ground
03	+DB0	◄─►	+Data Bus 0
04	−DB0	◄─►	−Data Bus 0
05	+DB1	◄─►	+Data Bus 1
06	−DB1	◄─►	−Data Bus 1
07	+DB2	◄─►	+Data Bus 2
08	−DB2	◄─►	−Data Bus 2
09	+DB3	◄─►	+Data Bus 3
10	−DB3	◄─►	−Data Bus 3
11	+DB4	◄─►	+Data Bus 4
12	−DB4	◄─►	−Data Bus 4
13	+DB5	◄─►	+Data Bus 5
14	−DB5	◄─►	−Data Bus 5
15	+DB6	◄─►	+Data Bus 6
16	−DB6	◄─►	−Data Bus 6
17	+DB7	◄─►	+Data Bus 7
18	−DB7	◄─►	−Data Bus Parity 7
19	+DBP	◄─►	+Data Bus Parity (odd parity)
20	−DBP	◄─►	−Data Bus Parity (odd parity)
21	DIFFSENS	?	?

Pin	Name	Dir	Description
22	GND	——	Ground
23	res		reserved
24	res		reserved
25	TERMPWR	◄—►	Termination Power
26	TERMPWR	◄—►	Termination Power
27	res		reserved
28	res		reserved
29	+ATN	◄—	+Attention
30	−ATN	◄—	−Attention
31	GND	——	Ground
32	GND	——	Ground
33	+BSY	◄—►	+Bus is busy
34	−BSY	◄—►	−Bus is busy
35	+ACK	◄—	+Acknowledge
36	−ACK	◄—	−Acknowledge
37	+RST	◄—►	+Reset
38	−RST	◄—►	−Reset
39	+MSG	—►	+Message
40	−MSG	—►	−Message
41	+SEL	◄—►	+Select
42	−SEL	◄—►	−Select
43	+C/D	—►	+Control or Data
44	−C/D	—►	−Control or Data
45	+REQ	—►	+Request
46	−REQ	—►	−Request
47	+I/O	—►	+In/Out
48	−I/O	—►	−In/Out
49	GND	——	Ground
50	GND	——	Ground

Note: Direction is Device relative Bus (other Devices).

▮ Universal Serial Bus (USB)

Developed by Compaq, Digital Equipment Corp, IBM PC Co., Intel, Microsoft, NEC and Northern Telecom.

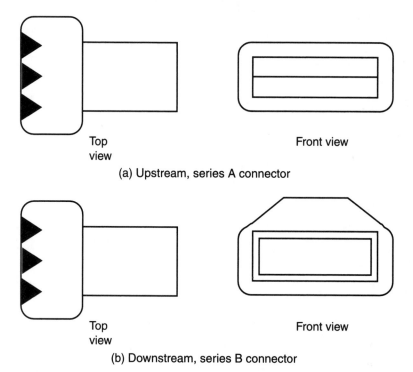

Top
view   Front view

(a) Upstream, series A connector

Top
view   Front view

(b) Downstream, series B connector

4-PIN MALE at the controller;
4-PIN FEMALE at the peripherals.

Pin	Name	Description
1	VCC	+5 V DC
2	D–	Data –
3	D+	Data +
4	GND	Ground

▌ VESA Local Bus (VLB)

VLB = VESA Local Bus.
VESA = Video Electronics Standards Association.

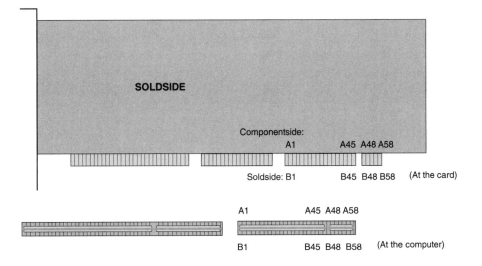

58-PIN EDGE CONNECTOR MALE at the card;
58-PIN EDGE CONNECTOR FEMALE at the computer.

Pin	Name	Description
A1	D1	Data 1
A2	D3	Data 3
A3	GND	Ground
A4	D5	Data 5
A5	D7	Data 7
A6	D9	Data 9
A7	D11	Data 11
A8	D13	Data 13
A9	D15	Data 15
A10	GND	Ground
A11	D17	Data 17
A12	VCC	+5 V DC

Pin	Name	Description
A13	D19	Data 19
A14	D21	Data 21
A15	D23	Data 23
A16	D25	Data 25
A17	GND	Ground
A18	D27	Data 27
A19	D29	Data 29
A20	D31	Data 31
A21	A30	Address 30
A22	A28	Address 28
A23	A26	Address 26
A24	GND	Ground
A25	A24	Address 24
A26	A22	Address 22
A27	VCC	+5 V DC
A28	A20	Address 20
A29	A18	Address 18
A30	A16	Address 16
A31	A14	Address 14
A32	A12	Address 12
A33	A10	Address 10
A34	A8	Address 8
A35	GND	Ground
A36	A6	Address 6
A37	A4	Address 4
A38	WBACK#	Write Back
A39	BE0#	Byte Enable 0
A40	VCC	+5 V DC
A41	BE1#	Byte Enable 1
A42	BE2#	Byte Enable 2
A43	GND	Ground
A44	BE3#	Byte Enable 3
A45	ADS#	Address Strobe

Pin	Name	Description
A48	LRDY#	Local Ready
A49	LDEV	Local Device
A50	LREQ	Local Request
A51	GND	Ground
A52	LGNT	Local Grant
A53	VCC	+5 V DC
A54	ID2	Identification 2
A55	ID3	Identification 3
A56	ID4	Identification 4
A57	LKEN#	
A58	LEADS#	Local Enable Address Strobe
B1	D0	Data 0
B2	D2	Data 2
B3	D4	Data 4
B4	D6	Data 6
B5	D8	Data 8
B6	GND	Ground
B7	D10	Data 10
B8	D12	Data 12
B9	VCC	+5 V DC
B10	D14	Data 14
B11	D16	Data 16
B12	D18	Data 18
B13	D20	Data 20
B14	GND	Ground
B15	D22	Data 22
B16	D24	Data 24
B17	D26	Data 26
B18	D28	Data 28
B19	D30	Data 30
B20	VCC	+5 V DC
B21	A31	Address 31

Pin	Name	Description
B22	GND	Ground
B23	A29	Address 29
B24	A27	Address 27
B25	A25	Address 25
B26	A23	Address 23
B27	A21	Address 21
B28	A19	Address 19
B29	GND	Ground
B30	A17	Address 17
B31	A15	Address 15
B32	VCC	+5 V DC
B33	A13	Address 13
B34	A11	Address 11
B35	A9	Address 9
B36	A7	Address 7
B37	A5	Address 5
B38	GND	Ground
B39	A3	Address 3
B40	A2	Address 2
B41	n/c	Not connected
B42	RESET#	Reset
B43	DC#	Data/Command
B44	M/IO#	Memory/IO
B45	W/R#	Write/Read
B48	RDYRTN#	Ready Return
B49	GND	Ground
B50	IRQ9	Interrupt 9
B51	BRDY#	Burst Ready
B52	BLAST#	Burst Last
B53	ID0	Identification 0
B54	ID1	Identification 1
B55	GND	Ground
B56	LCLK	Local Clock
B57	VCC	+5 V DC
B58	LBS16#	Local Bus Size 16

Drives (Disk/Tape/CD)

▌ 3.5" Power

Used for floppies.

Pin	Name	Color	Description
1	+5V	Red	+5 V DC
2	GND	Black	+5 V Ground
3	GND	Black	+12 V Ground (Same as +5 V Ground)
4	+12V	Yellow	+12 V DC

■ 5.25" Power

Used for hard disks and 5.25" peripherals.

```
┌─────────────┐
│ ●  ●  ●  ● │
└─────────────┘
  1  2  3  4
```
(At the powersupply cable)

```
┌─────────────┐
│ ●  ●  ●  ● │
└─────────────┘
  4  3  2  1
```
(At the peripheral)

Pin	Name	Color	Description
1	+12V	Yellow	+12 V DC
2	GND	Black	+12 V Ground (Same as +5 V Ground)
3	GND	Black	+5 V Ground
4	+5V	Red	+5 V DC

■ ATA Internal

ATA = AT bus Attachment.
Developed by Western Digital, Conner and Seagate.

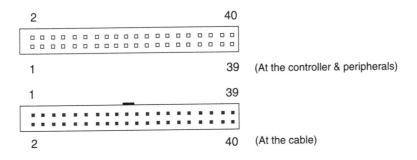

2   40

1   39   (At the controller & peripherals)

1   39

2   40   (At the cable)

40-PIN IDC MALE at the controller and peripherals;
40-PIN IDC FEMALE at the cable.

Pin	Name	Dir	Description
1	/RESET	→	Reset
2	GND	——	Ground
3	DD7	◄►	Data 7
4	DD8	◄►	Data 8
5	DD6	◄►	Data 6
6	DD9	◄►	Data 9
7	DD5	◄►	Data 5
8	DD10	◄►	Data 10
9	DD4	◄►	Data 4
10	DD11	◄►	Data 11
11	DD3	◄►	Data 3
12	DD12	◄►	Data 12
13	DD2	◄►	Data 2
14	DD13	◄►	Data 13
15	DD1	◄►	Data 1
16	DD14	◄►	Data 14
17	DD0	◄►	Data 0
18	DD15	◄►	Data 15
19	GND	——	Ground

Pin	Name	Dir	Description
20	KEY		Key (Pin missing)
21	DMARQ	?	DMA Request
22	GND	——	Ground
23	/DIOW	→—	Write Strobe
24	GND	——	Ground
25	/DIOR	→—	Read Strobe
26	GND	——	Ground
27	IORDY	←—	I/O Ready
28	SPSYNC:CSEL	?	Spindle Sync or Cable Select
29	/DMACK	?	DMA Acknowledge
30	GND	——	Ground
31	INTRQ	←—	Interrupt Request
32	/IOCS16	?	IO Chip Select 16
33	DA1	→—	Address 1
34	PDIAG	?	Passed Diagnostics
35	DA0	→—	Address 0
36	DA2	→—	Address 2
37	/IDE_CS0	→—	(1F0–1F7)
38	/IDE_CS1	→—	(3F6–3F7)
39	/ACTIVE	→—	LED driver
40	GND	——	Ground

Note: Direction is Controller relative Devices (Hard disks).

ESDI

ESDI = Enhanced Small Device Interface;
Developed by Maxtor in the early 1980s as an upgrade and improvement
to the ST506 design.

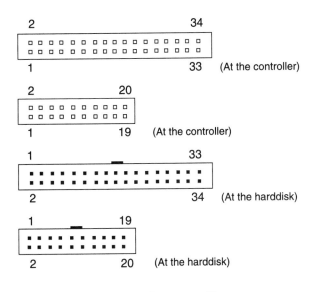

34-PIN IDC MALE at the controller;
20-PIN IDC MALE at the controller.

34-PIN IDC FEMALE at the hard disk;
20-PIN IDC FEMALE at the hard disk.

Control Connector

Pin	Name	Description
2		Head Sel 3
4		Head Sel 2
6		Write Gate
8		Config/Stat Data
10		Transfer Acknowledge
12		Attention
14		Head Sel 0
16		Sect/Add MK Found
18		Head Sel 1
20		Index
22		Ready

Pin	Name	Description
24		Transfer Request
26		Drive Sel 1
28		Drive Sel 2
30		Drive Sel 3
32		Read Gate
34		Command Data

Note: All odd are GND, Ground.

Data Connector

Pin	Name	Description
1		Drive Selected
2		Sect/Add MK Found
3		Seek Complete
4		Address Mark Enable
5		(reserved, for step mode)
6	GND	Ground
7		Write Clock+
8		Write Clock–
9		Cartridge Changed
10		Read Ref Clock+
11		Read Ref Clock–
12	GND	Ground
13		NRZ Write Data+
14		NRZ Write Data–
15	GND	Ground
16	GND	Ground
17		NRZ Read Data+
18		NRZ Read Data–
19	GND	Ground
20	GND	Ground

■ IDE Internal

IDE = Integrated Drive Electronics.
Developed by Compaq and Western Digital.
Newer version of IDE goes under the name ATA = AT bus Attachment.

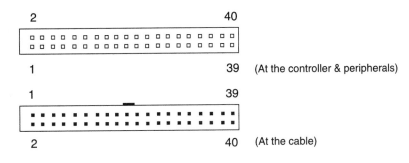

2   40

1   39   (At the controller & peripherals)

1   39

2   40   (At the cable)

40-PIN IDC MALE at the controller and peripherals;
40-PIN IDC FEMALE at the cable.

Pin	Name	Dir	Description
1	/RESET	→	Reset
2	GND	—	Ground
3	DD7	↔	Data 7
4	DD8	↔	Data 8
5	DD6	↔	Data 6
6	DD9	↔	Data 9
7	DD5	↔	Data 5
8	DD10	↔	Data 10
9	DD4	↔	Data 4
10	DD11	↔	Data 11
11	DD3	↔	Data 3
12	DD12	↔	Data 12
13	DD2	↔	Data 2
14	DD13	↔	Data 13
15	DD1	↔	Data 1
16	DD14	↔	Data 14
17	DD0	↔	Data 0
18	DD15	↔	Data 15

Pin	Name	Dir	Description
19	GND	——	Ground
20	KEY		Key
21	n/c		Not connected
22	GND	——	Ground
23	/IOW	——▶	Write Strobe
24	GND	——	Ground
25	/IOR	——▶	Read Strobe
26	GND	——	Ground
27	IO_CH_RDY	◀——	
28	ALE	——▶	Address Latch Enable
29	n/c		Not connected
30	GND	——	Ground
31	IRQR	◀——	Interrupt Request
32	/IOCS16		IO Chip Select 16
33	DA1	——▶	Address 1
34	n/c		Not connected
35	DA0	——▶	Address 0
36	DA2	——▶	Address 2
37	/IDE_CS0	——▶	(1F0–1F7)
38	/IDE_CS1	——▶	(3F6–3F7)
39	/ACTIVE	——▶	Led driver
40	GND	——	Ground

Note: Direction is Controller relative Devices (Hard disks).

■ Internal Disk Drive

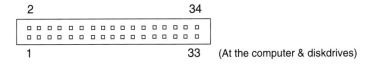

2   34

1   33   (At the computer & diskdrives)

34-PIN IDC MALE at the computer and disk drives.

Pin	Name	Dir	Description
2	/REDWC	⟶	Density Select
4	n/c		reserved
6	n/c		reserved
8	/INDEX	⟵	Index
10	MOTEA	⟶	Motor Enable A
12	/DRVSB	⟶	Drive Sel B
14	/DRVSA	⟶	Drive Sel A
16	/MOTEB	⟶	Motor Enable B
18	/DIR	⟶	Direction
20	/STEP	⟶	Step
22	/WDATE	⟶	Write Data
24	/WGATE	⟶	Floppy Write Enable
26	/TRK00	⟵	Track 0
28	/WPT	⟵	Write Protect
30	/RDATA	⟵	Read Data
32	/SIDE1	⟶	Head Select
34	/DSKCHG	⟶	Disk Change

Notes: Direction is Computer relative Diskdrive.
All odd pins are GND, Ground.
Can be an edge connector on old PCs.

▌ Mitsumi CD-ROM

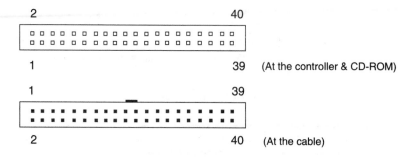

40-PIN IDC MALE at the controller and CD-ROM;
40-PIN IDC FEMALE at the cable.

Pin	Name	Description
1	A0	Address Bit 0
2	GND	Ground
3	A1	Address Bit 1
4	GND	Ground
5	n/c	Not connected
6	GND	Ground
7	n/c	Not connected
8	GND	Ground
9	n/c	Not connected
10	GND	Ground
11	n/c	Not connected
12	GND	Ground
13	INT	Interrupt
14	GND	Ground
15	REQ	Data request for DMA
16	GND	Ground
17	ACK	Data Acknowledge for DMA
18	GND	Ground
19	RE	Read Enable
20	GND	Ground

Pin	Name	Description
21	WE	Write Enable
22	GND	Ground
23	EN	Bus Enable
24	GND	Ground
25	DB0	Data Bit 0
26	GND	Ground
27	DB1	Data Bit 1
28	GND	Ground
29	DB2	Data Bit 2
30	GND	Ground
31	DB3	Data Bit 3
32	GND	Ground
33	DB4	Data Bit 4
34	GND	Ground
35	DB5	Data Bit 5
36	GND	Ground
37	DB6	Data Bit 6
38	GND	Ground
39	DB7	Data Bit 7
40	GND	Ground

▪ Panasonic CD-ROM

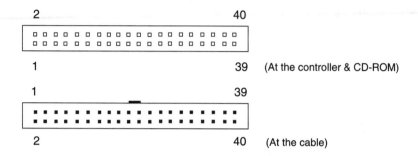

2   40

1   39   (At the controller & CD-ROM)

1   39

2   40   (At the cable)

40-PIN IDC MALE at the controller and CD-ROM;
40-PIN IDC FEMALE at the cable.

Pin	Name	Description
1	GND	Ground
2	RESET	CD-Reset
3	GND	Ground
4	GND	Ground
5	GND	Ground
6	MODE0	Operation Mode Bit 0
7	GND	Ground
8	MODE1	Operation Mode Bit 1
9	GND	Ground
10	WRITE	CD-Write
11	GND	Ground
12	READ	CD-Read
13	GND	Ground
14	ST0	CD-Status Bit 0
15	GND	Ground
16	n/c	No connection
17	GND	Ground
18	n/c	No connection
19	GND	Ground
20	ST1	CD-Status Bit 1
21	GND	Ground

Pin	Name	Description
22	EN	CD-Data Enable
23	GND	Ground
24	ST2	CD-Status Bit 2
25	GND	Ground
26	S/DE	CD-Status/Data Enable
27	GND	Ground
28	ST3	CD-Status Bit 3
29	GND	Ground
30	GND	Ground
31	D7	CD-Data 7
32	D6	CD-Data 6
33	GND	Ground
34	D5	CD-Data 5
35	D4	CD-Data 4
36	D3	CD-Data 3
37	GND	Ground
38	D2	CD-Data 2
39	D1	CD-Data 1
40	D0	CD-Data 0

▌ Sony CD-ROM

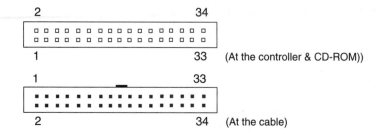

2   34

1   33   (At the controller & CD-ROM))

1   33

2   34   (At the cable)

34-PIN IDC MALE at the controller and CD-ROM;
34-PIN IDC FEMALE at the cable.

Pin	Name	Description
1	RESET	Reset
2	GND	Ground
3	DB7	Data Bit 7
4	GND	Ground
5	DB6	Data Bit 6
6	GND	Ground
7	DB5	Data Bit 5
8	GND	Ground
9	DB4	Data Bit 4
10	GND	Ground
11	DB3	Data Bit 3
12	GND	Ground
13	DB2	Data Bit 2
14	GND	Ground
15	DB1	Data Bit 1
16	GND	Ground
17	DB0	Data Bit 0
18	GND	Ground
19	WE	Write Enable
20	GND	Ground

Pin	Name	Description
21	RE	Read Enable
22	GND	Ground
23	ACK	Data Acknowledge for DMA
24	GND	Ground
25	REQ	Data Request for DMA
26	GND	Ground
27	INT	Interrupt
28	GND	Ground
29	A1	Address Bit 1
30	GND	Ground
31	A0	Address Bit 0
32	GND	Ground
33	EN	Bus Enable
34	GND	Ground

■ ST506/412

Developed by Seagate. Also known as MFM or RLL, since these are the encoding methods used to store data. Seagate originally developed it to support their ST506 (5 MB) and ST412 (10 MB) drives.

The first drives used an encoding method called MFM (Modified Frequency Modulation). Later a new encoding method was developed, RLL (Run Length Limited). RLL had the advantage that it was possible to store 50% more with it. But it required better drives. This is almost never a problem. Often called 2,7 RLL because the recording scheme involves patterns with no more than 7 successive zeros and no less than 2.

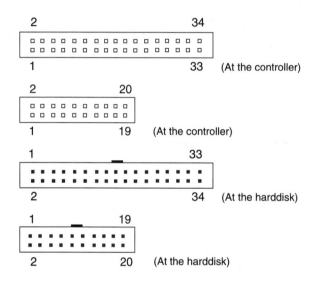

34-PIN IDC MALE at the controller;
20-PIN IDC MALE at the controller.

34-PIN IDC FEMALE at the hard disk;
20-PIN IDC FEMALE at the hard disk.

Control Connector

Pin	Name	Description
2		Head Sel 8
4		Head Sel 4
6		Write Gate
8		Seek Complete
10		Track 0

Pin	Name	Description
12		Write Fault
14		Head Sel 1
16	RES	reserved
18		Head Sel 2
20		Index
22		Ready
24		Step
26		Drive Sel 1
28		Drive Sel 2
30		Drive Sel 3
32		Drive Sel 4
34		Direction In

Note: All odd pins are GND, Ground.

Data Connector

Pin	Name	Description
1		Drive Selected
2	GND	Ground
3	RES	reserved
4	GND	Ground
5	RES	reserved
6	GND	Ground
7	RES	reserved
8	GND	Ground
9	RES	reserved
10	RES	reserved
11	GND	Ground
12	GND	Ground
13		Write Data+
14		Write Data−
15	GND	Ground
16	GND	Ground
17		Read Data+
18		Read Data−
19	GND	Ground
20	GND	Ground

Joysticks and Mice

■ Macintosh Mouse

Available on Macintosh Mac Plus and earlier.

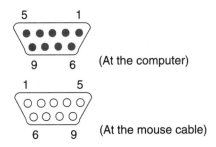

(At the computer)

(At the mouse cable)

9-PIN D-SUB FEMALE at the computer;
9-PIN D-SUB MALE at the mouse cable.

Pin	Name	Dir	Description
1	CGND	——	Chassis ground
2	+5V	——▶	+5 V DC
3	CGND	——	Chassis ground
4	X2	◀——	Horizontal movement line (connected to VIA PB4 line)
5	X1	◀——	Horizontal movement line (connected to SCC DCDA line)
6	n/c		Not connected
7	SW–	◀——	Mouse button line (connected to VIA PB3)
8	Y2	◀——	Vertical movement line (connected to VIA PB5 line)
9	Y1	◀——	Vertical movement line (connected to SCC DCDB line)

Note: Direction is Computer relative Mouse.

▌ Mouse (PS/2)

(At the computer)

6-PIN MINI-DIN FEMALE (PS/2 STYLE) at the computer.

Pin	Name	Dir	Description
1	DATA	←→	Key Data
2	n/c		Not connected
3	GND	——	Gnd
4	VCC	→—	Power, +5 V DC
5	CLK	→—	Clock
6	n/c		Not connected

Note: Direction is Computer relative Mouse.

■ PC Gameport

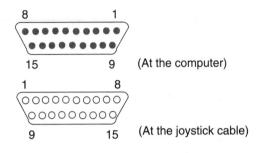

(At the computer)

(At the joystick cable)

15-PIN D-SUB FEMALE at the computer;
15-PIN D-SUB MALE at the joystick cable.

Pin	Name	Dir	Description
1	+5V	→	+5 V DC
2	/B1	←	Button 1
3	X1	←	Joystick 1 - X
4	GND	—	Ground
5	GND	—	Ground
6	Y1	←	Joystick 1 - Y
7	/B2	←	Button 2
8	+5V	→	+5 V DC
9	+5V	→	+5 V DC
10	/B4	←	Button 4
11	X2	←	Joystick 2 - X
12	GND	—	Ground
13	Y2	←	Joystick 2 - Y
14	/B3	←	Button 3
15	+5V	→	+5 V DC

Notes: Direction is Computer relative
Joystick. Use 100-kΩ resistor.

■ PC Gameport + MIDI

Some sound cards have some MIDI signals included in their gameport.
Ground and VCC have been used for this.

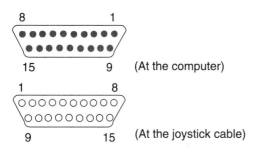

8   1

15   9   (At the computer)

1   8

9   15   (At the joystick cable)

15-PIN D-SUB FEMALE at the computer;
15-PIN D-SUB MALE at the joystick cable.

Pin	Name	Dir	Description
1	+5V	→	+5 V DC
2	/B1	←	Button 1
3	X1	←	Joystick 1 - X
4	GND	—	Ground
5	GND	—	Ground
6	Y1	←	Joystick 1 - Y
7	/B2	←	Button 2
8	+5V	→	+5 V DC
9	+5V	→	+5 V DC
10	/B4	←	Button 4
11	X2	←	Joystick 2 - X
12	MIDITXD	→	MIDI Transmit
13	Y2	←	Joystick 2 - Y
14	/B3	←	Button 3
15	MIDIRXD	←	MIDI Receive

Notes: Direction is Computer relative Joystick.
Use 100-kΩ resistor.

Keyboards

■ Keyboard (5 PC)

(At the computer)

5-PIN DIN 180° (DIN41524) FEMALE at the computer.

Pin	Name	Description	Technical
1	CLOCK	Clock	CLK/CTS, Open-collector
2	DATA	Data	RxD/TxD/RTS, Open-collector
3	n/c	Not connected	Reset on some very old keyboards
4	GND	Ground	
5	VCC	+5 V DC	

▌ Keyboard (6 PC)

```
 6 ⌒ 5
4 (• •) 3
   • ▪ •
 2 ⌣ 1    (At the computer)
```

6-PIN MINI-DIN FEMALE (PS/2 STYLE) at the computer.

Pin	Name	Dir	Description
1	DATA	◄►	Key Data
2	n/c		Not connected
3	GND	──	Ground
4	VCC	─►	Power, +5 V DC
5	CLK	─►	Clock
6	n/c		Not connected

Note: Direction is Computer relative Keyboard.

▌ Keyboard (XT)

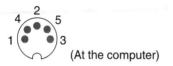

(At the computer)

5-PIN DIN 180° (DIN41524) FEMALE at the computer.

Pin	Name	Description	Technical
1	CLK	Clock	CLK/CTS, Open-collector
2	DATA	Data	RxD, Open-collector
3	/RESET	Reset	
4	GND	Ground	
5	VCC	+5 V DC	

■ Macintosh Keyboard

Available on Macintosh Mac Plus and earlier.

RJ-11 FEMALE CONNECTOR at the computer;
RJ-11 MALE CONNECTOR at the keyboard.

Pin	Name	Dir	Description
1	CGND	——	Chassis ground
2	KBD1	?	Keyboard clock
3	KDB2	?	Keyboard data
4	+5V	—→	+5 V DC

Note: Direction is Computer relative Keyboard.

Networking

■ AUI

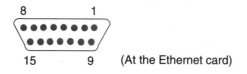

(At the Ethernet card)

15-PIN D-SUB FEMALE at the Ethernet card.

Pin	Description
1	Control in circuit shield
2	Control in circuit A
3	Data out circuit A
4	Data in circuit shield
5	Data in circuit A
6	Voltage common
7	?
8	Control out circuit shield
9	Control in circuit B
10	Data out circuit B
11	Data out circuit shield
12	Data in circuit B
13	Voltage plus
14	Voltage shield
15	?

▮ Ethernet 10/100Base-T

Same connector and pinout for both 10Base-T and 100Base-TX.

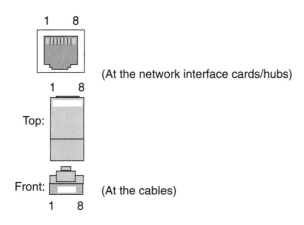

(At the network interface cards/hubs)

Top:

Front: (At the cables)

RJ-45 FEMALE CONNECTOR at the network interface cards/hubs;
RJ-45 MALE CONNECTOR at the cables.

Pin	Name	Description
1	TX+	Transceive Data+
2	TX−	Transceive Data−
3	RX+	Receive Data+
4	n/c	Not connected
5	n/c	Not connected
6	RX−	Receive Data−
7	n/c	Not connected
8	n/c	Not connected

Note: TX and RX are swapped on
Hubs.

▌ Ethernet 100Base-T4

100Base-T4 uses all four pairs. 100Base-TX only uses two pairs.

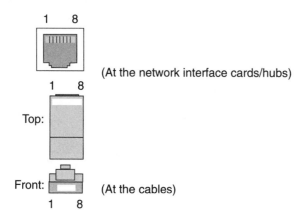

(At the network interface cards/hubs)

Top:

Front: (At the cables)

RJ-45 FEMALE CONNECTOR at the network interface cards/hubs;
RJ-45 MALE CONNECTOR at the cables.

Pin	Name	Description
1	TX_D1+	Transceive Data+
2	TX_D1–	Transceive Data–
3	RX_D2+	Receive Data+
4	BI_D3+	Bidirectional Data+
5	BI_D3–	Bidirectional Data–
6	RX_D2–	Receive Data–
7	BI_D4+	Bidirectional Data+
8	BI_D4–	Bidirectional Data–

Note: TX and RX are swapped on Hubs.
Don't know about Bidirectional data.

Parallel Ports

▌ Centronics

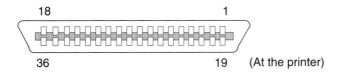

36-PIN CENTRONICS FEMALE at the printer.

Pin	Name	Dir	Description
1	/STROBE	←	Strobe
2	D0	↔	Data Bit 0
3	D1	↔	Data Bit 1
4	D2	↔	Data Bit 2
5	D3	↔	Data Bit 3
6	D4	↔	Data Bit 4
7	D5	↔	Data Bit 5
8	D6	↔	Data Bit 6
9	D7	↔	Data Bit 7
10	/ACK	→	Acknowledge
11	BUSY	→	Busy
12	POUT	→	Paper Out
13	SEL	→	Select
14	/AUTOFEED	←	Autofeed
15	n/c		Not used
16	0 V	—	Logic Ground
17	CHASSIS GND	—	Shield Ground
18	+5 V PULLUP	→	+5 V DC (50 mA max)
19	GND	—	Signal Ground (Strobe Ground)
20	GND	—	Signal Ground (Data 0 Ground)
21	GND	—	Signal Ground (Data 1 Ground)
22	GND	—	Signal Ground (Data 2 Ground)
23	GND	—	Signal Ground (Data 3 Ground)

Pin	Name	Dir	Description
24	GND	——	Signal Ground (Data 4 Ground)
25	GND	——	Signal Ground (Data 5 Ground)
26	GND	——	Signal Ground (Data 6 Ground)
27	GND	——	Signal Ground (Data 7 Ground)
28	GND	——	Signal Ground (Acknowledge Ground)
29	GND	——	Signal Ground (Busy Ground)
30	/GNDRESET	——	Reset Ground
31	/RESET	←	Reset
32	/FAULT	→	Fault (Low when off line)
33	0 V	——	Signal Ground
34	n/c		Not used
35	+5 V	→	+5 V DC
36	/SLCT IN	←	Select In (Taking low or high sets printer on line or off line, respectively)

Note: Direction is Printer relative Computer.

■ ECP Parallel

ECP = Extended Capabilities Port.

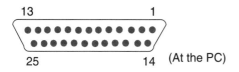

25-PIN D-SUB FEMALE at the PC.

Pin	Name	Dir	Description
1	nStrobe	⟶	Strobe
2	data0	⟷	Address, Data or RLE Data Bit 0
3	data1	⟷	Address, Data or RLE Data Bit 1
4	data2	⟷	Address, Data or RLE Data Bit 2
5	data3	⟷	Address, Data or RLE Data Bit 3
6	data4	⟷	Address, Data or RLE Data Bit 4
7	data5	⟷	Address, Data or RLE Data Bit 5
8	data6	⟷	Address, Data or RLE Data Bit 6
9	data7	⟷	Address, Data or RLE Data Bit 7
10	/nACK	⟵	Acknowledge
11	Busy	⟵	Busy
12	PError	⟵	Paper End
13	Select	⟵	Select
14	/nAutoFd	⟶	Autofeed
15	/nFault	⟵	Error
16	/nInit	⟶	Initialize
17	/nSelectIn	⟶	Select In
18	GND	—	Signal Ground
19	GND	—	Signal Ground
20	GND	—	Signal Ground
21	GND	—	Signal Ground
22	GND	—	Signal Ground
23	GND	—	Signal Ground
24	GND	—	Signal Ground
25	GND	—	Signal Ground

Note: Direction is Computer relative Device.

▮ Parallel (PC)

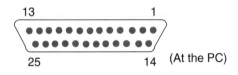

(At the PC)

25-PIN D-SUB FEMALE at the PC.

Pin	Name	Dir	Description
1	/STROBE	→	Strobe
2	D0	→	Data Bit 0
3	D1	→	Data Bit 1
4	D2	→	Data Bit 2
5	D3	→	Data Bit 3
6	D4	→	Data Bit 4
7	D5	→	Data Bit 5
8	D6	→	Data Bit 6
9	D7	→	Data Bit 7
10	/ACK	←	Acknowledge
11	BUSY	←	Busy
12	PE	←	Paper End
13	SEL	←	Select
14	/AUTOFD	→	Autofeed
15	/ERROR	←	Error
16	/INIT	→	Initialize
17	/SELIN	→	Select In
18	GND	—	Signal Ground
19	GND	—	Signal Ground
20	GND	—	Signal Ground
21	GND	—	Signal Ground
22	GND	—	Signal Ground
23	GND	—	Signal Ground
24	GND	—	Signal Ground
25	GND	—	Signal Ground

Note: Direction is Computer relative Device.

Serial Ports

∎ Commodore C64/C16/C116/+4 Serial I/O

Available on the Commodore C64, C16, C116, and +4 computers.

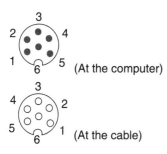

(At the computer)

(At the cable)

6-PIN DIN (DIN45322) FEMALE at the computer;
6-PIN DIN (DIN45322) MALE at the cable.

Pin	Name	Description
1	/SRQIN	Serial SRQIN
2	GND	Ground
3	ATN	Serial ATN In/Out
4	CLK	Serial CLK In/Out
5	DATA	Serial DATA In/Out
6	/RESET	Reset

■ Cisco Console Port

Used to configure a Cisco router.

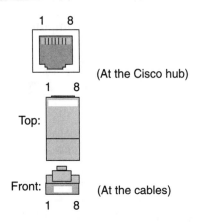

(At the Cisco hub)

Top:

Front: (At the cables)

RJ-45 FEMALE CONNECTOR at the Cisco routers;
RJ-45 MALE CONNECTOR at the cables.

Pin	Name	Description	Dir
1	RTS	Request To Send	→
2	DTR	Data Terminal Ready	→
3	TXD	Transceive Data	→
4	n/c	Not connected	
5	n/c	Not connected	
6	RXD	Receive Data	←
7	DSR	Data Set Ready	←
8	CTS	Clear To Send	←

▌ Macintosh RS-422

It's possible to connect RS-232 peripheral to the RS-422 port available on Macintosh computers. Use RXD– as RXD, TXD– as TXD; ground RXD+; leave TXD+ unconnected; use GPi as CD.

(At the computer)

8-PIN MINI-DIN FEMALE at the computer.

Pin	Name	Dir	Description
1	HSKo	⟶	Output Handshake
2	HSKi/CLK	⟵	Input Handshake or External Clock
3	TXD–	⟶	Transmit Data (–)
4	GND	—	Ground
5	RXD–	⟵	Receive Data (–)
6	TXD+	⟶	Transmit Data (+)
7	GPi	⟵	General-Purpose Input
8	RXD+	⟵	Receive Data (+)

Notes: Direction is DTE (Computer) relative DCE (Modem). GPi is connected to SCC Data Carrier Detect (or to Receive/Transmit Clock if the VIA1 SYNC signal is high). Not connected on the Macintosh Plus, Classic, Classic II, LC, LC II, or IIsi.

■ Macintosh Serial

Available on Macintosh Mac 512KE and earlier.

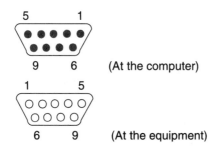

9-PIN D-SUB FEMALE at the computer;
9-PIN D-SUB MALE at the mouse cable.

Pin	Name	Dir	Description
1	GND	——	Ground
2	+5V	→	+5 V DC. Don't use this one; it may be converted into output handshake in later equipment.
3	GND	——	Ground
4	Tx+	→	Transmit Data, positive-going component
5	Tx–	→	Transmit Data, negative-going component
6	+12V	→	+12 V DC
7	DSR/HSK	←	Handshape input. Signal name depends on mode: Used for Flow Control or Clock In.
8	Rx+	←	Receive Data, positive-going component
9	Rx–	←	Receive Data, negative-going component

Note: Direction is Computer relative Equipment.

▌ Infrared: Motherboard IrDA

For motherboards with an IrDA-compliant Infrared Module connector.

1　2　3　4　5

●　●　●　●　●

5-PIN IDC MALE at the motherboard.

Pin	Name	Description
1	+5V	Power
2	n/c	Not connected
3	IRRX	IR Module data receive
4	GND	System GND
5	IRTX	IR Module data transmit

▌RS-232

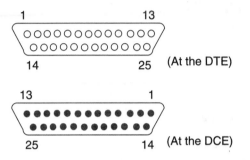

(At the DTE)

(At the DCE)

25-PIN D-SUB MALE at the DTE (computer);
25-PIN D-SUB FEMALE at the DCE (modem).

Pin	Name	ITU-T	Dir	Description
1	GND	101	——	Shield Ground
2	TXD	103	→	Transmit Data
3	RXD	104	←	Receive Data
4	RTS	105	→	Request to Send
5	CTS	106	←	Clear to Send
6	DSR	107	←	Data Set Ready
7	GND	102	——	System Ground
8	CD	109	←	Carrier Detect
9				reserved
10				reserved
11	STF	126	→	Select Transmit Channel
12	S.CD	122	←	Secondary Carrier Detect
13	S.CTS	121	←	Secondary Clear to Send
14	S.TXD	118	→	Secondary Transmit Data
15	TCK	114	←	Transmission Signal Element Timing
16	S.RXD	119	←	Secondary Receive Data
17	RCK	115	←	Receiver Signal Element Timing
18	LL	141	→	Local Loop Control
19	S.RTS	120	→	Secondary Request to Send
20	DTR	108.2	→	Data Terminal Ready
21	RL	140	→	Remote Loop Control

Pin	Name	ITU-T	Dir	Description
22	RI	125	←	Ring Indicator
23	DSR	111	→	Data Signal Rate Selector
24	XCK	113	→	Transmit Signal Element Timing
25	TI	142	←	Test Indicator

Notes: Direction is DTE (Computer) relative DCE (Modem). Do not connect SHIELD (1) to GND (7).

▌ RS-422

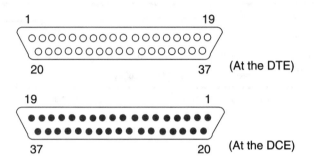

1   19
(At the DTE)
20   37

19   1
(At the DCE)
37   20

37-PIN D-SUB MALE at the DTE (computer);
37-PIN D-SUB FEMALE at the DCE (modem).

Pin	Name	Dir	Description
1	GND	——	Shield Ground
2	SRI	←	Signal Rate Indicator
3	n/c		Spare
4	SD	→	Send Data
5	ST	→	Send Timing
6	RD	←	Receive Data
7	RTS	→	Request To Send
8	RR	←	Receiver Ready
9	CTS	←	Clear To Send
10	LL	→	Local Loopback
11	DM	←	Data Modem
12	TR	→	Terminal Ready
13	RR	←	Receiver Ready
14	RL	→	Remote Loopback
15	IC	←	Incoming Call
16	SF/SR	→	Select Frequency/Select Rate
17	TT	→	Terminal Timing
18	TM	←	Test Mode
19	GND	——	Ground
20	RC	——	Receive Twisted-Pair Common
21	GND	——	Spare Twisted-Pair Return

Pin	Name	Dir	Description
22	/SD	———	Send Data TPR
23	GND	———	Send Timing TPR
24	GND	———	Receive Timing TPR
25	/RS	———	Request To Send TPR
26	/RT	———	Receive Timing TPR
27	/CS	———	Clear To Send TPR
28	IS	◄—	Terminal In Service
29	/DM	———	Data Mode TPR
30	/TR	———	Terminal Ready TPR
31	/RR	———	Receiver TPR
32	SS	—►	Select Standby
33	SQ	◄—	Signal Quality
34	NS	—►	New Signal
35	/TT	———	Terminal Timing TPR
36	SB	◄—	Standby Indicator
37	SC	———	Send Twisted Pair Common

Note: Direction is DTE (Computer) relative DCE (Modem).

■ Serial (PC 9)

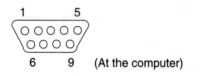

1   5

6   9   (At the computer)

9-PIN D-SUB MALE at the computer.

Pin	Name	Dir	Description
1	CD	←—	Carrier Detect
2	RXD	←—	Receive Data
3	TXD	—→	Transmit Data
4	DTR	—→	Data Terminal Ready
5	GND	——	System Ground
6	DSR	←—	Data Set Ready
7	RTS	—→	Request To Send
8	CTS	←—	Clear To Send
9	RI	←—	Ring Indicator

Note: Direction is DTE (Computer) relative DCE (Modem).

■ Serial (PC 25)

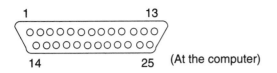

1   13

14   25   (At the computer)

25-PIN D-SUB MALE at the computer.

Pin	Name	Dir	Description
1	SHIELD		Shield Ground
2	TXD	⟶	Transmit Data
3	RXD	⟵	Receive Data
4	RTS	⟶	Request To Send
5	CTS	⟵	Clear To Send
6	DSR	⟵	Data Set Ready
7	GND		System Ground
8	CD	⟵	Carrier Detect
9	n/c		
10	n/c		
11	n/c		
12	n/c		
13	n/c		
14	n/c		
15	n/c		
16	n/c		
17	n/c		
18	n/c		
19	n/c		
20	DTR	⟶	Data Terminal Ready
21	n/c		
22	RI	⟵	Ring Indicator
23	n/c		
24	n/c		
25	n/c		

Note: Direction is DTE (Computer) relative DCE (Modem). Do not connect SHIELD (1) to GND (7).

Index